D1077406

Dr Norman Vincent Peale's deep and abiding faith in the power of great thoughts to provide lifelong courage and confidence led to this unique anthology.

In these pages Dr Peale has collected the works of inspired writers, the thoughts of great men, and anecdotes about remarkable people. The result is truly a treasury of COURAGE and CONFIDENCE.

From the Bible to Shakespeare, from Theodore Roosevelt to Albert Schweitzer to Dr Peale himself, here is something to lift the spirit of every reader and guide him toward peace of mind and the will to live the fullest possible life.

The material in this book is arranged in twelve sections; each offers a different approach to such individual concerns as how to banish fear, loving and being loved, the art of thankfulness, the power of prayer and how to find happiness. But, above all, this anthology was meant to serve as a stimulant to activate the mind creatively, as an instrument to deepen spiritual life – as a treasury of faith.

Norman Vincent Peale titles available in Vermilion

The Power of Positive Thinking
The Power of Positive Living
The Amazing Results of Positive Thinking
The Positive Way to Change Your Life
The Power of Positive Thinking for Young People
Stay Alive All Your Life
Courage and Confidence
You Can if You Think You Can

COURAGE AND CONFIDENCE

An Anthology edited by

NORMAN VINCENT PEALE

VERMILION

LONDON

Courage and Confidence: An Anthology

3 5 7 9 10 8 6 4 2

First published in Great Britain 1970 by George Allen & Unwin
Published in Cedar 1992. Reprinted 1993, 1994, 1995, 1996.

This edition published in the United Kingdopm in 1998 by Vermillion
an imprint of Ebury Press
The Random House Group Ltd.
20 Vauxhall Bridge Road
London SW1V 2SA

Random House Australia (Pty) Limited
20 Alfred Street, Milsons Point, Sydney,
New South Wales 2061, Australia

Random House New Zealand Limited
18 Poland Road, Glenfield,
Auckland 10, New Zealand

Random House South Africa (Pty) Limited
Endulini, 5a Jubilee Road, Parktown 2193, South Africa

The Random House Group Limited Reg. No. 954009
www.randomhouse.co.uk

A CIP catalogue record for this book is available from the British
Library

ISBN 0 7493 1341 2

Printed and bound in Great Britain by Cox & Wyman Ltd, Reading,
Berkshire

Papers used by Vermillion are natural, recyclable products made from
wood grown in sustainable forests.

Acknowledgments

Grateful acknowledgment is made to the following publishers, authors, agents, and individuals for the use of the protected material indicated.

Abingdon Press, for material from *Remember Now* by Walter Dudley Cavert; *Lord of All* by John Trevor Davies; *The Modern Rival of Christian Faith* by Georgia Harkness; *Abundant Living* and *Christ at the Round Table* by E. Stanley Jones; and *Prescriptions for Anxiety* by Leslie D. Weatherhead.

Mrs Eustace L. Adams, for 'A Little Parable for Mothers' by Temple Bailey.

American Tract Society and Methuen & Company, Ltd, London, for several poems from *Bees in Amber* by John Oxenham.

Dr Marcus Bach, for an excerpt from his book, *The Will to Believe.*

Dr Preston Bradley, for his 'Grace Before Reading a Book.'

The Christian Athlete, for a quote by Frank Kapral.

Margaret Conklin, Literary Executor of the Estate of Sara Teasdale, for 'The Philosopher' by Sara Teasdale.

Dodd, Mead & Company, Inc, for 'Blue Dusk,' 'Buttons and Trash,' 'In Such an Age,' and 'Prepare a Place' from *Creator Man* by Angela Morgan. Copyright 1929 by Dodd, Mead & Company, Inc. Renewal copyright 1956 by Angela Morgan.

Dodd, Mead & Company, Inc and McClelland and Stewart, Limited, for 'Vestigia' from *Bliss Carman's Poems*. Copyright 1931 by Dodd, Mead & Company, Inc.

Doubleday & Company, Inc, for excerpts from *Lessons for Life* by Robert I. Kahn, copyright © 1963 by Robert I. Kahn; *Midstream* by Helen Keller, copyright 1929 by Helen Keller and The Crowell Publishing Company; *Peace in the Heart* by Archibald Rutledge, copyright 1927, 1928, 1929, 1930 by Archibald Rutledge; and *Move Ahead with Possibility Thinking* by Robert H. Schuller, copyright © 1967 by Robert H. Schuller.

Doubleday & Company, Inc, Mrs George Bambridge, and Macmillan and Co, Ltd, for 'If,' copyright 1910 by Rudyard Kipling, from *Rewards and Fairies* by Rudyard Kipling.

Doubleday & Company, Inc and Curtis Brown, Ltd, for material from *Modern Parables* by Fulton Oursler. Copyright 1950 by Fulton Oursler.

Doubleday & Company, Inc and Robert Hale & Company, for material from *At Ease* by Dwight D. Eisenhower. Copyright © 1967 by Dwight D. Eisenhower.

Doubleday & Company, Inc and *Reader's Digest*, tor 'A String of Blue Beads' by Fulton Oursler. Copyright 1951 by the Estate of Fulton Oursler.

Doubleday & Company, Inc and A. P. Watt & Son, for material from *How to Live on Twenty-Four Hours a Day* by Arnold Bennett. Copyright 1910 by Doubleday & Company, Inc.

E. P. Dutton & Co, Inc, for material from *Happiness* by William Lyon Phelps. Copyright 1927 by E. P. Dutton & Co, Inc; renewal © 1955 by Dryden L. Phelps.

Norma Millay Ellis, for an excerpt from 'Renascence,' copyright 1912, 1940 by Edna St Vincent Millay, and for 'God's World,' copyright 1913, 1940 by Edna St Vincent Millay; both from *Collected Poems* by Edna St Vincent Millay, published by Harper & Row, Publishers.

First Church of Christ, Scientist, Maywood, Illinois, for 'I Am Still Rich' from *Home Roads and Far Horizons* by Thomas Curtis Clark.

Guideposts and the authors, for 'The Mystery of the Crumpled Notepaper' by George A. Straley; 'No End to Love' by Martin Buxbaum; 'A Test of Trust' by Evelyn Wick Smith; 'Be Bold – and Mighty Forces Will Come to Your Aid' by Arthur Gordon; 'A Gift of the Heart' by Norman Vincent Peale; 'The Heart of Prayer – Why Men Pray' by John Sherrill; 'I Believe in Prayer' by Edward Rickenbacker; 'How to Have a Better Family Life' by Margaret Peale Everett; and 'How to be a Better Husband' by Ruth S. Peale.

Harper & Row, Publishers, for excerpts from *Stake Your Claim* by Emmet Fox, copyright 1952 by Harper & Row, Publishers, Incorporated; *No Escape from Life* by John Sutherland Bonnell, copyright © 1958 by John Sutherland Bonnell; and 'The Ethics of Reverence for Life' from Vol. 1, No. 2 of *Christendom* by Albert Schweitzer, copyright 1936 by Willett, Clark and Co.

Harper & Row, Publishers and Hodder & Stoughton, Ltd, for 'Indifference' from *The Sorrows of God* by G. A. Studdert Kennedy. Copyright 1924 by Harper & Brothers. Renewed 1952 by Emily Studdert Kennedy.

Harper & Row, Publishers and SCM Press Ltd, for material from *The Meaning of Persons* by Paul Tournier.

Harvard University Press, for material from *Living Again* by Charles Reynold Brown.

Elmer G. Homrighausen, for material from 'Faith – the Knowledge Grown Confident,' originally published in *The Christian Herald*.

Herbert Hoover Foundation, for 'I See No Doom Down an Alley' by Herbert Hoover, originally published in *This I Believe*, edited by Edward P. Morgan, published by Simon & Schuster, Inc.

Houghton Mifflin Company, for material from *Forty Years for Labrador* by Sir Wilfred Grenfell.

Leonard C. Hudson and Joe D. Batten, for material from *Dare to Live Passionately* by Leonard C. Hudson and Joe D. Batten.

Elizabeth Kunkel, for material from *Creation Continues* by Fritz Kunkel.

Adelaide Love, for her poem, 'A Mother's Prayer.'

McGraw-Hill Book Company, for material from *Mine Eyes Have Seen* by Daniel A. Poling.

The Macmillan Company, for material from *When Life Gets Hard* by James Gordon Gilkey, copyright 1945 by The Macmillan Company; and *The Radiant Life* by Rufus M. Jones, copyright 1944 by The Macmillan Company.

The Macmillan Company and A. C. Black, Ltd, for material from *The Philosophy of Civilization*, Part Two, by Albert Schweitzer.

The Macmillan Company and William Heinemann, Ltd, for material from *The Brothers Karamazov* by Fyodor Dostoevsky, translated by Constance Garnett.

The Macmillan Company, Macmillan & Co Ltd, and The Trustees of the Tagore Estate, and Macmillan and Co of Canada, Ltd, for material from *Personality* and from *Collected Poems and Prayers* by Rabindranath Tagore.

The Macmillan Company and The Society of Authors as literary representatives of the Estate of John Masefield, for an extract from *Saturday Review* and for one line from 'The Widow in the Bye Street,' copyright 1912 by The Macmillan Company, copyright 1940 by John Masefield, from *Poems* by John Masefield.

Macmillan & Co Ltd, for material from Henri Amiel's *Journal*, translated by Mrs Humphrey Ward.

Virgil Markham, for five poems by Edwin Markham.

Joan M. Mills and *Reader's Digest*, for 'Good-by, Childhood' by Joan Mills. Copyright 1968 by the Reader's Digest Association, Inc, from the May 1968 *Reader's Digest*.

Raymond Moley, for material he wrote on Herbert Hoover, for *Newsweek*, November 7, 1964.

Harold Ober Associates, for 'The Angry Sinner' by Leon Ware. Copyright 1953 by Leon Ware.

The Open Church Foundation, for 'Slow Me Down, Lord' by Orin L. Crain.

Mrs Reginald Orcutt, for material from *The Conquest of Fear* by Basil King.

Fulton Oursler, Jr, for 'The Nightmare' from *Light Along the Shore* by Fulton Oursler.

Bonaro W. Overstreet, for her material from *This I Believe*, edited by Edward P. Morgan, published by Simon & Schuster, Inc.

Helen Channing Pollock, for material from 'Shining Armor' by Channing Pollock.

Prentice-Hall, Inc, for material from *Prayer Can Change Your Life* by William R. Parker and Elaine St Johns Dare, copyright © 1957 by William R. Parker and Elaine St Johns Dare; *The Success System That Never Fails* by W. Clement Stone, copyright © 1962 by Prentice-Hall, Inc; *Live at Peace with Your Nerves* by Walter C. Alvarez, MD, copyright © 1958 by Walter C. Alvarez, MD; *Now or Never – The Promise of the Middle Years* by Smiley Blanton and Arthur Gordon, copyright © 1959 by Smiley Blanton and Arthur Gordon; *Let Go and Let God* by Albert E. Cliffe, copyright 1951 by Albert E. Cliffe; *How I Raised Myself from Failure to Success in Selling* by Frank Béttger, copyright 1949 by Prentice-Hall, Inc; and *How to Live 365 Days a Year* by John A. Schindler, MD.

Prentice-Hall, Inc and The Updegraff Press Ltd, for material from *Try Giving Yourself Away* by David Dunn. Copyright © 1965 by Prentice-Hall, Inc.

Reader's Digest, for 'The Bible's Timeless – and Timely – Insights' by Smiley Blanton, MD, copyright © 1966 by the Reader's Digest Association, Inc, from the August 1966 *Reader's Digest*; 'A Gift from the Heart' by Norman Vincent Peale, copyright © 1967 by the Reader's Digest Association, Inc, from the January 1968 *Reader's Digest*; and 'Prayer Is Power' by Alexis Carrel, MD, copyright 1941 by the Reader's Digest Association, Inc, from the March 1941 *Reader's Digest*.

Henry Regnery Company, for material from *Collected Verse* by Edgar A. Guest.

Fleming H. Revell Company, for material from *Turbulent World, Tranquil God* by Reuben K. Youngdahl; *God's Psychiatry* by Charles L. Allen; and *It Will Be Daybreak Soon* by Archibald Rutledge.

Fleming H. Revell Company and the Lutterworth Press, for material from *Prayer, the Mightiest Force in the World* by Frank C. Laubach.

Fleming H. Revell Company and Peter Davies Ltd, for material from *Mr Jones, Meet the Master* by Peter Marshall.

Fleming H. Revell Company and Marshall, Morgan and Scott, Ltd, for material from *Prayer Changes Things* by Charles L. Allen.

Fleming H. Revell Company and James Clark & Co, Ltd, for material from *Passion for Souls* by John Henry Jowett.

Mrs J. P. Scott, for 'Oh, Close My Hand upon Beatitude' by Dorothy Canfield Fisher.

Charles Scribner's Sons, for 'Bedtime', copyright 1914 by Charles Scribner's Sons; renewal copyright 1942 by Tertius van Dyke, from *Grand Canyon and Other Poems* by Henry van Dyke, and for 'Four Things' from *The Builders* by Henry van Dyke.

Charles Scribner's Sons and The Cresset Press, for material from *My Host the World* by George Santayana. Copyright 1953 by Charles Scribner's Sons.

Charles Scribner's Sons and the SCM Press, Ltd, for material from *The New Being* by Paul Tillich. Copyright 1955 by Paul Tillich.

Simon & Schuster, Inc and Laurence Pollinger Limited, for material from *Love or Perish* by Smiley Blanton, M.O. Copyright © 1955, 1956 by Smiley Blanton.

Vincent Stuart and J. M. Watkins, Ltd, for material from *Meister Eckhart* translated by Franz Pfeiffer.

Elizabeth Gray Vining, for her material from *This I Believe*, edited by Edward P. Morgan, published by Simon & Schuster, Inc.

Ralph L. Woods, for 'The Atheist Who Went to the Mountain.'

Contents

Introduction

It is my sincere hope that this book will inspire you and lift your spirit. Getting these many fascinating items together in this anthology has done that for me, and I trust that reading them will do the same for you. The power of great thoughts to quicken and motivate one's life is incalculable.

I should like to begin this book with an appropriate thought from Dr Preston Bradley, an old friend and a distinguished minister in the city of Chicago.

Grace Before Reading a Book

Eternal Father, as we open the pages of this book we have chosen to read, we would express our gratitude for all the noble thoughts which the mind of man has given to the world.

We are grateful for the opportunity afforded us by good books to become companions of great minds and hearts. May we keep our minds always open and receptive to truth and beauty, knowing that these finally are manifested in our character.

May we treat this book as we respect and admire a friend. May we always choose for our reading moments books which will elevate our hearts, ennoble our minds, and lift our spirits.

For all the good things which come our way, we are grateful and, most of all, dear Father, may we be worthy of them. Amen.

For years I and my associates have been compiling lists of books in which dedicated and inspired writers present thoughts and experiences with which everyone can identify and thereby gain insight, strength, and guidance. Everyone should really have his own library of spiritual, inspirational, and self-help books. If you faithfully read and study such books until they become a part of you, the help that comes will give you courage, confidence, and the power to live more victoriously.

One of the most victorious men, spiritually and in every way, I have ever known was my friend, the late Ely Perry of Kinston, North Carolina. He never ceased to amaze me by his insights, his depth of understanding, and his zest for life. I found his secret when I visited his home and saw there the most comprehensive spiritual and in-spirational library I have ever seen in a private collection. Moreover, that he knew every book intimately was clearly evident, for each one was filled with notations on the margins. 'I use a book as a tool to grow myself bigger and I lend them out to help other people,' he explained. He gave away hundreds of pocket copies of Henry Drummond's classic, *The Greatest Thing in the World*. Ely Perry was a shining example of the astonishing development of personality that can come through the help of books.

And then, of course, there is poetry, little read today in comparison with earlier years. Dr Smiley Blanton, one of America's greatest psychiatrists, wrote a charming book on *The Healing Power of Poetry*. He found, in his work with patients, that emotional troubles could be helped by the healing properties in great poetry.

To a large extent our lives are made by thoughts and ideas. We become finally what we think. Over the years the things we read and hear and hold in our thoughts condition our minds and ultimately our lives. If we put into consciousness that which inspires and uplifts, it stands to reason that we shall tend to become inspired and uplifted persons. If, on the contrary, we saturate the mind with inferior and tawdry material the total effect will very likely be in kind. And the choice, as it should be, is our own. We determine the type of thing we shall feed to our minds, thereby affecting the nature of the personality.

This, of course, is not intended to imply that the modern person should read only that which is high minded and of an idealistic nature. The citizen of the world must know what goes on in the world. He should not be unaware of the varying types of thought and action which might be contrasted as evil with good. He cannot, as the saying is, be 'out of it'. But, because he must be cognizant of these elements, it does not mean he must paper his mind with them. Indeed, their very existence is all the more reason he should furbish his mind with the best thoughts of the greatest minds. Such mental and spiritual decoration will, we might hope, assist the individual not only to enjoy the beautiful things of this world but also to become a salutary influence in the gradual improvement of mankind's existence. For the kind of ideas people have determine people, and the kind of people we have determines the kind of world we have.

My mother literally read everything she could get her hands on. Indeed, I have never known a more voracious and thorough reader. Her reading covered the whole spectrum of literary interests: poetry, history, essays, short stories, fiction, non-fiction. She finished one book only to reach for the next one. She devoured magazines. She was, I am sure, easily one of the best-read persons in her area of western

Ohio, and her facility in conversation covering a wide range of subjects was remarkable. Her books were marked and marked again, and any sentence that was good was underscored. It had to be good to be thus emphasized, for her discrimination was acute. She could recite reams of poetry. She had a photographic memory and could read a page of prose and repeat it almost verbatim. She loved to share what she read. Excitedly, she would exclaim, 'Just listen to this,' and she would read it with gusto. She was always pretty low on money but as much as she could spare went for good books because she said, 'I want my children to be surrounded with the best things ever written. Maybe some of it will lodge in their minds and stay with them always to add to their lives.'

How I wish she might have compiled this anthology. What a rich mine of inspiring, stimulating material it would have been. She was a thinker; she might even be called a natural-born philosopher, a person who loved to deal with ideas and who dealt with them expertly and sensitively.

In a sense this *is* my mother's anthology, for it was she who introduced me to some of the writers quoted in this book. Much of the prose and poetry and not a few of the quotations which appear on these pages came to me from her, and I hope to pass them down to my children, for they are, I believe, priceless bits of truth.

Upon deciding to assemble an anthology to be called *Courage and Confidence*, I found enough material for several such books. I had to become highly selective, with the result that what I chose for this book really seems to me the best, although there is other excellent material that I could not include for lack of space.

Because a book must have some semblance of order, I divided the material into twelve categories. Some of it fell readily under a designated subject, but some didn't. So, standing before a table with twelve piles of material, I dropped some pieces at random into one pile or another. If, therefore, in a chapter you encounter an item that seems to have no particular relevance to the subject of that chapter, just say, 'Oh, that's one of those things he didn't know what to do with.' You see, I have included some things just because they are beautiful or important in themselves and so become relevant.

There is a real and definitive purpose in preparing this collection, and the material has been carefully selected and organized for the distinct purpose of helping the reader along twelve lines of thought which I believe cover the basic problems of most of us.

There are various ways in which such a book as this may be used most profitably. One way is to pick it up and leaf through it at random, reading such pieces as may strike your fancy, especially the short items. This tidbit method may serve to bring you some interesting, perhaps helpful, thoughts and is not to be disparaged. It is not, however, the most productive way to make use of the book.

Another method, one of a more substantial nature, is to begin with this introduction and read the book straight through, taking as much per reading as time and inclination allow. This is a more inclusive and efficient way to master any book, and it has the added advantage of permitting the reader to judge which parts seem of greatest value and to which he may later return for more intensive study.

There is yet another method of using this collection, and that is to regulate your reading by the chapter headings, applying the book to the particular need which you may feel at a given moment. But this method need not rule out either of the above-mentioned usages. In fact, the three reading methods referred to are all of value, though the first would seem to be more superficial than the other two which are suggested.

This anthology was prepared to be of practical service to the reader, and to go beyond the intellectual pleasure of reading for reading's sake. Its deeper purpose is to help overcome anxiety, to assist living with peace of mind, and to provide a source of courage and faith. It is designed to help one to get outside the narrow confines of his own prejudices and personal interests, and to become a participant in the affairs of men, to join with others in creating a better way of life for everyone.

It is hoped that the book may serve not only as a stimulant to activate the mind creatively, but also as an instrument to deepen the spiritual life. There is a definite golden thread of faith in God running through the material incorporated in this volume. This emphasis is deemed vital to the good life on earth. And it is a treasury of courage and confidence because it is first a treasury of faith.

NORMAN VINCENT PEALE

P.S. If you would like more of the philosophy and technique of living suggested in Norman Vincent Peale's *Courage and Confidence*, you might be interested in receiving monthly my inspirational messages in *PLUS: The Magazine of Positive Thinking*. To receive a sample copy, you have only to write to the Foundation for Christian Living, P.O. Box FCL, Pawling, New York 12564, U.S.A.

Chapter 1

How to Achieve Your Goals

To experience the satisfaction and enjoyment of success in life, a definitive goal is essential. Many people fail at this vital point. The goal must be definite and specific, not in any sense vague or fuzzy. And to prove attainable, its image needs to be sharpened and re-sharpened continually, so that it stands out vividly in your thoughts. You must know, at all times, precisely and for certain what it is you want to accomplish and achieve. Strong and organized purposefulness towards a definite objective will focus your powers into a strong motivation in attainment of your goal.

A frustrated young man once consulted me about his repeated failures. 'Success completely eludes me. I want to get somewhere,' he said rather dully.

'Good,' I replied, 'and exactly where do you want to get?'

His reply was a masterpiece of inconclusiveness: 'Well, I don't know for sure; never figured that one out. But I'm not happy the way it is. I think I'm entitled to a better break. I want to get somewhere.'

'Well, what can you do the best? What particular skills or leaning toward certain abilities do you possess? What do you think you're cut out for?'

He pondered this question. 'I don't believe I have any particular skills. In fact, I have no idea what I'm cut out for or what I can do the best. Never thought of it.'

I tried again. 'Let me ask you, what would you like to do? If you were told you could have any job you wanted or any achievement, what would you choose? Tell me, just what do you want to do?'

Again a vagueness and a lack of direction were revealed. 'I can't tell you. Really, I just don't know what I like best,' he replied sort of desperately. 'It never occurred to me to ask myself questions like these. I just take the next job that comes along. And I haven't liked any of them very much, to tell you the truth.'

'But yet you want to get somewhere?'

He nodded. It was obvious that a minor motivation, though not a very strong one, was working within this apathetic person; but it lacked cohesion, sharpness, objectivity. I said, 'You want to get somewhere, but you don't know just where. And you don't know what you like to do or what you can do best. Look – you must fix on a goal, then sharpen and clarify it. Hold it in your conscious mind until it sinks by a process of intellectual and spiritual osmosis into your subconscious. Then you will have it because it will have you, all of you. You will begin to move toward that goal on a direct road; not to a vague "somewhere", but to a definitive, specific objective.'

This defeated man did begin moving toward the accomplishment of specific goals. His personality fused into a driving force that pushed him forward when he learned to know what he wanted from life.

To definiteness of goal must, of course, be added enthusiasm, persistence, and hard work. These will be dealt with in another chapter. But perhaps more important than all else is spiritual guidance, from which one derives those deeper insights which are so necessary in reaching goals.

Let me tell you about one of my favorite personalities, whose life teaches pre-eminently how to reach goals.

I met one of the world's great positive thinkers in the wilderness of Judea, where, in the long ago, John the Baptist preached. His name is Musa Alami and he has made the desert to blossom as the rose – a desert that in all the history of the world had never blossomed before. He succeeded because he believed that he could, and he kept at it until he did, which, of course, is the way you succeed at anything.

Musa, an Arab boy, was educated at Cambridge, went back to Palestine where he became a well-to-do man – well-to-do, that is, by Middle Eastern standards. Then, in political turmoil, he lost everything, including his home.

He went beyond Jordan to the edge of Jericho. Stretching away on either side was the great, bleak, arid desert of the Jordan valley. In the distance to the left, shimmering in the hot haze, loomed the mountains of Judea, and to the right the mountains of Moab.

With the exception of a few oases, nothing had ever been cultivated in this hot and weary land, and everyone said that nothing could be, for how could you bring water to it? To dam the Jordan River for irrigation was too expensive and, besides, there was no money to finance such a project.

'What about underground water?' asked Musa Alami. Long and loud they laughed. Whoever heard of such a thing? There was no water under that hot, dry desert. Ages ago it had been covered by Dead Sea water; now the sand was full of salt, which added further to the aridity.

He had heard of the amazing rehabilitation of the California desert through subsurface water. He decided that he could find water here also. All the old-time Bedouin sheiks said it couldn't be done; government officials agreed, and so, solemnly, did the famous scientists from abroad. There was absolutely no water there. That was that.

But Musa was unimpressed. He thought there was. A few poverty-stricken refugees from the nearby Jericho Refugee Camp helped him as he started to dig. With well-drilling equipment? Not on your life. With pick and shovel. Everybody laughed as this dauntless man and his ragged friends dug away day after day, week after week, month after month. Down they went, slowly, deep into the sand into which no man since creation had plumbed for water.

For six months they dug; then one day the sand became wet and finally water, life-giving water, gushed forth. The Arabs who had gathered round did not laugh or cheer; they wept. Water had been found in the ancient desert!

A very old man, sheik of a nearby village, heard the amazing news. He came to see for himself. 'Musa,' he asked, 'have you really found water? Let me see it and feel it and taste it.'

The old man put his hand in the stream, splashed it over his face, put it on his tongue. 'It is sweet and cool,' he said. 'It is good water.' Then, placing his aged hands on the shoulders of Musa Alami, he said, 'Thank God. Now, Musa, you can die.' It was the simple tribute of a desert man to a positive thinker who did what everyone said could not be done.

Now, several years later, Musa Alami has fifteen wells supplying a ranch nearly three miles long and two miles wide. He raises vegetables, bananas, figs, citrus fruit, and boys. In his school he is growing citizens of the future, farmers and technicians, experts in the trades. Imitating Musa, others have also dug until forty thousand acres are under cultivation and the green is spreading over the sands.

I asked this amazing man what kept him going, kept him believing when everyone said it couldn't be done. 'There was no alternative. It had to be done,' he said, then added, 'God helped me.'

As twilight turned the mountains of Moab and the Judean hills to red and gold, I sat watching a huge stream of water gush from the heart of the desert. And as it splashed into a deep, wide pool, it seemed to say, 'It can be done, it can be done!' So, don't let your difficulties get you down and do not believe those croakers who say you cannot do it. Remember Musa Alami, positive thinker of the wilderness of Judea.

It seems that work and more work are important in achieving goals.

O Lord, thou givest us everything, at the price of an effort.

LEONARDO DA VINCI

Some more on work:

There is a perennial nobleness, and even sacredness, in work. Were a man ever so benighted, or forgetful of his high calling, there is always hope in him who actually and earnestly works; in idleness alone is there perpetual despair. Consider how, even in the meanest sort of labor, the whole soul of a man is composed into real harmony. He bends himself with free valor against his task; and doubt, desire, sorrow, remorse, indignation, despair itself, shrink murmuring, far off into their caves. The glow of labor in him is a purifying fire, wherein all poison is burnt up; and of smoke itself there is made a bright and blessed flame.

Blessed is he who has found his work; let him ask no other blessedness; he has a life purpose. Labor is life. From the heart of the worker rises the celestial force, breathed into him by Almighty God, awakening him to all nobleness, to all knowledge. Has thou valued patience, courage, openness to light, or readiness to own thy mistakes? In wrestling with the dim, brute powers of Fact, thou wilt continually learn. For every noble work, the possibilities are diffused through immensity – undiscoverable, except to Faith.

Man, son of Heaven! is there not in thine inmost heart a spirit of active method, giving thee no rest till thou unfold it? Complain not. Look up, wearied brother. See thy fellow-workmen surviving through eternity – the sacred band of immortals!

THOMAS CARLYLE

And motivation helps also!

I was six years old and scared. Selling newspapers on Chicago's tough South Side wasn't easy, especially with the older kids taking over the busy corners, yelling louder, and threatening me with clenched fists. The memory of those dim days is still with me, for it's the first time I can recall turning a disadvantage into an advantage. It's a simple story, unimportant now . . . and yet it was a beginning.

Hoelle's Restaurant was near the corner where I tried to work, and it gave me an idea. It was a busy and prosperous place that presented a frightening aspect to a child of six. I was nervous, but I walked in hurriedly and made a lucky sale at the first table. Then diners at the second and third tables bought papers. When I started for the fourth, however, Mr Hoelle pushed me out the front door.

But I had sold three papers. So when Mr Hoelle wasn't looking, I walked back in and called at the fourth table. Apparently, the jovial customer liked my gumption; he paid for the paper and gave me an extra dime before Mr Hoelle pushed me out once again. But I had.

already sold four papers and got a 'bonus' dime besides. I walked into the restaurant and started selling again. There was a lot of laughter. The customers were enjoying the show. One whispered loudly, 'Let him be,' as Mr Hoelle came toward me. About five minutes later, I had sold all my papers.

The next evening I went back. Mr Hoelle again ushered me out the front door. But when I walked right back in, he threw his hands in the air and exclaimed, 'What's the use!' Later, we became great friends, and I never had trouble selling papers there again.

Years later, I used to think of that little boy, almost as if he were not me but some strange friend from long ago. Once, after I had made my fortune and was head of a large insurance empire, I analyzed that boy's actions in the light of what I had learned. This is what I concluded:

1. He needed the money. The newspapers would be worthless to him if they weren't sold; he couldn't even read them. The few pennies he had borrowed to buy them would also be lost. To a six-year-old, this catastrophe was enough to motivate him – to make him keep trying. Thus, he had the necessary inspiration to action.

2. After his first success in selling three papers in the restaurant, he went back in, even though he knew he might be embarrassed and thrown out again. After three trips in and out, he had the necessary technique for selling papers in restaurants. Thus, he gained the know-how.

3. He knew what to say, because he had heard the older kids yelling out the headlines. All he had to do, when he approached a prospective customer, was to repeat in a softer voice what he had heard. Thus, he possessed the requisite activity knowledge.

I smiled as I realized that my 'little friend' had become successful as a newsboy by using the same techniques that later flowered into a system for success that enabled him, and others, to amass fortunes. But I'm getting ahead of myself. For now, just remember those three phrases: inspiration to action, know-how, and activity knowledge. They are the keys to the system.

W. CLEMENT STONE

Do your best. There is no goal achieved better than that.

TRUE NOBILITY

Who does his task from day to day
And meets whatever comes his way,
Believing God has willed it so,
Has found real greatness here below.

Who guards his post, no matter where,
Believing God must need him there,
Although but lowly toil it be,
Has risen to nobility.

For great and low there's but one test:
'Tis that each man shall do his best.
Who works with all the strength he can
Shall never die in debt to man.

EDGAR A. GUEST

Know where you are going.

The great thing in the world is not so much where we stand, as in what direction we are moving.

OLIVER WENDELL HOLMES

Tough-mindedness is a good achiever.

The only way that we can truly build deep, sustaining confidence is to test and practice the use of the principles of tough-minded living on real problems. We can sit in a library and read every book that exists on positive thinking or on tough-minded living or on problem-solving and this will do us very little good until we encounter problems; just as the weight lifter, just as the would-be body-builder will develop no muscle at all by simply sitting and looking at a set of bar bells; just as the would-be singer can gain nothing by simply studying music and never exercising the voice. In just this way, we cannot add to this toughness and the strength of our minds by simply reading about what we should do until we are faced with some taxing, stretching requirements to develop this new muscle of the mind. Again, let me use the example of the athlete; the man who wants to be a good pole vaulter, who stands and contemplates that high bar, sets it at about ten feet, grips his bamboo pole and then stands there in the sun and reads all the material he can find about pole vaulting – this man will never get over that bar. If he's a beginner and he sets that bar up there at ten feet, he'll probably knock it off dozens and dozens of times. But only in that way will he build up the proper muscle, the proper co-ordination, the proper confidence to ultimately clear that bar.

For this precise reason, then, we must seek out problems and convert them to challenges! We need to welcome problems with arms open. Embrace them because this can well be some of the finest parts of living. Many older people look back on the years they spent wondering how they would meet the expenses of raising a family, coping with the problems, the illnesses – in some instances the vexations of their children – they look back now and think 'those were the most developmental, the most rewarding, the most wonderful years of my life. If I could only have recognized it then.'

What they're saying, in effect, is, that they should have welcomed problems. Encountering a steady stream of problems day after day made their lives warm and meaningful. It gave them confidence. It helped insure that their later years would be years of serenity. Welcome problems, reach out for them, charge into them and convert them in your mind immediately to challenges. The negative way to look at a problem is to think of it as a problem. Search it out, isolate it as a problem, then in your mind convert it to a challenge, determine the steps that you will need to surmount it just as the pole vaulter needs to first determine steps and then work at it. Only in this way do you develop the skill, the co-ordination, the mind, the muscle and the confidence to really get it done.

JOE D. BATTEN AND LEONARD C. HUDSON

Never give up on the strenuous life.

I wish to preach not the doctrine of ignoble ease but the doctrine of the strenuous life; the life of toil and effort; of labor and strife; to preach that highest form of success which comes not to the man who desires mere easy peace but to the man who does not shrink from danger, from hardship, or from bitter toil, and who out of these wins the splendid ultimate triumph.

No country can long endure if its foundations are not laid deep in the material prosperity which comes from thrift, from business energy and enterprise, from hard unsparing effort in the fields of industrial activity; but neither was any nation ever yet truly great if it relied upon material prosperity alone. All honor must be paid to the architects of our material prosperity; . . . But our debt is yet greater to the men whose highest type is to be found in a statesman like Lincoln, a soldier like Grant. They showed by their lives that they recognized the law of work, law of strife; they toiled to win a competence for themselves and those dependent upon them; but they recognized that there were yet other and even loftier duties – duties to the nation and duties to the race.

I preach to you, then, my countrymen, that our country calls not for the life of ease, but for the life of strenuous endeavor. Let us therefore boldly face the life of strife, resolute to do our duty well and manfully; resolute to uphold righteousness by deed and by word;

resolute to be both honest and brave, to serve high ideals, yet to use practical methods. Above all, let us shrink from no strife, moral or physical, within or without the nation, provided we are certain that the strife is justified; for it is only through strife, through hard and dangerous endeavor, that we shall ultimately win the goal of true national greatness.

THEODORE ROOSEVELT

Each object overcome is one less on your way. Check them off one by one.

> Success is to be measured not so much
> by the position that one has reached
> in life as by the obstacles which he has
> overcome while trying to succeed.
>
> BOOKER T. WASHINGTON

Good use of time is important too.

Time is the inexplicable raw material of everything. With it, all is possible; without it, nothing. The supply of time is truly a daily miracle, an affair genuinely astonishing when one examines it.

You wake up in the morning, and lo! your purse is magically filled with twenty-four hours of the unmanufactured tissue of the universe of your life! It is yours. It is the most precious of possessions. . . . No one can take it from you. It is unstealable. And no one receives either more or less than you receive.

In the realm of time there is no aristocracy of wealth, and no aristocracy of intellect. Genius is never rewarded by even an extra hour a day. And there is no punishment. Waste your infinitely precious commodity as much as you will, and the supply will never be withheld from you. . . . Moreover, you cannot draw on the future. Impossible to get into debt! You can only waste the passing moment. You cannot waste tomorrow; it is kept for you. You cannot waste the next hour; it is kept for you.

I have said the affair was a miracle. Is it not?

You have to live on this twenty-four hours of daily time. Out of it you have to spin health, pleasure, money, content, respect, and the evolution of your immortal soul. Its right use, its most effective use, is a matter of the highest urgency and of the most thrilling actuality. All depends on that. Your happiness – the elusive prize that you are all clutching for, my friends – depends on that.

If one cannot arrange that an income of twenty-four hours a day shall exactly cover all proper items of expenditure, one does muddle one's whole life indefinitely.

We shall never have any more time. We have, and we have always had, all the time there is.

ARNOLD BENNETT

Nothing will ever be attempted if all possible objections must first be removed.

SAMUEL JOHNSON

And so is faith important.

If ye have faith as a grain of mustard seed, ye shall say unto this mountain, Remove hence to yonder place; and it shall remove: and nothing shall be impossible unto you.

MATTHEW 17: 20

Make the most of yourself, for that is all there is to you.

RALPH WALDO EMERSON

And stay in there fighting.

It is not the critic who counts; not the man who points out how the strong man stumbled, or where the doer of deeds could have done better. The credit belongs to the man who is actually in the arena; whose face is marred by dust and sweat and blood; who strives valiantly; who errs and comes short again and again; who knows the great enthusiasms, the great devotions, and spends himself in a worthy cause; who at the best knows in the end the triumph of high achievement; and who at the worst, if he fails, at least fails while daring greatly; so that his place shall never be with those cold and timid souls who know neither victory nor defeat.

THEODORE ROOSEVELT

Appropriate for a poet, the best advice I ever had came to me in the form of a sententious little quatrain. It has been of inestimable value to me, and, so I have been told, to hundreds of others to whom I have passed it on.

I was only seventeen or eighteen. I had quit my life as a seaman and was working in a carpet factory in Yonkers, New York, while trying to learn to write. Having just read Keats and Shelley for the first time, I was on fire to be a poet, but, as everyone knows who has tried to compose a poem, the new task I had set myself was far more difficult than climbing masts or painting decks. I had almost despaired when I came upon this homespun sentiment:

> Sitting still and wishing
> Makes no person great.
> The good Lord sends the fishing,
> But you must dig the bait.

This easily remembered stanza somehow gave me the courage I needed to go on. I dug bait for months – and finally caught a publisher who accepted my first poem.

JOHN MASEFIELD

What a word is persistence, and how terribly necessary!

PERSISTENCE

> Nothing in the world
> can take the place of persistence.
> Talent will not;
> nothing is more common than
> unsuccessful men with talent.
> Genius will not;
> unrewarded genius is almost a proverb.
> Education will not;
> the world is full of educated derelicts.
> Persistence and determination
> alone are omnipotent.
> The slogan 'Press On' has solved
> and always will solve
> the problems of the human race.

CALVIN COOLIDGE

Instead of saying that man is the creature of circumstances, say that man is the architect of circumstances.

THOMAS CARLYLE

TWO WAYS

> To every soul there openeth
> A high way and a low;
> The high soul climbs the high way
> The low soul gropes the low,
> And in between, on the misty flats,
> The rest drift to and fro.

> To every soul there openeth
> A high way and a low;
> And every man decideth
> Which way his soul shall go.
>
> JOHN OXENHAM

Get your thinking in order.

Nurture great thoughts for you will never go higher than your thoughts.

BENJAMIN DISRAELI

Be sure your goal is a right one, for if it isn't, it's a wrong one, and nothing wrong ever turns out right.

Beware of what you want for you will get it.

RALPH WALDO EMERSON

Don't do things the wrong way. Learn the right way. It's easier because it's right.

Always take hold of things by the smooth handle.

THOMAS JEFFERSON

I can do all things through Christ which strengtheneth me.

PHILIPPIANS 4: 13

This is the basic assurance of two things:

(1) a right goal;
(2) the sustaining strength to accomplish that goal.

There's more in you than you realize.

The kingdom of God is within you.

LUKE 17: 21

Hast thou not known? hast thou not heard, that the everlasting God, the Lord, the Creator of the ends of the earth, fainteth not, neither is weary? there is no searching of his understanding. He giveth power to the faint; and to them that have no might he increaseth strength. Even the youths shall faint and be weary, and the young men shall utterly fall: But they that wait upon the Lord shall renew their strength; they shall mount up with wings as eagles; they shall run, and not be weary; and they shall walk, and not faint.

ISAIAH 40: 28–31

Don't let problems be the main thing.

Shift your emphasis from problems to challenges. The relationship of this concept to tension is very close. When you have problems you worry about them. When you have challenges, you are working, applying and attacking this plan to get results. The shift in thinking from problems to challenges is important in making tension an asset. Don't let your unsolved problems pursue you, make your decisions and forget them, and then do your job as well as you can.

The essential difference between the unhappy, neurotic type person and the happy, normal person is the difference between get and give. The unhappy person is concerned with: the world is against me, what's in it for me, what are people doing to me, and so forth. When your central theme in life is getting you usually do get headaches. But the happy person is looking toward what he can do, what he can give, what he can accomplish.

JOE D. BATTEN AND LEONARD C. HUDSON

Let us, then, try what love will do; for
if men once see we love them, we should
soon find they would not harm us. . . .
Force may subdue, but love gains; and he
that forgives first, wins the laurel.

WILLIAM PENN

Be not simply good; be good for something.

HENRY DAVID THOREAU

Think a dynamic future – work in a dynamic present.

We should all be concerned about the future because we will have to spend the rest of our lives there.

CHARLES F. KETTERING

When you get low in spirit and discouraged, remember this:

The lowest ebb is the turn of the tide.

HENRY WADSWORTH LONGFELLOW

We believe that the power behind us is greater than the task ahead.

MOTTO OVER A CHURCH IN MISSOURI

DUTY

So nigh is grandeur to our dust,
So near is God to man,
When Duty whispers low, 'Thou must,'
The youth replies, 'I can.'

RALPH WALDO EMERSON

Obstacles in the pathway of the weak become stepping stones in the pathway of the strong.

THOMAS CARLYLE

Try hard, real hard, and you'll have a great ally.

To the man who himself strives earnestly, God also lends a helping hand.

AESCHYLUS

Great minds have purposes, others have wishes. Little minds are tamed and subdued by misfortune; but great minds rise above them.

WASHINGTON IRVING

FAILURES

'Tis better to have tried in vain,
Sincerely striving for a goal,
Than to have lived upon the plain
An idle and a timid soul.

'Tis better to have fought and spent
Your courage, missing all applause,
Than to have lived in smug content
And never ventured for a cause.

For he who tries and fails may be
The founder of a better day;
Though never his the victory,
From him shall others learn the way.

EDGAR A. GUEST

A wise man will make more opportunities than he finds.

FRANCIS BACON

THE BUILDERS

All are architects of fate.
    Working in these walls of Time;
Some with massive deed and great,
    Some with ornaments of rhyme.

Nothing useless is, or low;
    Each thing in its place is best;
And what seems but idle show
    Strengthens and supports the rest.

For the structure that we raise,
    Time is with materials filled;
Our todays and yesterdays
    Are the blocks with which we build.

Truly shape and fashion these;
    Leave no yawning gaps between;
Think not, because no man sees,
    Such things will remain unseen.

In the elder days of Art,
    Builders wrought with greatest care
Each minute and unseen part;
    For the gods see everywhere.

Let us do our work as well,
    Both the unseen and the seen;
Make the house where gods may dwell
    Beautiful, entire, and clean,

Else our lives are incomplete
    Standing in these walls of Time,
Broken stairways, where the feet
    Stumble, as they seek to climb.

Build today, then, strong and sure,
    With a firm and ample base;
And ascending and secure
    Shall tomorrow find its place.

Thus alone can we attain
  To those turrets, where the eye
Sees the world as one vast plain,
  And one boundless reach of sky.
          HENRY WADSWORTH LONGFELLOW

Self-confidence is the first requisite to great undertakings.
          SAMUEL JOHNSON

Take a step at a time toward your goal.

The journey of a thousand miles begins with one step.
          LAO-TSE

Chapter 2

Meeting Trouble When It Comes

It is inadvisable to go out, as they say, looking for trouble. For when you make it a point of looking for trouble, you are pretty likely to find it. It will flow to you if it finds you hospitable to it.

David Keppel wrote a little verse years ago:

> Better never trouble trouble
> Until trouble troubles you
> For you only make your trouble
> ' Double trouble when you do
> And your trouble like a bubble
> That you're troubling about
> May be nothing but a cipher
> With the rim rubbed out.

But all pretty philosophy to the contrary notwithstanding, trouble does come and sometimes it seems to come all at once and lots of it. So much so and so true is this that a basic necessity of every human being is assuredly to know how to meet trouble if and when it comes.

Since much trouble in life is self-manufactured, caused not by conditions or by other people but by ourselves, it is wise to condition the mind to the non-production of trouble.

Once, playing golf with Lowell Thomas, he made a statement to me that has lingered in my mind. We were preparing to drive from a tee alongside a deep woods which ran the entire length of the fairway. Just in front was a deep ravine. Lowell turned rather extremely to the left, the woods on his right, but an even fairway to the left of the ravine and addressed the ball.

He drove the ball cleanly away from the woods and safely at the side of the ravine for over two hundred yards. Picking up his tee, he remarked, 'It's always best to shoot away from trouble.'

Some people have more trouble than others simply because they do not shoot away from trouble. They think in terms of trouble, or they are careless, or their acts are not designed wisely, and so they draw trouble to themselves.

Others think positively and conduct themselves in such a manner that they hedge themselves around with fortuitous circumstances and literally beat back trouble. But there is no assurance that trouble will not enter into the life of every man. He must then have resources built into him over long days when things were fortuitous, when favorable winds and smooth seas were kind to the craft of his life.

He who does not prepare for storms when no storms are indicated is lacking in the plain preparatory wisdom required by any rational person. The fact is that storms and troubles will come. They may be delayed, even long delayed, but ultimately they will come. So therefore one must buttress oneself inwardly, prepare oneself in the spirit, condition oneself in the mind, so that when trouble does finally come he´or she will have the equipment and the resources with which to handle it constructively.

For example, a friend, aged forty, began having eye trouble. His doctors sent him to the best specialists in New York. After many examinations and much treatment, he learned the score – he was going blind. Seemingly nothing could arrest the deterioration of his eyes.

He went back to his hotel room thirty stories above the street. Completely depressed, he looked down. In only a matter of seconds his body could hurtle to the street. That would be the end of his trouble. But for years he had built strength into himself, a strength equal to this trouble. He drew upon the wealth of faith he had built up within himself. It was enough. He came out of his depression and adjusted, though he never did regain his sight. In fact, he is one of the best adjusted people I know. He is a truly happy man.

In this chapter we have assembled some thoughts that will help in your own build-up for that time when trouble comes, enough to see you through.

An unknown poet says it well:

> When things gó wrong as they sometimes will,
> When the road you're trudging seems all uphill,
> When the funds are low and the debts are high,
> And you want to smile, but you have to sigh,
>
> When care is pressing you down a bit,
> Rest if you must, but don't you quit.
> Life is queer with its twists and turns,
> As every one of us sometimes learns,
> And many a failure turns about

When he might have won had he stuck it out.
Don't give up though the pace seems slow –
You may succeed with another blow!

Success is failure turned inside out –
The silver tint of the clouds of doubt,
And you never can tell just how close you are,
It may be near when it seems so far.

So stick to the fight when you're hardest hit –
It's when things seem worst that you must not quit.

AUTHOR UNKNOWN

God understands trouble, so talk it over with Him.

May our prayer,–O Christ, awaken all Thy human reminiscences, that we may feel in our hearts the sympathizing Jesus. Thou hast walked this earthly vale and has not forgotten what it is to be tired, what it is to know aching muscles, as Thou didst work long hours at the carpenter's bench. Thou has not forgotten what it is to feel the sharp stabs of pain, or hunger or thirst. Thou knowest what it is to be forgotten, to be lonely. Thou dost remember the feel of hot and scalding tears running down Thy cheeks.

O, we thank Thee that Thou wert willing to come to earth and share with us the weaknesses of the flesh, for now we know that Thou dost understand all that we are ever called upon to bear. We know that Thou, Our God, art still able to do more than we ask or expect. So bless us, each one, not according to our deserving, but according to the riches in glory of Christ Jesus, our Lord. AMEN.

PETER MARSHALL

It's whom you know that determines your strength in trouble.

A professor of English once delivered a brilliant lecture on 'The Literary Excellence of the Twenty-third Psalm' to the Literary Society of the church where he had been brought up as a boy. The old Scots minister, who had been his pastor and teacher in his youth, was the chairman. At the close of the lecture the distinguished speaker asked the old minister to read the psalm. He did so, as he had so often through the years to the members of that congregation, in their sorrows and troubles. A hush followed the heartfelt recital by the white-headed old man. Then the lecturer rose and quietly said, 'I may know the psalm – but he knows the Shepherd.'

JOHN TREVOR DAVIES

The touch of God's hands helps when trouble comes.

During the war a boy was brought into the hospital badly wounded. Word was sent to the mother that the boy was dying. She came to the hospital and begged to see him, but the doctors said that he was just hovering between life and death and that the slightest excitement might kill him. Besides, he was unconscious and would not know her. She promised that she would not speak to him or make the slightest noise, but begged to sit by the side of his bed and be with him. The doctor relented and gave permission for her to sit there without a word. She sat by her boy with her heart bursting. His eyes were closed. She gently put her hand upon his brow. Without opening his eyes the boy whispered, 'Mother, you have come.' The touch of that mother's hand was self-verifying to the boy. He knew it. When Christ puts his hand upon the fevered brow of our souls, we know the meaning of that touch and say from the inmost depths, 'My Saviour, you have come.'

E. STANLEY JONES

I seem to recall an old Russian proverb, 'The hammer shatters glass but forges steel.' So just what trouble does to you depends upon what is in you.

The tests of life are to make, not break us. Trouble may demolish a man's business but build his character. The blow at the outward man may be the greatest blessing to the inner man. If God, then, puts or permits anything hard in our lives, be sure that the real peril, the real trouble, is what we shall lose if we flinch or rebel.

MALTBIE D. BABCOCK

In this old favorite, Kipling gives an answer to trouble.

IF

If you can keep your head when all about you
    Are losing theirs and blaming it on you;
If you can trust yourself when all men doubt you.
    But make allowance for their doubting too;
If you can wait and not be tired by waiting,
    Or being lied about, don't deal in lies,
Or being hated don't give way to hating,
    And yet don't look too good, nor talk too wise;

If you can dream – and not make dreams your master;
    If you can think – and not make thoughts your aim,

If you can meet with Triumph and Disaster
  And treat those two impostors just the same;
If you can bear to hear the truth you've spoken
  Twisted by knaves to make a trap for fools,
Or watch the things you gave your life to, broken,
  And stoop and build 'em up with worn-out tools;

If you can make one heap of all your winnings
  And risk it on one turn of pitch-and-toss,
And lose, and start again at your beginnings
  And never breathe a word about your loss;
If you can force your heart and nerve and sinew
  To serve your turn long after they are gone,
And so hold on when there is nothing in you
  Except the Will which says to them: 'Hold on!'

If you can talk with crowds and keep your virtue,
  Or walk with Kings - nor lose the common touch,
If neither foes nor loving friends can hurt you,
  If all men count with you, but none too much;
If you can fill the unforgiving minute
  With sixty seconds' worth of distance run,
Yours is the Earth and everything that's in it,
  And - which is more - you'll be a Man, my son!
                                        RUDYARD KIPLING

          Two men looked through prison bars -
          One saw mud, the other stars.
                                        AUTHOR UNKNOWN

Wise words from the great Shakespeare:

          Sweet are the uses of adversity;
          Which, like the toad, ugly and venomous,
          Wears yet a precious jewel in his head;
          And this our life, exempt from public haunt,
          Finds tongues in trees, books in the running brooks,
          Sermons in stones, and good in every thing.
                                        WILLIAM SHAKESPEARE

One way to handle trouble is to get busy.

Don't waste life in doubts and fears; spend yourself on the work before you, well assured that the right performance of this hour's duties will be the best preparation for the hours or ages that follow it.

RALPH WALDO EMERSON

Markham has the same idea:

> For all your days prepare,
>   And meet them ever alike:
> When you are the anvil, bear –
>   When you are the hammer, strike.

EDWIN MARKHAM

You can take it – anything.

How powerful is man! He is able to do all that God wishes him to do. He is able to accept all that God sends upon him.

MARCUS AURELIUS

A thrilling story about one man who was able to take it and why:

When the situation looks hopeless, keep hoping. When everything looks impossible, refuse to accept defeat.

I learned this lesson the night I outraced the tornado. I was back home in Iowa only one week after my first year in college. Throughout the afternoon my Dad and I could hear an awesome roar that sounded high in the darkened western sky. It was an eerie sound – like many freight trains rumbling above the clouds. 'Sounds like we're in for a hailstorm,' Dad predicted. He was worried about his prize roses. In a desperate attempt to protect them, we rounded up empty pails and wooden boxes to cover every treasured bush. It was six o'clock now. We had finished our evening meal in haste. From the vantage point of our front lawn we could see more than a mile across the rolling farm land. The sun was lost now, seemingly swallowed by the black monstrous storm that was prowling the western sky. Slowly, with an alarming stillness, like a creeping tiger crawling up on a sleeping prey, the storm crept closer. Gusts of hot wind blew dry dust on the country road. The old box elder began bending before the mounting winds. Out in the pasture I could hear a cow bellow frantically, calling her little calf to come to her side for safety. I could see my riding horse standing in the green pasture. He seemed to sense impending disaster. He cut a commanding picture, standing erect, with his head held high; his graceful neck arched; his tail, lifted slightly blowing wildly in the wind; his ears pricking the air for sounds of danger.

Suddenly a black lump, about the size of the sun, bulged out of the black sky. In an instant it telescoped into a long gray funnel snaking its way down to the ground. For a moment it hung suspended like a slithering serpent about to strike a death sting on helpless victims below. Dad called Mom: 'It's a tornado, Jennie!'

I asked excitedly, 'Are you sure it's a real tornado, Dad?' My first emotion was delightful excitement. This would be something to tell the fellows when I'd return to Hope College in the fall. The funnel seemed so small I couldn't imagine the fury that could be unleashed from such a funny cloud.

'Call Mother, son, and tell her to take whatever she can grab and come to the car. We've got to get out of here – right away!'

A moment later we were driving crazily down the road. We lived on the east end of a dead-end road and had to drive a mile west, directly into the path of the oncoming tornado to reach a side road that would head south and away from the path of the storm. We made it. Two miles south, we parked our car on the crest of the hill and watched the wicked twister spend its killing power. As quickly and quietly as it had dropped, it lifted and disappeared. It was all over. The storm was gone. The air was deathly still, but the danger was past. Gentle raindrops now began to fall. The tail end of the dark sky dropped a soothing shower of cool rain, as if heaven was pouring a soothing balm on fresh wounds.

We could go home now. (Oh, God, will we find our house?) We reached the crossroads, only to find a long line of cars. Curious sightseers, sensing that something terrible had happened, already were gathering. They were looking at the complete destruction of a neighboring farm. Wondering if our house had been spared, we drove down the lonely road that led to our secluded farm. Wires from broken telephone poles crisscrossed the road. We came to the base of the hill that hid the view of our house. We could always see the peak of our barn rise above the hill. But not now. We knew before we went over the hill that our barn was gone. Now we were on the top of the hill. We saw it. Everything was gone. Where only a half hour before there were nine buildings, freshly painted, now there were none. Where there was life, there was the silence of death. It was all gone. It was all dead. We were dazed; our brains reeled. Only white foundations remained, lying on a clean patch of black ground. There was no debris. Everything had simply been sucked up and carried away. A dead pig was lying in the driveway. Three little pigs, still living, sucked the breasts of their dead mother. We could hear the sickening moan of dying cattle, the hiss of gas escaping from a portable tank of butane used to provide fuel for our stove. Then I saw my riding horse – lying dead with a fourteen-foot long two-by-four piercing his belly.

Stunned, we sat in our car. My father was past sixty and had worked hard for twenty-six years to try to win this farm. The mortgage was about due. This seemed to kill all chances of ever saving the place from the creditors. I looked at my dad, sitting horror-eyed in the front seat – my dad, white-haired, underweight from overwork, hands blue, desperately gripping the steering wheel. Suddenly these calloused hands with bulging blood vessels began hitting the steering wheel of the car, and Dad cried, 'It's all gone! Jennie! Jennie, it's all gone! Twenty-six years, Jennie, and it's all gone in ten minutes.' Dad got out of the car, ordering us to wait. We could see him walking with his cane around the clean-swept, tornado-vacuumed farmyard. We found out later our house had been dropped in one smashed piece a half mile out in the pasture. We had a little sign in the kitchen – one of these molded plaster mottoes that you hang on the wall. It was a simple verse that said, 'Keep looking to Jesus.' My dad found and carried to the car the top broken half that said simply: 'Keep looking . . . ' Well, this was God's message to Dad – Keep looking! Keep looking!

Don't quit now. Don't sell out. Dig in and hold on. And he did! People thought that my dad was finished, but he was not. He was not finished because he would not give up. He had faith with hanging-on power! There's one ingredient that mountain-moving faith, miracle-generating faith, earth-shaking faith, problem-solving faith, situation-changing faith must have, and that ingredient is HOLDING power. So Dad didn't quit.

Two weeks later we found in a nearby town an old house that was being torn down. A section of it was still left for sale, for fifty dollars. So we bought this remnant and took it apart, piece by piece. We saved every nail. We saved every shingle. And from these pieces we built a new little house on the old home farm! Piece by piece, additional farm buildings were built. Nine farms were demolished in that tornado, but my father was the only farmer to rebuild a completely demolished farm. A few years later prices rose sharply. Farm products prospered. Within five years the mortgage was paid off. My father died a successful man! 'No man having put his hand to the plow and looking back is fit for the kingdom of God.'

Somebody said:

'Great people are just ordinary people with an extraordinary amount of determination.' Most people who succeed in the face of seemingly impossible conditions are people who simply don't know how to quit.

When unexpected damage wreaks havoc with your dreams, then what? Never dwell on what you have lost. If you do, you will be discouraged and defeated. Look not at what you have lost but at what you have left.

ROBERT H. SCHULLER

Think this one over. When you get that quietness, nothing can upset you.

When he giveth quietness, who then can make trouble?

JOB 34: 29

How many of your troubles never really came?

I am an old man and have known a great many troubles, but most of them never happened.

MARK TWAIN

Many have told me of the rich rewards they have received from a time of illness, suffering, and enforced inactivity. It is a time to think. John Greenleaf Whittier wrote:

> Drop Thy still dews of quietness,
>   Till all our strivings cease;
> Take from our souls the strain and stress,
> And let our ordered lives confess
>   The beauty of Thy peace.

In a time of quietness we have a chance to rest, an opportunity to evaluate life more properly, to develop a sympathy for other people. We learn that the world can keep going without us, and that gives us a wholesome sense of humility. When we are sick we gain some other values, such as a greater appreciation of God's gift of health, and a realization of the higher purposes of life; we lose some of our selfish independence and develop our appreciation of and dependence upon others; we become aware of and thankful for the achievements of medicine and science. Most important of all, sickness can become a time when we develop a stronger faith and become surer of God.

Once there was a woman who was trying to turn on the light in a telephone booth. A passerby said, 'Lady, if you will shut the door, the light will come on.' In a sickroom we can shut the door to the outside world for a time. We are not required to carry on all our daily responsibilities and, in shutting the door, we often experience the light of the Lord coming on.

St Paul wonderfully wrote, 'I am persuaded, that neither death, nor life, nor angels, nor principalities, nor powers, nor things present, nor things to come, Nor height, nor depth, nor any other creature, shall be able to separate us from the love of God, which is in Christ Jesus our Lord' (Romans 8: 38–39). This is his way of saying that no matter what may come, you can still hold on to God and you need never step outside the circle of His love.

In a time of illness and trouble we worry about the things we might lose – especially our chance to live on in this life – but nothing, not even death, can take away from us our most precious possession – the warm, comforting, sustaining love of God. This assurance takes from us the strain and undue worry; it gives us a sense of security and well-being.

George Matheson beautifully wrote:

> There is an Eye that never sleeps,
> Beneath the wind of night.
> There is an Ear that never shuts,
> When sinks the beams of light.
> There is an Arm that never tires,
> When human strength gives way.
> There is a Love that never fails,
> When earthly loves decay.

In a time of illness – a time of helplessness and near-despair – we can lean back easier on that 'arm that never tires' and we find it sufficient. During the last war, someone noted a sign in front of a church in London which said, 'If your knees are shaking, kneel on them.'

One other thought – as we kneel we find the strength to hold on. Emerson said that a man is a hero not because he is braver than anyone else but because he is braver for ten minutes longer. Put your hand in His hand and God will give you the help to keep you brave as long as necessary.

CHARLES L. ALLEN

Difficulties and troubles have their value.

Many men owe the grandeur of their lives to their tremendous difficulties.

CHARLES H. SPURGEON

Storms make oaks take deeper root.

GEORGE HERBERT

The gem cannot be polished without friction, nor man perfected without trials.

CONFUCIUS

Emerson always says it well:

Most of the shadows of this life are caused by standing in one's own sunshine.

RALPH WALDO EMERSON

When it is dark enough, men see the stars.

RALPH WALDO EMERSON

Maybe your trouble came from making a mistake.

The man who does things makes many mistakes, but he never makes the biggest mistake of all – doing nothing.

BENJAMIN FRANKLIN

No matter if everything seems shattered by trouble you can put life together again.

During the war, the rose window in the great Rheims cathedral was shattered into bits by an indirect hit. The parishioners lovingly got down on their hands and knees to gather together all the tiny pieces of broken glass. When the war was over, they hired the most skilled workmen available to rebuild it, piece by piece, from the gathered fragments. Today's rose window in Rheims is more beautiful than it ever was. So God can take our broken lives and reshape them as we pray, 'Lord, please forgive my mistakes of this day.'

REUBEN K. YOUNGDAHL

Did you ever stop to think how successful a failure can be?

The most vital test of a man's character is not how he behaves after success, but how he sustains defeat. The tributes which have appeared on all sides since the passing of Herbert Hoover have noted the massive public service which he contributed to his country and the world since he left the White House in March 1933. He was then a frustrated and indescribably wearied man, after nearly four years of bitter battle against an economic disaster for which even his former enemies now realize he was not responsible. . . .

I remember best a moment when Herbert Hoover rose magnificently above defeat. It was at the Gridiron Club dinner only a month after election. The spirit of that occasion was pregnant with anticipation of a new regime. Almost unrestrained confidence emanated from those who were attached in one way or another to the fortunes of the coming

Administration. But even this Roosevelt orientation was stemmed for the moment by the unforgettable message of the man who had lost.

At this time, nothing could provide a better tribute to the statesman whose life ebbed away two weeks ago than what he said that night in 1932. His first words carried a message of dry humor:

'You will expect me to discuss the late election. Well, as nearly as I can learn, we did not have enough votes on our side. During the campaign I remarked that this Administration had been fighting on a thousand fronts; I learned since the campaign that we were fighting on 21 million fronts.'

He continued: 'I notice in the press a generous suggestion that my countrymen owe to me some debt. I have said in part elsewhere that, on the contrary, the obligation is mine. My country gave me, as it gives every boy and every girl, a chance. It gave me schooling, the precious freedom of equal opportunity for advancement in life, for service and honor. In no other land could a boy from a country village without inheritance or influential friends look forward with un-bounded hope. It gave me a certain measure of success in my profession. It conferred upon me the honor of administering the world's response to the appeal of hundreds of millions of afflicted people during and after the war. It gave me high place in the war councils of the nation. My country called upon me to represent it in the reconstruction of human and economic relations between former enemies on the continent of Europe after the armistice. It gave me an opportunity for service in the Cabinets of two Presidents. It gave me the highest honor that comes to man – the Presidency of the United States. For this fullness of life, for the chance to serve in many emergencies, I am indebted to my country beyond any human power to repay.

'Only a few rare souls in a century, to whose class I make no pretension, count much in the great flow of this Republic. The life stream of this nation is the generations of millions of human particles acting under the impulses of advancing ideas and national ideals gathered from a thousand springs. These springs and rills have gathered into great streams which have nurtured and fertilized this great land over these centuries. Its dikes against dangerous floods are cemented with the blood of our fathers. . . .

'We are but transitory officials in government whose duty is to keep these channels clear and to strengthen and extend these dikes. What counts toward the honor of public officials is that they sustain the national ideals upon which are patterned the design of these channels of progress and the construction of these dikes of safety.'

RAYMOND MOLEY

Trouble makes life bigger if your attitude toward it is a large one.

Defeat may serve as well as victory
To shake the soul and let the glory out.
When the great oak is straining in the wind,
The boughs drink in new beauty and the trunk
Sends down a deeper root on the windward side.
Only the soul that knows the mighty grief
Can know the mighty rapture. Sorrows come
To stretch out spaces in the heart for joy.

EDWIN MARKHAM

Take your troubles to church and leave them there.

The sexton of the big city church was frankly puzzled. Every week for several months he had been finding a sheet of blue-lined notepaper, crumpled into a small wad, lying in a corner of the same rear-row pew.

For some time he had attached no significance to the find; people were always leaving odd things in a church – handbags, spectacle cases, chewing gum. Once he had found a pair of unused theatre tickets for a not quite proper show.

But one Monday morning he smoothed out one of the little wads of paper and read several pencilled words, written one under the other like a shopping list: Clara – ill; Lester – job; Rent.

After that, the sexton began looking for the paper wads. They were always there, after every Sunday morning service. He opened them all and read them. Then he began to watch for the person who sat in that particular corner of the pew.

It was a woman, he discovered – middle-aged, plain but kind-faced, unassuming. She was always alone. The sexton sought out the rector, told him what he had observed, and handed him the collection of note sheets. The rector read the cryptic words with furrowed brow.

On the next Sunday he contrived to greet the woman at the church door as she was leaving, and asked her kindly if she would wait for him a moment in the vestry. In the privacy of that room he showed her the creased pages of blue-lined notepaper, and inquired gently if they had any meaning for the church.

Tears welled in the woman's eyes. She hesitated, then said softly: 'They have meaning for me. You'll think it's silly, I guess – but sometime ago I saw a sign among the advertising posters in a streetcar. It said, "Take your troubles to church with you." My troubles are written on those pieces of paper. I wrote them down during the week and brought them here on Sunday mornings – and left them. I felt that God was taking care of them.'

'God is taking care of them,' the rector said softly, 'and I shall ask Him to keep on doing so. Please continue to bring your troubles here.'

On his way out of the church the rector paused to pick up the freshly wadded note that had been left there that morning. Smoothing it out, he saw that it contained three words: 'John – in Korea.'

GEORGE A. STRALEY

Let God guide when trouble comes. He will never let you down.

God shall be my hope,
My stay, my guide and lantern to my feet.

WILLIAM SHAKESPEARE

Do your duty and leave the rest to Providence.

STONEWALL JACKSON

All troubles end.

Now I want you to think that in life troubles will come, which seem as if they never would pass away. The night and storm look as if they would last forever; but the calm and the morning cannot be stayed; the storm in its very nature is transient. The effort of nature, as that of the human heart, ever is to return to its repose, for God is Peace.

GEORGE MACDONALD

Chapter 3

How to Use the Power of Prayer

The most effective way to make use of the power of prayer is simply to pray. Reading about prayer, discussing prayer, hearing about prayer will bring few results unless you actually pray. To use the power of prayer, pray; pray in depth and pray without ceasing.

I once sat with Madame Chiang Kai-shek and listened in fascination as she recounted the dangers of her life in China. Marveling at her undefeatable spirit, I asked how she managed to retain composure and hope throughout such a difficult life. She said, 'It is the time I spend each morning with the Lord.' I asked her how much time daily she spent in prayer, and she told me it seemed to be from one to two hours every day.

A bit of solace or courage may result from shallow or superficial prayer, but the great continuing power that sustains and strengthens comes from prayer in depth. Some years ago, I had an unforgettable conversation about prayer with the famous singer Roland Hayes. He quoted his aged grandfather, who he said had little formal schooling but was profoundly versed in religious faith. 'Some prayers,' said the wise old man, 'just ain't got no suction. They don't go down deeply enough. They don't take hold.'

This interesting remark brought to mind an old friend, a man supremely knowledgeable in the ways of God, the late Harlowe B. Andrews of Syracuse, New York. 'Pray big prayers,' he advised, 'big prayers that have big faith, big expectation in them.' And he added, 'Think little and you will get little results. So think big, pray big, act big, love big, live big.'

Perhaps the biblical injunction to 'pray without ceasing', which refers to a continuous, earnest, never-let-up form of prayer, may be another way of emphasizing that the immense power of prayer is not lightly come by. Continuous in-depth praying is required to develop power in prayer.

Personally, I owe an enormous debt of gratitude to the famous missionary Frank Laubach for a method of prayer that has greatly enriched my life. It is a practical application of the 'pray without ceasing' principle. The idea is to employ fractional moments during the day for 'quick' prayers. Examples might be a fragmentary prayer while waiting for a bus, a word of prayer while waiting for the party you are telephoning to answer, asking a blessing upon your conversation, brief prayer during a taxi ride or while sitting in an office waiting room. Such prayer fragments add up to a surprising time total.

Still another procedure is that of 'shooting' prayers at apparently worried or unhappy people on the street or bus or in a restaurant. Look for someone who is obviously tired, worried, or unhappy and beam a prayer toward that individual, suggests Dr Laubach. I have often seen such persons react by their faces brightening, by startled glances in my direction, or some other indication that the prayer had in some way reached them. And, of course, the effect upon the person who sends out such 'flash' prayers is bound to be significant.

Practice these procedures and you will increasingly pray so much so that you will secure new power and peace in this atmosphere of prayer. The effect of your prayers upon other people will be incalculable, both to you and to those for whom the prayers are offered.

Anyone who consciously endeavors to discover new uses for the power of prayer will develop spiritually. Joy and strength will come to him and through him to those whose lives he touches.

I have been gathering evidences of the power of prayer for many years, and some are given in this chapter. There are also some splendid expressions concerning the helpfulness of prayer in the practical affairs of daily life. I hope they will be of as much value to you as they have to me.

What is prayer? Here is one answer.

Let this mind be in you, which was also in Christ Jesus.

PHILIPPIANS 2: 5

Prayer works both ways – and it works.

Trouble and perplexity drive us to prayer, and prayer driveth away trouble and perplexity.

PHILIPP MELANCHTHON

I have been driven many times to my knees by the overwhelming conviction that I had nowhere else to go. My own wisdom, and that of all about me seemed insufficient for the day.

ABRAHAM LINCOLN

Lord of Lords, grant us the good whether we pray for it or not, but evil keep from us, even though we pray for it.

PLATO

God warms His hands at man's heart when he prays.

JOHN MASEFIELD

> O Thou by whom we come to God,
> The Life, the Truth, the Way –
> The path of prayer Thyself hath trod,
> Lord, teach us how to pray.

ANONYMOUS

Certain thoughts are prayers. There are moments when, whatever be the attitude of the body, the soul is on its knees.

VICTOR HUGO

There is Something in us, deeper than hands or feet, that finds the way to the Central Reality, and when we arrive we know it.

RUFUS M. JONES

Eleanor Roosevelt always carried the following prayer in her purse:

Our Father, who has set a restlessness in our hearts and made us all seekers after that which we can never fully find . . . keep us at tasks too hard for us, that we may be driven to Thee for strength.

The great spiritual moments in life are when we touch the ultimate – when we feel and know God.

> I, that still pray at morning and at eve,
> Loving those roots that feed us from the past,
> And prizing more than Plato things I learned
> At that best academe, a mother's knee,
> Thrice in my life perhaps have truly prayed,
> Thrice, stirred below my conscious self, have felt
> That perfect disenthrallment which is God;

JAMES RUSSELL LOWELL

And how may we feel Him ? Peter Marshall gives some answers:

All of us need to touch Christ for some reason or other.
As the Church offers this wonderful new life – this peace of mind and heart – this healing of mind and soul and body in Christ's name – perhaps she ought more and more to give instructions with her soul medicine.
You are justified in looking for directions on the lid or some instructions for taking a manual of operation.

Perhaps I can make some suggestions which will be helpful.

First, give God a chance. Take your problem, whatever it may be, to Him in prayer. Tell Him all about it – just as if He didn't know a thing. In the telling be absolutely honest and sincere. Hold nothing back. . . .

Then the second step is to believe that God will hear you. Remember that He heard the poor woman who only touched the hem of His garment. Believe with all your faith that He cares what happens to you. You must believe that. You can't doubt it when you look at the Cross.

Next, you must be willing to wait patiently for the Lord. He does not answer every prayer on Sunday afternoon! You may have to wait until Friday. But wait. God is never in a hurry.

Then when He speaks to you – as He will – do what He tells you. He may not tell you audibly. You may not hear your voices – as did Joan of Arc. You may not see any writing in the sky or have any unusual experience. God could, if He wanted, send you messages in that way, but that is not His usual method.

It generally comes through your own conscience – a sort of growing conviction that such and such a course of action is the one He wants you to take. Or it may be given you in the advice of friends of sound judgment – those who love you most.

God speaks sometimes through our circumstances and guides us, closing doors as well as opening them.

He will let you know what you must do, and what you must be.

He is waiting for you to touch Him.

The hand of faith is enough. Your trembling fingers can reach Him as He passes.

> Reach out your faith – touch Him,
> He will not ask, 'Who touched me?'
> He will know.
>
> PETER MARSHALL

Why should we pray? What good does it do?

In the first place, prayer is a way of increasing our sensitivity to the spiritual aspects of life. From this point of view, it is very much like exercise. A man's muscles become responsive by training. . . . Exercise of any sort enlarges the capacity to understand, to appreciate, to react.

The soul is stretched and enlarged by prayer just as the body is stretched and enlarged by physical exercise. 'O Lord, open my eyes that I may see truth and beauty in all Thy world, and Thy spirit in all things.'

In the second place, prayer is good because it helps us conquer and control our appetites.

And, finally, prayer is a way of aspiration. It is a way of lifting ourselves, of getting a higher look, of transcending self. For when a man looks at life only from inside himself, or only from within the walls of his home, or profession, seeing the world as though it were all in terms of his special interests, then he is 'too full of himself to have any room for God.' But in prayer, he sees life as God sees it, and relates his own little life and his own little needs to the needs and life of humanity. He lifts himself by prayer, and achieves a high spiritual stature.

ROBERT I. KAHN

More things are wrought by prayer
Than this world dreams of. Wherefore let thy voice
Rise like a fountain for me night and day.
For what are men better than sheeps or goats
That nourish a blind life within the brain,
If, knowing God, they lift not hands of prayer
Both for themselves and those who call them friend?
For so the whole round earth is every way
Bound by gold chains about the feet of God.

ALFRED, LORD TENNYSON

Why do we pray? Because we have needs? Yes, of course. But isn't there a deeper reason? May not the desire to pray be that deep inner longing we have as children of God?

Lord, thou madest us for thyself, and we
can find no rest till we find rest in thee.

ST AUGUSTINE

One great thinker says we pray because we cannot help doing so.

We hear in these days of scientific enlightenment a great deal of discussion about the efficacy of *Prayer*. Many reasons are given why we should *not* pray. Others give reasons why we *should* pray. Very little is said of the reason we *do* pray. The reason is simple. We pray because we cannot help praying.

WILLIAM JAMES

Amazing things happen when we pray.

Lord, what a change within us one short hour
Spent in Thy presence will avail to make —

What heavy burdens from our bosom take,
What parched grounds refresh as with a shower!
We kneel, and all around us seems to lower;
We rise, and all, the distant and the near,
Stands forth in sunny outline, brave and clear;
We kneel, how weak; we rise, how full of power!
Why, therefore, should we do ourselves this wrong,
Or others, – that we are not always strong;
That we are overborne with care,
That we should ever weak or heartless be,
Anxious or troubled, when with us is prayer,
And joy and strength and courage are with Thee?

RICHARD TRENCH

Just remember always that God loves you. Talk to Him, knowing of His kindly feelings for you.

Dear Lord! Kind Lord!
Gracious Lord! I pray
Thou wilt look on all I love
Tenderly today!

Weed their hearts of weariness
Scatter every care
Down a wake of angel-wings
Winnowing the air.

And with all the needy
O divide, I pray,
This vast treasure of content
That is mine today.

JAMES WHITCOMB RILEY

A point of view worth pondering:

I have lived to thank God that all my prayers have not been answered.

JEAN INGELOW

Prayer is the soul's sincere desire
Uttered or expressed,
The motion of a hidden fire
That trembles in the breast.

Prayer is the burden of a sigh,
The falling of a tear,
The upward glancing of an eye,
When none but God is near.

Prayer is the simplest form of speech
That infant lips can try,
Prayer, the sublimest strains that reach
The Majesty on high.

O thou by whom we come to God –
The life, the truth, the way –
The path of prayer thyself hast trod,
Lord, teach us how to pray!

JAMES MONTGOMERY

Make prayer a regulative and regular part of your daily life, and it will change things that need changing.

At one time the sculptor, Rodin, was approached by an extremely enthusiastic tourist who had viewed his major works in Paris. 'Oh, Mr Rodin,' she fluttered. 'Is it difficult work to sculpt?'

'Not at all, Madam,' replied the master. 'You simply buy a block of marble and chip away what you don't want.' Simple? Yes! Easy? No!

Each of us must realize that, within our own block of marble, imprisoned by the fogs of our making that hem us in and stand between us and our true Self, stands the Son of God, just as surely as the magnificent statues of Rodin were already complete both within his material and in the mind of the sculptor. The process then is one of freeing this Self which was made in the image and likeness of God. This will not be accomplished overnight for the reasons that our prayer techniques will not be perfected overnight. Demons, doubts, unwanted bits and pieces must be chipped away, sacrificed gladly to Love's healing power through prayer as soon as recognized, until we stand free.

Prayer is simple, yes, but it is not an easy art – except sometimes for little children who are completely trusting. For most of us this most rewarding skill, as with all others, will never be mastered on a hit or miss basis. *Prayer must be made a regular and regulative part of life. . . .*

We must be patient with ourselves if we would master prayer. Dedication and deep desire reinforce our will and carry us through arid periods when prayer does not come easily and we had rather not. If we are tempted to abandon regular prayer in moments when we are feeling fine or, conversely, when inspiration is lacking and we feel we have no talent for it, we can recall the little girl who fell out of bed during the night.

Her mother heard the crash, rushed in alarm and picked her up, crooning sympathy. 'I'm all right, Mommy,' said the child. 'I just fell asleep too close to where I got in.'

We must pray regularly not only to develop skill but so that it becomes a regulative part of our lives and we do not fall asleep too close to where we got in. No psychiatrist or psychologist or any other therapist would expect a patient to be helped if he came to the clinic irregularly or only a few times. Very probably he would dismiss the patient. There is a follow through, a gradual enfoldment, in all therapeutics.

Regular prayer helps one to identify oneself gradually with the spirit of Love – the spirit of Christ – the mind that was in Christ Jesus. It establishes internal controls which begin to give us spontaneously the responses we need. For this reason we must bring as much sincerity as we now possess to our prayers.

By praying regularly the last thing at night before retiring, and the first thing in the morning, always with an emphasis on Love, our prayer power will begin to increase measurably. Even in our present imperfect condition, still in the 'presence of our enemies' – our doubts and demons – we will find we are growing toward that most Holy state which Brother Lawrence called 'the practice of the Presence of God.'

WILLIAM R. PARKER AND ELAINE ST JOHNS DARE

Prayer is more than words. It's listening, seeing, feeling, as well.

VESTIGIA

I took a day to search for God
And found him not. But as I trod
 By rocky ledge, through woods, untamed
 Just where one scarlet lily flamed,
I saw his footprint in the sod.

Then suddenly, all unaware,
Far off in the deep shadows, where
 A solitary hermit thrush
 Sang through the holy twilight-hush –
I heard his voice upon the air.

And even as I marveled how
God gives us heaven here and now,

In a stir of wind that hardly shook
The poplar leaves beside the brook –
    His hand was light upon my brow.

At last with evening I turned
Homeward, and thought what I had learned
    And all that there was still to probe –
    I caught the glory of his robe
Where the last fires of sunset burned.

Back to the world with quickening start
I look and longed for any part
    In making saving beauty be –
    And from that kindling ecstasy
I knew God dwelt within my heart.

                    BLISS CARMAN

A MOTHER'S PRAYER

Lord Jesus, You who bade the children come
And took them in Your gentle arms and smiled,
Grant me unfailing patience through the days
To understand and help my little child.

I would not only give his body care
And guide his young dependent steps along
The wholesome ways, but I would know his heart,
Attuning mine to childhood's griefs and song.

Oh, give me vision to discern the child
Behind whatever he may do or say,
The wise humility to learn from him
The while I strive to teach him day by day.

                    ADELAIDE LOVE

THE ANGRY SINNER

Ben Huckins shifted restlessly in his pew seat. His was an enterprising nature and to have to sit quietly for an hour, without participating, went against the grain. He didn't like any game where he couldn't carry the ball.

His eyes roamed around the church. It was an old building, and there was a crack that started on the wall behind the pulpit and angled up toward the roof. Wouldn't happen today – not if they'd used Huckins Mix. He turned to follow the course of the crack and Evelyn's sharp elbow dug into his ribs.

He didn't understand how she could sit so quietly, her gloved hands in her lap, her pretty head cocked a little as she listened intently to the sermon. She was always happy Sunday morning – getting breakfast, seeing that the boys were cleaned up for Sunday school, dressing herself carefully, getting them all off in time. She always worked on him a little, too, trying to get him to come, but she wasn't successful unless it rained, like today, and his weekly tennis game was canceled.

He settled himself doggedly to listen to the balance of the sermon. The Reverend Paul Burdick was young, but in the two years he'd been pastor he'd made a good impression on the community.

Ben eyed him now, wondering what made a minister. Dr Burdick was a bachelor, big, broad-shouldered, and as tanned as one of Ben's truck drivers.

The sermon ended, the congregation sang a hymn, and Ben got ready to leave. But Dr Burdick had an announcement to make.

'As you know,' he said, smiling, 'I'm taking a month's vacation, but in the meantime, until I return, I hope the congregation will give some thought to what we might do about a youth hut on the piece of land left the church by Mr Harkness.

'Our town sorely needs a meeting place for the young people – for the Boy and Girl Scouts, the various youth organizations. The building wouldn't need to be elaborate, but building costs being what they are, it would probably take a considerable sum. I want to ask you all to join me in a prayer that we may be able to utilize Mr Harkness' generosity for our children's benefit.'

Dr Burdick bent his head and the congregation followed suit. All but Ben Huckins. He stared at the big man while his deep voice rumbled in prayer. Ben knew that piece of land down by the river. It's never been worth much, and when the state condemned part of it for a levee, Harkness had been paid a lot more than the whole piece was worth. Generosity indeed! He must have snorted, because Evelyn's elbow dug into his ribs again.

When they were finally out in the foyer, she put her gloved hand on his arm. 'Ben, would you mind if I asked Dr Burdick to dinner?'

'O.K. Day's spoiled anyway.'

'*Ben!*'

He winced a little because he hadn't really meant it. He grinned. 'Sorry, honey. Sure, it's O.K. by me.'

Having the minister to dinner certainly improved the boys' table manners. Ben grinned sympathetically once at Ricky, the ten-year-old. Ricky started a sickly smile and then froze as Dr Burdick glanced at him.

'Play football, Ricky?'

'Oh, sure. Yes, sir . . . a little,' he added hesitantly, as if wondering if the church approved.

'Great game, football. Used to enjoy it.'

Ricky's mouth dropped open. 'Did you play football ?'

'High school and two years of college.' Dr Burdick smiled, remembering. 'Played tackle.'

'Is that how you got the scar ?' Joey asked. 'Playing football ?'

'Joey!' Evelyn's face grew pink.

Dr Burdick laughed and gently touched his fingertips to the scar that began on his forehead at the right temple and ran back, faintly visible, through his hair.

'No,' he said ruefully, 'I got that at Iwo Jima. I was standing up when I should have been sitting down – way down. And I had my helmet off – something no Marine should ever do.'

'Well, how do you like that!' Ricky exclaimed, 'You, a fightin' Marine!'

'Ricky,' Evelyn said quickly, 'the Marines have chaplains, just like the other branches of service.'

Dr Burdick shook his head. 'I wasn't a chaplain, Mrs Huckins. I was a buck sergeant. But it was at Iwo that I decided.'

He smiled at Ben and added, 'As a matter of fact, I wouldn't have been surprised to find the whole division in theological college after the war.'

Ben chuckled. 'I know what you mean. I was in the Seabees. There were times when I needed more than a foxhole.'

The minister settled into a deep chair with a sigh of contentment while Ben stood at the window, apparently studying the sullen day.

'A fine family you have, Mr Huckins.'

Ben turned. 'Thanks.' He sank into a chair. 'Maybe I'm nosy,' he said, 'but after football and the Marine Corps, don't you rather miss the excitement ?'

Dr Burdick smiled. 'I'm afraid one of the reasons I went into the ministry was because I'd had enough excitement. And now I find that this is the most exciting thing in the world.'

Evelyn came in and they sat with their coffee. Dr Burdick smiled at Ben. 'You know, Mr Huckins, most ministers have to work on faith alone. There's no financial reserve – you just go along with your plans, praying and working, and when the time comes, whatever you need is there at hand.'

Ben laughed shortly. 'Wish it'd work for me.'

Dr Burdick smiled. 'The power of prayer is practically unexplored, Mr Huckins. Probably yours weren't answered because you didn't think they would be. You not only have to pray, you have to believe, too.'

Ben couldn't resist it. 'Like this youth hut?'

Dr Burdick nodded. 'That's right.'

Ben stretched out his legs. 'You mean seriously now, that you'll get that place by prayer alone?'

Dr Burdick's glance was steady, vaguely disturbing to Ben. As a matter of fact, the calm, quiet, assured gaze irritated him. By what right did this big young man sit there talking about prayer getting him what he wanted when he should be out hustling for it?

'I believe we will,' Dr Burdick said quietly. 'If the whole community joins in prayer, I'm sure we will.'

'That leaves you quite an out,' Ben said.

'*Ben!*'

Dr Burdick chuckled. 'It's all right, Mrs Huckins. Believing, really believing, is the hardest thing in the world to do. Even the disciples, who'd witnessed the greatest miracle of all time, didn't believe at first.'

Evelyn didn't have much to say to Ben when they were alone. She was too angry. 'Just because you couldn't play tennis today you don't have to take it out on everyone! Sometimes, I just don't understand you!'

'I don't understand him,' Ben returned shortly. Knowing that he hadn't behaved well only lent an edge to his voice. 'A big husky guy like that ought to be working for what he wants!'

She spun on her heels and went swiftly up the stairs, her back stiff, her head high.

She didn't come down; he didn't go up. Late in the afternoon he got into his rain clothes and went out in the car.

He turned down toward the river front. He found the lot old man Harkness had bequeathed to the church. An ugly mud levee cut across it at an angle, leaving an oddly shaped piece of land on which there were only weeds and scrub willows. He got out and paced it.

Some generosity! A building thirty by fifty would practically cover all the usable ground. He stopped suddenly, looking down at the mud. A slow, wry grin crossed his face. What a joke! What a first-class, down-to-earth, cash-on-the-barrelhead kind of joke!

He got back into his car and drove some distance to Earl Kenyon's house. There were a number of cars parked in front, so he drove on to a drugstore and went in to use the phone.

'Earl! Ben Huckins. Look: day after tomorrow I'm pouring a concrete slab thirty by fifty for a community youth hut. I'll supply the asbestos shingles and the wallboard, too. How about you donating the lumber?'

'Hey, wait a minute!' Earl gasped. 'What is this?'

'Call it a shakedown,' Ben said curtly. 'Do you or don't you want in?'

'Who you sore at?' Earl demanded. 'Thirty by fifty – that's a lot of lumber!'

'Never mind who I'm sore at,' Ben said. 'This is a rush job. Gotta be done – paint, wiring, plumbing – everything in a month.'

'Free?'

'Free. Are you in?'

'Well . . . sure . . . I guess so. I always like to help . . . But thirty by fifty . . .'

'And plywood for a locker room, plus kitchen cabinets.'

Earl groaned.

'What electrical contractor's had the best year?' Ben asked.

Earl snorted. 'All of 'em. Joe Pearce, maybe. He had that big job in Watertown.'

'Joe's my man, then. And Earl – this is top secret. Make sure everybody who works on the deal understands it.'

By the time he got home Evelyn was in the kitchen, fixing a snack of soup and toast for the boys, and he ate some, too. She didn't speak to him, and he didn't speak to her. He nursed his secret, gloating a little.

By the end of the week the slab was in, the studs up, the roof on, and the fireplace almost finished. Abe Decebaum stopped him on the street.

'Look,' Abe said, 'I live here. My kids belong to the Scouts. How come you don't come near me?'

Ben pushed his hat back on his head. 'How'd you find out?'

Abe grinned. 'Radar.'

Ben laughed, 'Abe, you're all right. I didn't come to you because, after all, the building's going to belong to our church.'

'O.K.,' Abe said. 'All the kids gonna use it – that's good enough for me. What do you need?'

'A stove, refrigerator, and a sink.'

'Me and my big mouth! O.K., Ben – you got 'em.'

He rode it like a bucking bronco. And it was done in time – just.

Dr Burdick returned from his trip late in the afternoon, and Ben made an appointment for after dinner. He took Evelyn along and they picked up the minister. Ben drove slowly, savoring the moment to come. When they turned down the dead-end street he began his little speech.

'You remember the rainy Sunday you were over to dinner, Doctor?' Ben asked.

'I remember it with pleasure.'

'You spoke about the youth hut – how we could get it by prayer,' Ben continued.

'That's right.'

'Well – that's one way, maybe. A way I don't know much about, I guess. But there's another way, too. Get out and hustle and sweat. That's my way. For my money, that's what gets things done. How do you like it, Doctor ?'

He had timed it perfectly. The car stopped in front of the youth hut whose white paint glistened in the moonlight. The lights were on and the front door open.

Dr Burdick got out of the car without a word. He went up the walk and took off his hat as he entered. He saw the opened kitchen, the locker room, the two bathrooms. He swallowed several times and turned slowly around, his eyes glistening. Only then was Ben conscious of Evelyn squeezing his arm so tight it hurt.

'Here's the key, Doctor,' Ben said.

Dr Burdick took the key and bent his head. When he looked up again his face was shining. His eyes held Ben's.

'A miracle,' he said softly.

Ben shook his head. 'No miracle. Just plain hard work by a lot of hard-working people.' He grinned triumphantly.

'I told you this was an exciting business,' Dr Burdick said gently, 'and I think it's a miracle. How else do you explain that a man who's had but little interest in the church should become God's instrument ? Only a man like you could have accomplished this in so short a time, Mr Huckins – so a man like you was selected.'

Ben's grin slowly faded. An odd, puzzled feeling crept over him.

'Why did you do this for us ?' Dr Burdick asked.

Ben looked past the man, at the big fireplace. He recognized the feeling now. It was awe.

'I . . . I got mad at you,' he said, almost to himself. 'I thought instead of just praying, you ought to be out doing something about it.'

Dr Burdick laughed softly. 'I was doing something about it, I guess. I was making the right man mad!'

LEON WARE

O Lord, I know not what I ought to ask of thee; thou only knowest what I need; thou lovest me better than I know how to love myself. O Father! give to thy child that which he himself knows not how to ask. I dare not ask either for crosses or consolations; I simply present myself before thee, I open my heart to thee. Behold my needs which I know not myself; see and do according to thy mercy. Smite or heal, depress or raise me up; I adore all thy purposes without knowing them; I am silent; I offer myself in sacrifice; I yield myself to thee; I would have no other desire than to accomplish thy will. Teach me to pray. Pray thyself in me.

FRANÇOIS DE SALIGNAC DE LA MOTHE FÉNELON

If God be for us, who can be against us?

ROMANS 8: 31

... in him we live, and move, and have our being.

ACTS 17: 28

Lord, make me an instrument of your peace
Where there is hatred ... let me sow love.
Where there is injury ... pardon.
Where there is doubt ... faith.
Where there is despair ... hope.
Where there is darkness ... light.
Where there is sadness ... joy.

O Divine Master, grant that I may not so much seek
To be consoled ... as to console,
To be understood ... as to understand;
To be loved ... as to love,
    For
It is in giving ... that we receive.
It is in pardoning, that we are pardoned,
It is in dying ... that we are born to eternal life.

ST FRANCIS OF ASSISI

The human soul is a silent harp in God's choir, whose strings need only to be swept by the divine breath to chime in with the harmonies of creation.

HENRY DAVID THOREAU

Prayer builds strength within against the stress of life.

Man must be arched and buttressed from within, else the temple wavers to the dust.

MARCUS AURELIUS

PRAYER IS POWER*

Prayer is not only worship; it is also an invisible emanation of man's worshipping spirit – the most powerful form of energy that one can generate. The influence of prayer on the human mind and body is as demonstrable as that of secreting glands. Its results can be measured in terms of increased physical buoyancy, greater intellectual vigor,

* Reprinted with permission from the March 1941 *Reader's Digest*, copyright, 1941, by Reader's Digest Association, Inc.

moral stamina, and a deeper understanding of the realities underlying human relationships.

'If you make a habit of sincere prayer, your life will be very noticeably and profoundly altered. Prayer stamps with its indelible mark our actions and demeanor. A tranquility of bearing, a facial and bodily repose are observed in those whose inner lives are thus enriched. Within the depths of consciousness a flame kindles. And man sees himself. He discovers his selfishness, his silly pride, his fears, his greeds, his blunder. He develops a sense of moral obligation, intellectual humility. Thus begins a journey of the soul toward the realm of grace.

Prayer is a force as real as terrestrial gravity. As a physician, I have seen men, after all other therapy has failed, lifted out of disease and melancholy by the serene effort of prayer. It is the only power in the world that seems to overcome the so-called 'laws of nature'; the occasions on which prayer has dramatically done this have been termed 'miracles.' But a constant, quieter miracle takes place hourly in the hearts of men and women who have discovered that prayer supplies them with a steady flow of sustaining power in their daily lives.

Too many people regard prayer as a formalized routine of words, a refuge for weaklings, or a childish petition for material things. We sadly undervalue prayer when we conceive it in these terms, just as we should underestimate rain by describing it as something that fills the birdbath in our garden. Properly understood, prayer is a mature activity indispensable to the fullest development of personality – the ultimate integration of man's highest faculties. Only in prayer do we achieve that complete and harmonious assembly of body, mind and spirit which gives the frail human reed its unshakable strength.

The words 'Ask and it shall be given to you' have been verified by the experience of humanity. True, prayer may not restore the dead child to life or bring relief from physical pain. But prayer, like radium, is a source of luminous, self-generating energy.

How does prayer fortify us with so much dynamic power? To answer this question (admittedly outside the jurisdiction of science), I must point out that all prayers have one thing in common. The triumphant hosannas of a great oratorio or the humble supplication of an Iroquois hunter begging for luck in the chase demonstrate the same truth: that human beings seek to augment their finite energy by addressing themselves to the Infinite source of all energy. When we pray, we link ourselves with the inexhaustible motive power that spins the universe. We ask that a part of this power be apportioned to our needs. Even in asking, our human deficiencies are filled and we arise strengthened and repaired.

But we must never summon God merely for the gratification of our whims. We derive most power from prayer when we use it, not as a petition, but as a supplication that we may become more like Him. Prayer should be regarded as practice of the Presence of God. An old peasant was seated alone in the last pew of the village church. 'What are you waiting for?' he was asked; and he answered, 'I am looking at Him and He is looking at me.' Man prays not only that God should remember him, but also that he should remember God.

How can prayer be defined? Prayer is the effort of man to reach God, to commune with an invisible being, creator of all things, supreme wisdom, truth, beauty, and strength, father and redeemer of each man. This goal of prayer always remains hidden to intelligence. For both language and thought fail when we attempt to describe God.

We do know, however, that whenever we address God in fervent prayer we change both soul and body for the better. It could not happen that any man or woman could pray for a single moment without some good result. 'No man ever prayed,' said Emerson, 'without learning something.'

One can pray everywhere. In the streets, the subway, the office, the shop, the school, as well as in the solitude of one's own room or among the crowd in a church. There is no prescribed posture, time or place.

'Think of God more often than you breathe,' said Epictetus the Stoic. In order really to mold personality, prayer must become a habit. It is meaningless to pray in the morning and to live like a barbarian the remainder of the day. True prayer is a way of life; the truest life is literally a way of prayer.

ALEXIS CARREL, MD

The helpfulness of people praying for you. What a force such prayers create.

I believe in the power of prayer. I know something of this power through having been on the receiving end. After the war I was asked to be the tutor to the Crown Prince of Japan. In this fascinating but delicate and sometimes difficult work I was doing, situations arose in which I had no precedent to follow, no rules that I could consult. I had to depend more than I had ever done before on intuition. I used to hear again and again of people who were praying for me.

More than once I found myself lifted up and carried over the critical point, and it may well be that the prayers of unknown people in far places were helping me in ways I could not know. We understand very little about this power of prayer, and it is possible to misuse it even with the highest motives. I think that I can only ask that God's will be done in regard to any situation and that people whom I want to help may come to seek Him and know His love and truth directly.

But by the very act of asking, if I do it sincerely and without reserve, I open myself as a channel for God's healing action.

ELIZABETH GRAY VINING

Do not pray for tasks equal to your powers.
Pray for powers equal to your tasks.

PHILLIPS BROOKS

Who rises from prayer a better man, his prayer is answered.

GEORGE MEREDITH

When Holman Hunt's painting *The Light of the World* was unveiled, an art critic thought he had found an error in this representation of Christ standing in a garden at midnight, holding a lantern in one hand and knocking on a door with the other hand.

'I say, Hunt,' said the critic, 'there is no handle on that door.'

'That is correct,' replied the artist. 'You see, that is the door to the human heart; it can only be opened from the inside.'

Good deeds are the best prayer.

SERBIAN PROVERB

He that prays much by night his face is fair by day.

ORACLE OF TATSUTA

Make truth thy prayer, faith thy prayer carpet.

ARJAN

Pray as though no work could help,
and work as though no prayer could help.

GERMAN PROVERB

When in prayer you clasp your hands,
God opens His.

GERMAN PROVERB

The first time I saw Brother Lawrence was upon the 3d of August, 1666. He told me that God had done him a singular favor in his conversion at the age of eighteen.

That in the winter, seeing a tree stripped of its leaves, and considering that within a little time the leaves would be renewed, and after that the flowers and fruit appear, he received a high view of the providence and power of God, which has never since been effaced from his soul. That this view had perfectly set him loose from the world, and kindled in him such a love for God that he could not tell whether it had increased during the more than forty years he had lived since. . . .

That we should establish ourselves in a sense of God's presence by continually conversing with Him. That it was a shameful thing to quiet His conversation to think of trifles and fooleries.

That we should feed and nourish our souls with high notions of God; which would yield us great joy in being devoted to Him. . . .

That when an occasion of practicing some virtue offered, he addressed himself to God, saying, Lord, *I cannot do this unless Thou enablest me*; and that then he received strength more than sufficient.

That when he had failed in his duty, he only confessed his fault, saying to God, *I shall never do otherwise if You leave me to myself; it is You who must hinder my falling, and mend what is amiss.* That after this he gave himself no further uneasiness about it. . . .

That his prayer was nothing else but a sense of the presence of God, his soul being at that time insensible to everything but divine love; and that when the appointed times of prayer were past, he found no difference, because he still continued with God, praising and blessing Him with all his might, so that he passed his life in continual joy; yet hoped that God would give him somewhat to suffer when he should grow stronger.

That we ought, once for all, heartily to put our whole trust in God, and make a total surrender of ourselves to Him, secure that he would not deceive us. . . .

That the whole substance of religion was faith, hope, and charity, by the practice of which we become united to the will of God; that all besides is indifferent, and to be used as a means that we may arrive at our end, and be swallowed up therein, by faith and charity.

That all things are possible to him who *believes*; that they are less difficult to him who *hopes*; that they are more easy to him who *loves*, and still more easy to him who perseveres in the practice of these three virtues.

That the end we ought to propose to ourselves is to become, in this life, the most perfect worshippers of God we can possibly be, as we hope to be through all eternity.

CONVERSATIONS AND LETTERS OF NICHOLAS HERMAN
OF LORRAINE, BROTHER LAWRENCE

Let me not pray to be sheltered from dangers, but to be fearless in facing them.

RABINDRANATH TAGORE

All of us are needed to save the world from the world's mightiest enemy, which is war itself.

'Prayer alone will not be enough,' you say. 'We need right deeds.' Precisely! But prayer is the door that opens our minds and the minds of our leaders to God, so that we and they may know what deeds are right. . . .

'If prayer can save the world,' asked a friend, 'why haven't the prayers of the devout done it already?'

Because their prayers have been a trickle, when we needed a river. The world at this moment is the *resultant of the total thought forces* which have struggled for supremacy. We had these world wars because wills all over the world have been at cross purposes with the will of God and with other wills. The people who were working and planning with God were fewer than those at cross purposes with God's will. Hundreds were praying, when we needed hundreds of millions. People prayed for a few minutes a week, when they should have been praying all week, all year 'without ceasing.'

We do not 'persuade God to try harder' when we pray; it is our world leaders, our statesmen and churchmen whom we persuade to try harder. We help God when we pray. When great numbers of us pray for leaders, a mighty invisible spiritual force lifts our minds and eyes toward God. His Spirit flows through our prayer to them, and He can speak to them directly.

We can do more for the world with prayer than if we could walk into Whitehall, London, or the Kremlin in Moscow, and tell those men what to do – far more! If they listened to our suggestions, we would probably be more or less wrong. But what God tells them, when they listen to Him, must be right. It is infinitely better for world leaders to listen to God than for them to listen to us.

Most of us can never enter the White House and offer advice to the President. Probably he will never have time to read our letters. But we can give him what is far more important than advice. We can give him a lift into the presence of God, make him hungry for divine wisdom, which is the grandest thing one man ever does for another. We can visit the White House with prayer *as many times a day* as we think of it, and every such visit makes us a channel between God and President.

This idea struck one minister like a thunderbolt:

'Man,' he exclaimed, 'if this is true at all, it is the mightiest truth in the universe! It means that enough of us praying *often enough* could make everybody in the whole world look up and listen to God. We could transform the world.'

He was right. Prayer is the mightiest power on earth. Prayer's power has been proven many millions of times. *Enough* of us, if we prayed *enough, could* save the world – if we prayed *enough!*

But the clergyman, in his enthusiasm, then went too far.

'If we could get Christians to stop and pray one minute a day, they could save the world.'

I do not think that would be enough. The sun could keep nothing alive shining one minute a day. Life itself is dependent on the sun's rays, yet not one ray of light in a million produces life. Not one raindrop in a million finds its way to the roots of a tree. Not a seed in a million germinates. Not a shovelful of dirt in a million turns up a diamond in Kimberley. ... So if we should find that our prayers do not always reach those for whom they are intended, but that every prayer probably reaches somebody somewhere, that is all we can ask, and more! Indeed, that fact is so powerful that if we of the Christian world pray persistently, and 'faint not,' as Jesus commanded, we *shall* transform the world. But occasional feeble, doubting prayers will get only feeble results. One minute a day will not save us!

So we must guard against expecting an easy victory. Prayer is powerful, but it is not the power of a sledge hammer that crushes with one blow. It is the power of sunrays and raindrops which bless, because there are so many of them. Instead of a minute a day, we Christians must learn to flash *hundreds of instantaneous prayers* at people near and far, knowing that many prayers may show no visible results, but that at least one of them will hit their mark. When you fill a swamp with stones, a hundred loads may disappear under the water before a stone appears on the surface, but all of them *are necessary*. ...

Prayer is likely to be undervalued by all but wise people because it is so silent and so secret. We are often deceived into thinking that noise is more important than silence. War sounds far more important than the noiseless growing of a crop of wheat, yet the silent wheat feeds millions, while war destroys them. Nobody but God knows how often prayers have changed the course of history. Many a man who prayed received no credit excepting in heaven. We are tempted to turn from prayer to something more noisy like speeches or guns, because our motives are mixed. We are interested in the making of a better world, of course, but we also want people to give us credit for what we have done.

Secret prayer for others all during the day is an acid test of our unselfishness. Our little selves must fade out, leaving a self-forgetting channel, through which God's warmth flows unhindered in lovely, unending prayer. The highest form of communion is not asking God for things for ourselves, but letting Him flow down through us, out over the world – in endless benediction. In the old Hebrew story Sodom needed ten good men to be saved. Now the world needs ten million. Anybody Christian enough to have read this far must be one of that ten million or there will not be enough to save our age.

FRANK C. LAUBACH

Chapter 4

Living Successfully Through Faith

The Holy Bible, wisest of all books, assigns high importance to faith: 'If you have faith as a grain of mustard seed ... nothing shall be impossible unto you.'

The implication is that while you may not have perfect faith (who does?), or considerable faith, or even faith as small as a tiny mustard seed, yet, if what you do have is real faith, then life will be predicated, not on an impossibility concept, but rather upon the fact of great possibilities. Faith strongly held can move you out of the area of the impossible into a way of life that is full of exciting possibilities.

This must not be taken to mean, however, that if you practice faith you are thereby going to get everything you desire. Nor does it mean you will be able to avoid difficulty, pain, or disappointment. Not at all. The real difference between faith and no faith is shown by how creatively you handle the troubles of life. Having even a mustard-seed category of faith, it will be quite impossible for the hard things, no matter how hard they may be, to defeat you. Indeed, your spiritual perception and control will be such that you will see and develop the vast possibilities that are almost invariably inherent in difficulties.

Faith is an educative process in that it teaches a proper philosophy of problems. Through it we learn God's procedures for giving to those who have faith in Him the real values of life. When God wishes to give you a value of inestimable worth, He is not so crude as to hand it to you on a silver platter as a 'come easy' kind of gift. God is aware that the valuation we place on the easy-got is much less than on that which comes the hard way. Accordingly, He often imbeds the greater value which He wants to give inside a big difficulty or problem; often the bigger the problem, the greater the value that is given. The individual who lacks faith will probably fail to find such values, because he will allow the difficulties in a problem to discourage him.

But it is definitely not so with the man of faith in depth. He is aware of God's methods. And, furthermore, he is a philosopher who knows that in some way every difficulty contains an inherent good. He clearly understands that every problem contains the seeds of its own solution. Because he believes that with faith nothing is impossible, he faces a problem expectantly, not fearfully. In fact, he approaches it positively rather than negatively with the excitement of impending discovery. He subjects a difficult problem to prayer and asks for guidance. His mind is put solely to the solution of the situation and is not distracted by anxiety about difficulties which the situation may contain. As a result, he finally breaks the problem apart and finds at its center the good that God placed there for him. Such a man has no doubt whatsoever that faith brings seeming impossibilities to pass, that it does for a fact 'move mountains.'

Those who have never cultivated faith of this character will most likely have a mental attitude that, instead of moving mountains, builds up mountainous difficulties. But those who have faith are able to say confidently to that mountain, 'Be removed,' and, finally, through their faith, it is.

As my late friend and colleague, the famous psychiatrist Dr Smiley Blanton, used to say, 'Faith is the answer.' In fact Dr Blanton and I wrote a book bearing that title.

In this chapter I have gathered together for your inspiration some fine insights and demonstrations of faith creatively at work in people's lives.

I should like to make a point which I believe is most important: faith can be a practical way of living and of melting problems in every phase of life.

One man told me of his method of applying faith to his business of sales work. Formerly shy and diffident, always apprehensive of his own inability, always fearful to make an approach to a prospect, he became a student of faith through the teachings in inspirational books. As a result, he worked out his own 'faith method that worked.'

It goes something like this:

1. He practices affirmations daily. 'I affirm that God's guiding presence is with me. I affirm that through Divine guidance I will take the right steps. I affirm that God's mind working on my mind is reducing error in me and building up rightness hence depreciating my tendency to make mistakes.'

2. He makes an effort to know all of his customers and prospects as friends and seeks every opportunity to help them, not for the purpose of making a sale, but 'to be on God's team,' by which he means to 'bear one another's burdens.' Every morning he puts a list of his customers on his desk and prays for each one by name with directed thought to any special needs of those persons.

3. He knows that he represents a needed and good product, and daily he brings up a mental image of himself as 'getting a fair share of the competitive selling and his competitors likewise.'

4. 'I try to live by faith,' he says, 'and it's amazing how the more I do that, the better everything seems to go.'

To get things done, an ounce of faith is worth a ton of experience. Kipling recounts how a battle was won by the fool raw recruits, the boys who stormed the fort like lunatics, while the old wise soldiers knew better and held back.

William Carey, the father of modern missions, was called a 'dreamer who dreams that he is dreaming.' The movement he inaugurated is one of the marvels of human achievement. He had something better than wisdom; he had faith.

There are plenty of people to do the possible. . . . The prizes are for those who perform the impossible. If a thing can be done, experience and skill can do it; if a thing cannot be done, only faith can do it.

And it is the quality of faith that counts. It is not of so much importance what you believe as how you believe. For faith is the peculiar elixir of youth. . . . Whoever has faith is young, no matter how old he is; whoever has lost faith is old, even at twenty-one.

DR FRANK CRANE

My Friends: No one, not in my situation, can appreciate my feeling of sadness at this parting. To this place, and the kindness of these people, I owe everything. Here I have lived a quarter of a century, and have passed from a young to an old man. Here my children have been born and one is buried. I now leave, not knowing when or whether I may return, with a task before me greater than that which rested upon Washington. Without the assistance of that Divine Being who ever attended him, I cannot succeed. With that assistance, I cannot fail. Trusting in Him who can go with me, and remain with you, and be everywhere for good, let us confidently hope that all will yet be well. To His care commending you, as I hope in your prayers you will commend me, I bid you an affectionately farewell.

ABRAHAM LINCOLN

(*On leaving Springfield, Illinois, for Washington, D.C.*)

My professional training was in science and engineering. That is a training in the search for truth and its application to the use of mankind. With the growth of science we have had a continuous contention from a tribe of atheistic and agnostic philosophers that there is an implacable conflict between science and religion, in which religion will be vanquished. I do not believe it.

I believe not only that religious faith will be victorious, but that it is vital to mankind that it shall be. We may differ in form and particulars in our religious faith. Those are matters which are sacred to each of our inner sanctuaries. It is our privilege to decline to argue them. Their real demonstration is the lives that we live.

But there is one foundation common to all religious faith.

Our discoveries in science have proved that all the way from the galaxies in the heavens to the constitution of the atom, the universe is controlled by inflexible laws. Somewhere a Supreme Power created these laws. At some period, man was differentiated from the beasts and was endowed with a spirit from which spring conscience, idealism and spiritual yearnings. It is impossible to believe that there is not here a divine touch and a purpose from the Creator of the Universe. I believe we can express these things only in religious faith.

From their religious faith, the Founding Fathers enunciated the most fundamental law of human progress since the Sermon on the Mount, when they stated that man received from the Creator certain inalienable rights and that these rights should be protected from the encroachment of others by law and justice.

HERBERT HOOVER

Certainly you cannot doubt when you know Jesus Christ. There has never been anyone like him. Believe and put your faith in him, in his words, his teachings. Truth cannot fail.

ONE SOLITARY LIFE

Here is a man who was born in an obscure village, the child of a peasant woman. He grew up in an obscure village. He worked in a carpenter shop until he was thirty, and then for three years he was an itinerant teacher. He never wrote a book. He never held an office. He never owned a home. He never had a family. He never went to college. He never traveled, except in his infancy, more than two hundred miles from the place where he was born. He never did one of the things that usually accompany greatness. He had no credentials but himself. While he was still a young man, the tide of popular opinion turned against him. His friends ran away. One of them denied him. He was turned over to his enemies. He went through the mockery of a trial. He was nailed upon a cross between two thieves. His executioners gambled for the only piece of property he had on earth, his seamless robe. When he was dead, he was taken down from the cross and laid in a borrowed grave through the courtesy of a friend. Nineteen wide centuries have come and gone, and today he is the centerpiece of the human race and the leader of all human progress. I am well within the mark when I say that all the armies that ever marched, all the navies that ever were built, all the parliaments that ever sat, and all the kings that ever reigned, put together, have not affected the life of man upon this earth as powerfully as has this one solitary personality.

AUTHOR UNKNOWN

I have lived, Sir, a long time, and the longer I live the more convincing proof I see of this truth – that God governs the affairs of men.

BENJAMIN FRANKLIN

Have a good healthy faith in yourself – you are greater than you think.

You are a distinctive and individual expression of a Creative Force. You are not a blueprint or a carbon copy or a ditto of anyone past, present or future. You are *you* and there is no one quite like you in the world.

You don't look exactly like anyone else, you don't live exactly like anyone else. There are things you can do better than anyone else can do them, and there are qualities and talents that no one else can possess in exactly the same way that you do. There are thoughts that are your own special revelation. That which makes you YOU is personal, unique and exclusive. All of this is a reflection of a world and a life *within*.

Talk about how to be a success! The successful person is simply the one who does his best with the things he can do better than anyone else.

Talk about living well! Who lives better than the one who is true to his own inner light?

Talk about being interesting! What is more interesting than the person who is being himself?

Talk about how to be happy! The happy, self-unfolded people are those who, with a will to believe in the world and the life within, have found that the secret of really getting the most out of life is to make the most of the qualities that are innately their own. . . .

This inner world grows as we will to believe in it. It is not through searching or feverish groping that we enter into it. It is through the gateway of our will to believe. You will to believe that because you are an individual expression of God there is purpose, real and meaningful, in your life, and you will to believe that to achieve this purpose you are also equipped with the talent and potential necessary for its achievement. Will to believe it!

There is that within each of us that makes us great – I do not mean greatness in the sense of getting one's name in the headlines or making a million, but greatness in the sense of coming to terms with God and life. We might call it getting hold of a guiding principle and making life count in terms of what we are and have and want to be. For it is the originality in each of us and not our uniformity which gives life its deepest meaning.

In this world within, your world, you are the most important figure. There is a place that no one else can fill. There is an influence that no one else can impart. There is a life that no one else can live quite as well as you can live it. What you do with your life within, in terms of self-realization, self-awareness, self-denial and self-expression, is the greatest challenge that can come to you.

MARCUS BACH

With faith you will be strong, and strong we must be to live in this particular world which, of course, is our world.

> Be strong!
> We are not here to play, to dream, to drift;
> We have hard work to do, and loads to lift;
> Shun not the struggle – face it; 'tis God's gift.

> Be strong!
> Say not, 'The days are evil. Who's to blame?'
> And fold the hands and acquiesce – oh shame!
> Stand up, speak out, and bravely, in God's name.

> Be strong!
> It matters not how deep intrenched the wrong,
> How hard the battle goes, the day how long;
> Faint not – fight on! Tomorrow comes the song.

MALTBIE D. BABCOCK

God isn't far off, in Heaven only – He is in you in the very spirit of your life.

I believe in God, whom I comprehend as Spirit, as Love, as the Source of all. I believe that He is in me and I in Him.

LEO TOLSTOY

The spiritual world is real. God is alive and real. And God is interested in our lives, every detail of them.

I believe in a spiritual world, not as something separate from this world, but as its innermost truth. With the breath we draw, we must feel this truth, that we are living in God. Born in this great world, full of the mystery of the infinite, we cannot accept our existence as a momentary outburst of chance, drifting on the current of matter toward an eternal nowhere. We cannot look upon our lives as dreams of a dreamer who has no awakening in all time. We have a personality to which matter and force are unmeaning unless related to something infinitely personal, whose nature we have discovered, in some measure, in human love, in the greatness of the good, in the martyrdom of heroic souls, in the ineffable beauty of nature, which can never be a mere physical fact not anything but an expression of personality.

RABINDRANATH TAGORE

If it is sometimes difficult to have faith in a better world because progress moves so slowly and evil seems so very strong, read this hymn of faith.

LIGHT SHINING OUT OF DARKNESS

God moves in a mysterious way
　His wonders to perform;
He plants His footsteps in the sea,
　And rides upon the storm.

Deep in unfathomable mines
　Of never-failing skill
He treasures up His bright designs,
　And works His sovereign will.

Ye fearful saints, fresh courage take;
　The clouds ye so much dread
Are big with mercy, and shall break
　In blessings on your head.

Judge not the Lord by feeble sense;
　But trust Him for His grace;
Behind a frowning providence
　He hides a smiling face.

His purposes will ripen fast,
　Unfolding every hour;
The bud may have a bitter taste,
　But sweet will be the flower.

Blind unbelief is sure to err,
　And scan His work in vain;
God is His own interpreter,
　And He will make it plain.

WILLIAM COWPER

Faith in yourself is a religious thing, for you are God's creation, His child. Believe in yourself and believe in Him.

Our first duty is not to hate ourselves; because to advance we must have faith in ourselves first and then in God. He who has no faith in himself can never have faith in God.

VIVEKANANDA

You do not need to know how or why faith works; it does work.

Why is it that the very term 'religious life' has come to voice the popular idea that religion is altogether divorced from ordinary life? That conception is the exact opposite of Christ's teachings. Faith, 'reason grown courageous,' as someone has called it, has become assurance to me now, not because the fight is easy and we are never worsted but because it has made life infinitely worth-while, so that I want to get all I can out of it, every hour.

God help us not to neglect the use of a thing – like faith – because we do not know how it works! It would be a criminal offense in a doctor not to use the X-ray even if he does not know how barium chloride makes Gamma rays visible. We must know that our opinions are not a matter of very great moment, except in so far as in what they lead us to do. I see no reason whatever to suppose that the Creator lays any stress on them either. Experience answers our problems – experience of faith and common sense. For faith and common sense, taken together, make reasonable service, which ends by giving us the light of life.

SIR WILFRED GRENFELL

Faith is not belief without proof,
but trust without reservations.

ELTON TRUEBLOOD

The world has a way of giving what is demanded of it. If you are frightened and look for failure and poverty, you will get them, no matter how hard you may try to succeed. Lack of faith in yourself, in what life will do for you, cuts you off from the good things of the world. Expect victory and you make victory. Nowhere is this truer than in business life, where bravery and faith bring both material and spiritual rewards.

DR PRESTON BRADLEY

Very often when I haven't faith in my faith, I have to have faith in His faith. He makes me believe in myself and my possibilities, when

I simply can't. I have to rise to His faith in me. A woman who was inwardly collapsed said to me, 'Well, I have no faith of my own, but I do have faith in your faith.' 'Good,' I replied, 'take faith in my faith as a first step, and then you will go on to something infinitely better – faith in His faith.' With faith in His faith you can do anything – anything that ought to be done.

There is a passage which touches your need. 'For the Eternal . . . will not let you go.' Faith is not merely your holding on to God – it is God holding on to you. He will not let you go! As Walt Whitman puts it, 'Not until the sun refuses to shine, do I refuse you.' Then keep saying to your soul, 'In quietness and in confidence shall be your faith' (Isaiah 30: 15). Then repeat to your soul these words: 'To say what ought to be cannot be is a brief and complete statement of atheism.' It is. Say to yourself, 'What ought to be can be, and I will make it so.' And you will. You will go beyond yourself.

E. STANLEY JONES

For verily I say unto you, That whosoever say unto this mountain, Be thou removed, and be thou cast into the sea; and shall not doubt in his heart, but shall believe that those things which he saith shall come to pass; he shall have whatsoever he saith.

Therefore I say unto you, What things soever ye desire, when ye pray, believe that ye receive them, and ye shall have them.

MARK 11: 23–24

The whole course of things goes to teach us faith. We need only obey. There is guidance for each of us, and by lowly listening we shall hear the right word. . . . Place yourself in the middle of the stream of power and wisdom which flows into you as life, place yourself in the full center of that flood, then you are without effort impelled to truth, to right, and a perfect contentment.

RALPH WALDO EMERSON

The most important thought I ever had was that of my individual responsibility to God.

DANIEL WEBSTER

If thou canst believe, all things are possible to him that believeth.

MARK 9: 23

Never let yourself become discouraged. Never give in to a negative, as easy as that may be to do. Remind yourself of the power you have, the power of faith.

Immense hidden powers seem to lurk in the unconscious depths of even the most common man – indeed, of all people without exception. It is these powers, when put under pressure, that are responsible for all great creative efforts. The men who make history are those who – consciously or unconsciously – turn the switch on the inner switchboards of human character. Pour out all your fears and anxieties, malicious joy and greed and hatred, and you will be astonished at the terrific amount of power which is pent up in your unconscious mind. We can release this power and transform it from negative into positive power, only by bringing into the open, into the light of consciousness, and by accepting ourselves as we are, even though the mountains of debts seem to crush us. This is the principle of honesty. And it is clear that it can be applied only if connected with the principle of faith.

FRITZ KUNKEL

True religion is betting your life that there is a God.

DONALD HANKEY

Four things a man must learn to do
If he would make his record true;
To think without confusion clearly;
To love his fellow-men sincerely;
To act from honest motives purely;
To trust in God and Heaven securely.

HENRY VAN DYKE

Sad is the day for any man when he becomes absolutely satisfied with the life he is living, the thoughts that he is thinking and the deeds that he is doing; when there ceases to be forever beating at the doors of his soul a desire to do something larger which he seeks and knows he was meant and intended to do.

PHILLIPS BROOKS

One of the commonest mistakes and one of the costliest is thinking that success is due to some genius, some magic – something or other which we do not possess. Success is generally due to holding on, and failure to letting go. You decide to learn a language, study music, take a course of reading, train yourself physically. Will it be success or failure? It depends upon how much pluck and perseverance that word 'decide' contains. The decision that nothing can overrule, the grip that nothing can detach will bring success. Remember the Chinese proverb, 'With time and patience, the mulberry leaf becomes satin.'

MALTBIE D. BABCOCK

Faith will turn any course, light any path, relieve any distress, bring joy out of sorrow, peace out of strife, friendship out of enmity, heaven out of hell. Faith is God at work.

F. L. HOLMES

Faith draws the poison from every grief, takes the sting from every loss, and quenches the fire of every pain; and only faith can do it.

J. G. HOLLAND

If ye abide in me, and my words abide in you, ye shall ask what ye will, and it shall be done unto you.

JOHN 15:7

According to your faith be it unto you.

MATTHEW 9:29

I could not say I believe. I know! I have had the experience of being gripped by something that is stronger than myself, something that people call God.

CARL JUNG

We live by Faith; but Faith is not the slave
    Of text and legend. Reason's voice and God's,
    Nature's and Duty's, never are at odds.
What asks our Father of His children, save
Justice and mercy and humility,
    A reasonable service of good deeds,
    Pure living, tenderness to human needs,
Reverence and trust, and prayer for light to see
The Master's footprints in our daily ways?
    No knotted scourge nor sacrificial knife,
    But the calm beauty of an ordered life
Whose very breathing is unworded praise! —
A life that stands as all true lives have stood
Firm-rooted in the faith that God is Good.

JOHN GREENLEAF WHITTIER

Not for one single day
Can I discern my way,
    But this I surely know —
Who gives the day·
Will show the way,
    So I securely go.

JOHN OXENHAM

WE MUST BELIEVE

'Lord, I believe: help Thou mine unbelief.'

We must believe –
Being from birth endowed with love and trust –
Born unto loving; – and how simply just
That love – that faith! – even in the blossom-face
The babe drops dreamward in its resting-place,
Intuitively conscious of the sure
Awakening to rapture ever pure
And sweet and saintly as the mother's own,
Or the awed father's, as his arms are thrown
O'er wife and child, to round about them weave
    And wind and bind them as one harvest-sheaf
Of love – to cleave to, and *forever* cleave. ...
              Lord, I believe:
                  Help Thou mine unbelief. ...

We must believe:
For still all unappeased our hunger goes,
From life's first waking, to its last repose:
The briefest life of any babe, or man
Outwearing even the allotted span,
Is each a life unfinished – incomplete:
For these, then, of th' outworn, or unworn feet
Denies one toddling step – O there must be
Some fair, green, flowering pathway endlessly
Winding through lands Elysian! Lord, receive
    And lead each as Thine Own Child – even the
        Chief
Of us who didst Immortal life achieve. ...
              Lord, I believe:
                  Help Thou mine unbelief.
                     JAMES WHITCOMB RILEY

The inner need of believing that this world of nature is a sign of something more spiritual and eternal than itself is just as strong and authoritative in those who feel it, as the inner need of uniform laws of causation ever can be in a professionally scientific head. ...

Our faculties of belief were not primarily given us to make orthodoxies and heresies withal; they were given us to live by. And to trust our religious demands means first of all to live in the light of them. ...

The part of wisdom as well as of courage is to *believe what is in the line of your needs*, for only by such belief is the need fulfilled. Refuse to believe, and you shall indeed be right, for you shall irretrievably perish. But believe, and again you shall be right, for you shall save yourself.

WILLIAM JAMES

Chapter 5

How to Find Health of Mind and Body

Find real health of mind and you will have gone a long way toward finding health of body also. As Dr Paul Tournier, the well-known Swiss physician, points out, health depends to a large extent on mental attitudes and even upon the spiritual condition of the personality.

If this is true, and we have no reason to doubt the thesis, it follows that anything which ministers helpfully to the mental, emotional, and spiritual well-being of the individual will be an important factor in health of mind and body.

You frequently hear people say, 'I am sick with worry.' That is much more than a mere expression designating intense anxiety. A person definitely can become sick of worry. One doctor has stated that fifty per cent of his patients have definite worry symptoms, and Dr Smiley Blanton said, 'Anxiety is the great modern plague.'

Resentment and hate and ill will also have their place in the ill-health picture. A physician said that a certain man who had nursed a long-time hate for another individual actually 'died of a grudgitis.' Naturally, he could not enter this officially as the cause of death, but he described how the patient's color 'sickened,' his eyes lost luster, his organs functioned with increasing sluggishness and his breath became extremely foul. 'His whole being deteriorated and left his organs lacking in resistance and prey to disease. Yes,' he insisted, 'the man died of a virulent long-held hate.'

That this is an extreme case is obvious, but think of the thousands of dull, listless, and lethargic people with aches and pains who drag through life low in energy and vitality, all because of a diseased emotional and spiritual condition. And, of course, such a condition undermines the body tone, leaving it open to the encroachment of disease. This is not to say that all sickness is emotionally induced. It must be remembered, however, that a distinguished Canadian physician had advanced the theory that stress is an active agent in all disease.

In the course of my own experience, I have noted not a few personal situations where unhealthy mental and spiritual attitudes gave rise to emotional conditions which in turn had pronounced physical manifestations. For example, a woman came up to me after I had preached a sermon with the blunt announcement, 'I itch terribly. Whatever shall I do about it?'

'Well, madam,' I replied, 'I've had all kinds of reactions to my poor sermons but this is the first time I can remember stimulating itching.'

'I've had it off and on for about three years, but it's particularly bad when I am in church. Look at my arm, see how it itches.' The exposed arm showed nothing except maybe a slight redness. I was curious as to why the itching was particularly noticeable when she came to church, and I had a counseling session with her. The only thing that emerged from our conversation came out strongly, and that was hatred of her sister, and I mean hatred, dark, vehement, and virulent.

It seemed that her older sister, so she claimed, was executor of their father's estate and had defrauded her of a considerable part of her rightful inheritance, although she admitted she had plenty to live on. I reasoned that, because she was a long-time church member, the hatred was compounded with a sense of guilt when she came to church and concluded that the itching must be a concomitant of the guilt-hate complex.

Becoming curious about the case, I received permission to discuss it with her physician. He was obviously interested when I told him of her hate confession. 'She never opened up on that with me,' he said. 'This woman possibly had what we might call an internal eczema. She has been scratching herself on the inside and producing an outward pseudo itching. I have a hunch that if she would drop the hatred she might get over it. At least it's worth trying.'

The doctor talked with the patient along this line and sent her back to me with the stern warning, 'You'll itch yourself into a breakdown if you don't straighten up your sick thought pattern.'

She was essentially a sensible person and spiritually sensitive, and she responded to the therapy we suggested. She forgave her sister, not without effort, but she exorcized the hate. The guilt feeling let up, and, believe it or not, the itching got less and less and finally ceased altogether. Apparently her changed attitude had a salutary effect on the grasping sister-executor, for she straightened out the financial situation to their mutual satisfaction.

In the chapter following are some thoughts designed to be helpful in effecting healthy attitudes to stimulate health of mind and body.

Hope awakens courage. He who can implant courage in the human soul is the best physician.

KARL VON KNEBEL

I should like to add one more beatitude to those of the gospels and to say, Blessed are they who heal us of self-despisings. Of all services which can be done to man, I know of none more precious.

MARK RUTHERFORD

Fret not thyself.
PSALM 37: I

Don't push – slow down to an unhurried pace.

> Slow me down, Lord!
> Ease the pounding of my heart by the quieting
> of my mind.
> Steady my hurried pace,
> With a vision of the eternal reach of time.
> Give me, amidst the confusion of my day,
> The calmness of the everlasting hills.
> Break the tension of my nerves
> With the soothing music of the singing streams
> That live in my memory.
> Help me to know the magical restoring power
> of sleep.
> Teach me the art of taking minute vacations of
> slowing down.
> To look at a flower;
> To chat with an old friend or make a new one;
> To pat a stray dog; to watch a spider build a
> web;
> To smile at a child; or to read from a good
> book.
> Remind me each day
> That the race is not always to the swift;
> That there is more to life than increasing its
> speed.
> Let me look upward into the towering oak
> And know that it grew great and strong
> Because it grew slowly and well.

ORIN L. CRAIN

I learned many things from Coach 'Biggie' Munn at Michigan State. I would like to tell you one story that Munn told to our team. One day he said to us, 'After every big storm plenty of broken oak limbs can be found lying on the ground. But you never find any branches from the fir trees. Oak trees are big and strong, but they stand stiff and straight. When the wind blows, they crack. But fir trees sway with the storm – and snap back afterward. Just remember: if you want to be king of the forest, you can't be too proud to bend with the wind.'

Somehow, this story related directly to me and the story of my experiences in life. My life was full of many storms that seemed to be trying to break me, make me give up. And the storms almost succeeded in winning out a number of times. But, gradually, I developed more and more ability to bend with the wind. I seemed to be able to draw on some inner strength in times of despair, in the face of obstacles to my success. I couldn't do it alone, I admit. Perhaps this is one of the reasons for my finally succeeding in sports. My early days in sports had helped me develop a humility that enabled me to ask for help and advice, and then follow that advice. I learned eventually to go to God for advice. And, as I matured, I began to be able to bend with the wind. When the wind of adversity was strong, I might be pushed backward to one side, but I managed to spring back. No, I don't think of myself as the king of the forest, but do think I have managed to become more like the fir tree than the oak.

Now as I look back, I can see more clearly than ever the value of the obstacles, the trials, the adversity in my life. Each hurdle I jumped ... each obstacle I managed to surmount ... each trial I went through ... made me more able to overcome the next. Just as the life of a Christian is not a smooth one, because God promises that there will be tribulations in this world, the life of an athlete is never smooth. A young person who desires to be successful in athletics must make up his mind that he is willing to travel a rocky road. He must set his sights high, and plan to do whatever is necessary to achieve that goal. With this determination to succeed, and the help of God, he can achieve his full potential in athletics.

It took me a while to recognize the leading of God in my life. I struggled against it for many years. When I finally accepted His will, I began to find that peace that can only come to a life lived close to Him. When this occurred, I did the only thing I could do – recommitted my life to Him.

FRANK KAPRAL

OUT IN THE FIELDS WITH GOD

The little cares that fretted me,
  I lost them yesterday,
Among the fields above the sea,
  Among the winds at play,

Among the lowing of the herds,
The rustling of the trees,
Among the singing of the birds,
The humming of the bees.

The foolish fears of what might pass
I cast them all away
Among the clover-scented grass
Among the new-mown hay,
Among the rustling of the corn
Where drowsy poppies nod,
Where ill thoughts die and good are born —
Out in the fields with God!

AUTHOR UNKNOWN

Important rules to watch in living. Keep life simple. Avoid watching for a knock in your motor. Learn to like work. Have a good hobby. Learn to be satisfied. Like people, say cheerful pleasant things. Turn the defeat of adversity into victory. Meet your problems with decision. Make the present moment a success. Always be planning something. Say 'nuts' to irritations.

JOHN A. SCHINDLER, MD

Most illnesses do not, as is generally thought, come like a bolt out of the blue. The ground is prepared for years, through faulty diet, intemperance, overwork, and moral conflicts, slowly eroding the subject's vitality. And when at last the illness suddenly shows itself, it would be a most superficial medicine which treated it without going back to its remote causes, to all that I call 'personal problems.'

There are personal problems in every life. There are secret tragedies in every heart.

'Man does not die,' a doctor has remarked. 'He kills himself.'

This book is devoted to the study of the very complex relationships which always exist between our personal problems and our health.

Every act of physical, psychological, or moral disobedience of God's purpose is an act of wrong living and has its inevitable consequences.

PAUL TOURNIER, MD

Now the day is over,
Night is drawing nigh;
Shadows of the evening
Steal across the sky;

Jesus give the weary
　　Calm and sweet respose;
With thy tenderest blessing
　　May our eyelids close.

Grant to little children
　　Visions bright of thee;
Guard the sailors tossing
　　On the deep, blue sea.

Comfort every sufferer
　　Watching late in pain;
Those who plan some evil
　　From their sins restrain.

Through the long night watches,
　　May thine angels spread
Their white wings above me,
　　Watching round my bed.

When the morning wakens,
　　Then may I arise
Pure, and fresh, and sinless
　　In thy holy eyes. Amen.
　　　　　　　　　　SABINE BARING-GOULD

The best advice I have ever found for worriers I got from the great Dr Austen Riggs. He used to say to a worried woman, 'First ask yourself, is this my problem? If it isn't, leave it alone.' For instance, suppose a mother has fretted herself into an illness because her daughter cannot make up her mind to accept the proposal of marriage from some fine, well-to-do man. Dr Riggs would tell the mother she is foolish because it is not her problem – it is the girl who must decide what to do.

The next question for a worrier is, 'If it is my problem, can I tackle it now?' If the person can get right at it and settle it, he should do so. Once he has it settled, he ought to leave it alone, and not open the subject again. Often worse than a poor decision is none at all, and still worse is a decision that, once made, is quickly changed for no good reason.

The third bit of advice from Dr Riggs is, 'If your problem could be settled by an expert in some field, go quickly to him and take his advice.' For instance, I remember a widow who was in a terribly nervous state trying to decide what to do with an old apartment house which was not paying well. I said, 'That's easy; go right off to your banker, your lawyer, perhaps your income tax expert, and then to a realtor who is an expert on apartment houses. Take the advice of these men and settle the matter quickly.'

WALTER C. ALVAREZ, MD

Another point I make to women is that they should try hard not to do their worrying at night. Problems ought to be thought out and settled during the day. Night is a time for sleeping. All worriers would do well to take the advice of the great physician Sir William Osler. He told his patients to live in 'day tight compartments'; in other words, never to brood over the mistakes of the past or to worry about what might happen on the morrow. As Thomas Carlyle said, our job is to do quickly and as well as we can the work that lies close to our hands.

Some worriers may wonder why I haven't yet spoken of the great comforts that many a worrier can find in religion. Actually I cannot hope to do this as well as any number of inspired men and women are doing, and so I won't try. I can sum up much of the faith of many a physician by quoting that wonderful old prayer, 'Oh Lord, if you will only reveal to me where I can get help, I will go and get it.' In other words, let a worried person go to a priest, minister, or rabbi for spiritual help or consolation, and to a physician for reassurance in regard to the state of the body.

WALTER C. ALVAREZ, MD

> Let nothing disturb thee,
> Nothing affright thee;
> All things are passing:
> God never changeth;
> Patient endurance
> Attaineth to all things;
> Who God possesseth
> In nothing is wanting;
> Alone God sufficeth.

ST TERESA

In the degree, however, that you come into a vital realization of your oneness with the Infinite Spirit of Life, whence all life in individual form has come and is continually coming, and in the degree that through this realization you open yourself to its divine inflow, you set into operation forces that will sooner or later bring even the physical body into a state of abounding health and strength. For to realize that this Infinite Spirit of Life can from its very nature admit of no disease, and to realize that this, then, is the life in you, by realizing your oneness with it, you can so open yourself to its more abundant entrance that the diseased bodily conditions – effects – will respond to the influences of its all-perfect power, this either quickly or more tardily, depending entirely on yourself. . . .

Many will receive great help, and many will be entirely healed by a, practice somewhat after the following nature: With a mind at peace, and with a heart going out in love to all, go into the quiet of your own interior self, holding the thought – I am one with the Infinite Spirit of Life, the life of my life. I then as spirit, I a spiritual being, can in my own real nature admit of no disease. I now open my body, in which disease has obtained a foothold, I open it fully to the inflowing tide of this Infinite Life, and it now, even now, is pouring in and coursing through my body, and the healing process is going on. Realize this so fully that you begin to feel a quickening and a warming glow imparted by the life forces to the body. Believe the healing process is going on. Believe it, and hold continually to it. Many people greatly desire a certain thing, but expect something else. They have greater faith in the power of evil than in the power of good, and hence they remain ill.

If a man will give himself to this meditation, realization, treatment or whatever term it may seem best to use, at stated times, as often as he may choose, and then continually hold himself in the same attitude of mind, thus allowing the force to work continually, he will be surprised how rapidly the body will be exchanging conditions of disease and inharmony for health and harmony. There is no particular reason, however, for this surprise, for in this way he is simply allowing the Omnipotent Power to do the work, which will have to do it ultimately in any case. . . .

We are rapidly finding today, and we shall find even more and more, as time passes, that practically all disease, with its consequent suffering, has its origin in perverted mental and emotional states and conditions. The mental attitude we take toward anything determines to a greater or lesser extent its effects on us. If we fear it, or if we antagonize it, the chances are that it will have detrimental or even disastrous effects on us. If we come into harmony with it by quietly recognizing and inwardly asserting our superiority over it, in the degree that we are able successfully to do this, in that degree will it carry with it no injury for us.

No disease can enter into or take hold of our bodies unless it find therein something corresponding to itself which makes it possible. And in the same way, no evil or undesirable conditions of any kind can come into our lives unless there is already in them that which invites it and so makes it possible for it to come. The sooner we begin to look within ourselves for the cause of whatever comes to us, the better it will be, for so much the sooner will we begin to make conditions within ourselves such that only good may enter. . . .

Full, rich and abounding health is the normal and the natural condition of life. Anything else is an abnormal condition, and abnormal conditions as a rule come through perversions. God never created sickness, suffering and disease; they are man's own creations. They come through his violating the laws under which he lives. So used are we to seeing them that we come gradually, if not to think of them as natural, then to look on them as a matter of course. . . .

The whole matter may then be summed up in the one sentence, 'God is well and so are you.' You must awaken to the knowledge of your real being. When this awakening comes, you will have, and you will see that you have, the power to determine what conditions are externalized in your body. You must recognize, you must realize yourself, as one with Infinite Spirit. God's will is then your will; your will is God's will, and 'with God all things are possible.' When we are able to do away with all sense of separateness by living continually in the realization of this oneness, not only will our bodily ills and weaknesses vanish, but all limitations along all lines.

RALPH WALDO TRINE

As far as the east is from the west, so far hath he removed our transgressions from us.

PSALM 103; 12

One morning as I was hurriedly dressing to begin a full and thrilling day I felt a pain in my back. I mentioned it to my wife, but was sure it would soon pass away. However, she insisted I see a physician, and he put me in a hospital.

In the hospital I was very unhappy. I had no time to be wasting there in bed. My calendar was full of good activities, and the doctor told me to cancel all my appointments for at least a month. A dear minister friend of mine came to see me. He sat down and very firmly said, 'Charles, I have only one thing to say to you – "He *maketh* me to lie down!" '

I lay there thinking about those words in the Twenty-third Psalm long after my friend had gone. I thought about how the shepherd starts the sheep grazing about four o'clock in the morning. The sheep walk steadily as they graze; they are never still.

By ten o'clock the sun is beaming down and the sheep are hot, tired, and thirsty. The wise shepherd knows that the sheep must not drink when it is hot, neither when their stomachs are filled with undigested grass.

So the shepherd makes the sheep lie down in green pastures, in a cool, soft spot. The sheep will not eat lying down, so they chew their cud, which is nature's way of digestion.

Study the lives of great people, and you will find every one of them drew apart from the hurry of life for rest and reflection. Great poems are not written in crowded streets, lovely songs are not written in the midst of clamoring multitudes; our visions of God come when we stop. The Psalmist said, 'Be still, and know that I am God' (Psalm 46: 10).

Elijah found God, not in the earthquake or the fire, but in 'a still small voice.' Moses saw the burning bush as he was out on the hillside. Saul of Tarsus was on the lonely, quiet road to Damascus when he saw the heavenly vision. Jesus took time to be alone and to pray.

This is perhaps the most difficult thing for us to do. We will work for the Lord, we will sing, preach, teach. We will even suffer and sacrifice. Lustily we sing, 'Work, for the night is coming,' 'Onward Christian soldiers,' 'Stand up, stand up for Jesus.'

We sometimes forget that before Jesus sent out His disciples to conquer the world, He told them to tarry for prayer and the power of God.

Sometimes God puts us on our backs in order to give us a chance to look up. 'He maketh me to lie down.' Many times we are forced, not by God, but by circumstances of one sort or another to lie down. That can always be a blessed experience. Even the bed of an invalid may be a blessing if he takes advantage of it!

> Take from our souls the strain and stress,
> And let our ordered lives confess –
> The beauty of thy peace.
>
> CHARLES L. ALLEN

> At the heart of the cyclone tearing the sky
> And flinging the clouds and the towers by,
>   Is a place of central calm:
> So here in the roar of mortal things,
> I have a place where my spirit sings,
>   In the hollow of God's Palm.
>
> EDWIN MARKHAM

Time spent on the knees in prayer will do more to remedy heart strain and nerve worry than anything else.

GEORGE DAVID STEWART

Your subconscious mind produces in your daily life evidence of the thoughts you send back to it. The constant repetition of fear, anxiety and worry thoughts will bring upon you the same thing multiplied many times over, but the constant practice of positive thinking, making affirmations hour by hour that God is now healing your fears and worries, will bring magnificent results.

How many times have you heard the phrase, 'Believe you can do it and you will do it'? Belief enables you to do things that were otherwise impossible, for the act of believing is the starting force which leads to accomplishment. The more you believe, the more power within comes to your aid. . . .

'For whosoever hath, to him shall be given, and he shall have more abundance.' This means that to him that hath faith shall be given the truth that will make him free of every negative thing. It means that more health, more happiness, more harmony in living will be added unto him. It does not mean wealth in dollars and cents. It does mean that if you will accept the suggestion that Jesus Christ was God and that His spirit lives within you, then by practicing His teachings, you will never doubt any more that you can overcome in the world everything negative that you can possibly have to face. . . .

First believe; then make use of the power of suggestion that Jesus Christ, who is now your captain and your pilot, has begun to give you strength, to give you ideas, and to give you happiness. Make this your belief, your affirmation, every hour of the day. . . .

Remember to look upon God as a friend. Remember also that all your life must be lived according to laws He has made. Believe that He is willing to give you now His Kingdom. Trust that He will solve every problem you have to face at this moment, if you will practice the magic of believing.

The way to get along in the world lies in the thought, the suggestion, that once you accept Christ by simply letting Him be the dominating factor in your life, and take Him at His word, believing that He is now showing you the way to a life free from error and a life more abundant, then the self-imposed prison you have lived in for so long will disappear.

Learn how to *let go* the negative suggestions of the human side of your nature, and learn how to *let God* bring happiness to you. You have the ability for successful living. You have the tools. The power you use is faith and the tools are your thoughts and ideas. Learn today how to use them, not for yourself but for God. Thus you will become a radiant, happy Christian, living in Christ and He in you, for you will have gained every righteous desire of your heart.

ALBERT E. CLIFFE

Never have I enjoyed youth so thoroughly as I have in my old age. In writing *Dialogues in Limbo*, *The Last Puritan*, and now all these descriptions of the friends of my youth and the young friends of my middle age, I have drunk the pleasure of life more pure, more joyful, than it ever was when mingled with all the hidden anxieties and little annoyances of actual living. Nothing is inherently and invincibly young except spirit. And spirit can enter a human being perhaps better in the quiet of old age and dwell there more undisturbed than in the turmoil of adventure. But it must be in solitude. I do not need or desire to hobnob artificially with other old men in order to revisit them in their salad days, and to renew my own. In Rome, in the eternal city, I feel nearer to my own past, and to the whole past and future of the world, than I should in any cemetery or in any museum of relics. Old places and old persons in their turn, when spirit dwells in them, have an intrinsic vitality of which youth is incapable; precisely the balance and wisdom that comes from long perspectives and broad foundations. Everything shines then for the spirit by its own light in its own place and time; but not as it shone in its own restless eyes. For in its own eyes each person and each place was the centre of a universe full of threatening and tempting things; but old age, having less intensity at the centre has more clearness at the circumference, and knows that just because spirit, at each point, is a private centre for all things, no one point, no one phase of spirit is materially a public centre for all the rest.

GEORGE SANTAYANA

When you have closed your doors, and darkened your room, remember never to say that you are alone, for you are not alone; God is within, and your genius is within – and what need have they of light to see what you are doing?

EPICTETUS

The world is too much with us; late and soon,
Getting and spending, we lay waste our powers;
Little we see in Nature that is ours;
We have given our hearts away, a sordid boon!
The sea that bares her bosom to the moon;
The winds that will be howling at all hours,
And are up-gathered now like sleeping flowers;
For this, for everything, we are out of tune;
It moves us not. – Great God! I'd rather be
A Pagan suckled in a creed outworn;
So might I, standing on this pleasant lea,
Have glimpses that would make me less forlorn;
Have sight of Proteus rising from the sea;
Or hear old Triton blow his wreathèd horn.

WILLIAM WORDSWORTH

Finish every day and be done with it. You have done what you could. Some blunders and absurdities no doubt crept in; forget them as soon as you can. Tomorrow is a new day; begin it well and serenely and with too high a spirit to be cumbered with your old nonsense. This day is all that is good and fair. It is too dear, with its hopes and invitations, to waste a moment on the yesterdays.

RALPH WALDO EMERSON

Ere thou sleepest, gently lay
Every troubled thought away;
Put off worry and distress
As thou puttest off thy dress;
Drop thy burden and thy care
In the quiet arms of prayer.
Lord thou knowest how I live,
All I've done amiss forgive;
All of good I've tried to do
Strengthen, bless and carry through;
All I love in safety keep
While in Thee I fall asleep.

HENRY VAN DYKE

To the quiet mind all things are possible. What is a quiet mind? A quiet mind is one which nothing weighs on, nothing worries, which, free from ties and from all self-seeking, is wholly merged into the will of God and dead as to its own. Such a one can do no deed however small but it is clothed with something of God's power and authority.

MEISTER ECKHART

Quiet minds cannot be perplexed or frightened, but go on in fortune or misfortune at their own private pace, like a clock in a thunderstorm.

ROBERT LOUIS STEVENSON

You cannot run away from a weakness; you must sometime fight it out or perish; and if that be so, why not now, and where you stand?

ROBERT LOUIS STEVENSON

Love your enemies, bless them that curse you, do good to them that hate you, and pray for them which despitefully use you, and persecute you.

MATTHEW 5:44

Have courage for the great sorrows of life and patience for the small ones; when you have laboriously accomplished your daily tasks, go to sleep in peace. God is awake.

VICTOR HUGO

And one cried unto another, and said, Holy, holy, holy, is the Lord of hosts; the whole earth is full of his glory.

ISAIAH 6: 3

And be renewed in the spirit of your mind.

EPHESIANS 4: 23

Is any sick among you? Let him call for the elders of the church; and let them pray over him. . . .

And the prayer of faith shall save the sick, and the Lord shall raise him up; and if he have committed sins, they shall be forgiven him.

JAMES 5: 14–15

Matthew, Mark, Luke, and John,
Bless the bed that I lie on.
Before I lay me down to sleep
I give my soul to Christ to keep.
Four corners to my bed,
Four angels there aspread,
Two to foot, and two to head,
And four to carry me when I'm dead.
I go by sea, I go by land.
The Lord made me with His right hand.

If any danger come to me,
Sweet Jesus Christ deliver me.
He's the branch and I'm the flower,
Pray God send me a happy hour,
And if I die before I wake,
I pray that Christ my soul will take.

ANONYMOUS

All men's miseries derive from not being able to sit quiet in a room alone.

BLAISE PASCAL

Thou wilt keep him in perfect peace, whose mind is stayed on thee.

ISAIAH 26: 3

Ere you lie down to sleep in the night, sit still awhile, and nurse again to life your gentler self. Forget the restless, noisy spirit of the day, and encourage to speech the soft voices within you that timidly whisper of the peace of the quiet night; and occasionally look out at the quiet stars. The night will soothe you like a tender mother, folding you against her soft bosom, and hiding you from the harm of the world. Though denied and rejected by men in the light of day, the night will not reject you and in the still of her soft shadows you are free. After the day's struggle there is no freedom like unfettered thoughts, no sound like the music of silence. And though behind you lies a road of dust and heat and discouragement, and before you the challenge and uncertainty of untried paths, in this brief hour you are master of all highways, and the universe nestles in your soul.

MAX EHRMANN

Chapter 6

How Hope and Courage Banish Fear

Can you imagine a person who has everything to make him happy and provide security and yet is always troubled and anxious? Unfortunately, there are many such in this world.

On a sun-kissed summer day a man of this kind drove out of his beautiful country home and down a road that wound over the hills. His mind was agitated by uncertainties, anxieties, and fears. He reviewed all the things he had which made such fears irrational. But then it came to him that he was still the timorous, shy, and fearful person he had been as a boy. Always his mother had expected disaster. Though it never came, she had infected her son to expect the same, and so always fear haunted him; anxiety lurked somewhere in every thought.

On this summer morning, as he drove he happened to notice a little road leading off along a small stream into the hills. On an impulse he took it and made an encounter that started a change in his life. He followed the road for two miles or so, finally coming to an intersection. No marker pointed the way. While he hesitated, a white-haired man came along on horseback. Stopping him to ask directions, he fell into conversation. 'Lots of trouble in the world these days,' said our friend in the car, for want of something else to say.

'Well, maybe,' said the man on the horse, 'but the other day I saw a statement I sort of liked – it went like this: "And he laid His right hand upon me, saying unto me, Fear not . . ." ' And he waved and started on.

'Hey, who said that?' the other man shouted.

'The Bible,' said the horseman.

The strange statement wouldn't leave the motorist. He looked it up and found it in Revelation 1: 17. 'Seems like a father putting his hand on your troubled head,' he thought. This curious incident started him on a search for other such statements that would 'take away my old insecurity and fear feelings.' He gave me several which are used in this chapter. These quotations helped him to find hope and courage and gradually lessen his fears.

What words they are: *hope, courage, fear !* Two of them make life wonderful. One of them blights human existence. How many people have we seen across many years who have suffered from unresolved fear. But, then, also how many have found release and relief through hope and courage.

And all three of these are mental attitudes that result from the kind of thoughts we think. The mental climate a person creates determines whether he shall have hope even when things seem hopeless, have courage even when apprehensive factors appear, or live in fear because of hopelessness and apprehension. You can think your way to hope and courage or you can think your way into the dark morass of fear and misery.

Hope and courage can be developed through practice. Deliberately start thinking hopeful and courageous thoughts. At first this will seem futile, even hypocritical, for you will feel that you are trying to act contrary to the way you really are. But it is not futile, for it will start a healthy process going, and it is not hypocritical, for you are making an effort to change yourself for the better.

You will have long-established mental habits to counteract and that is not easy. But it can be done. In fact, that in itself is a hopeful and courageous thought: *it can be done*. Say those four magic words until they start working in your consciousness.

Fear began in the first place as a thin trickle of thought across your mind, perhaps in childhood, in fact most probably in your early formative years. Continuing to develop, it finally cut a deep channel of thought into your mind. So dominating did it become that every thought you have about yourself, your health, your future, your family, was drained into this deep channel of fear and came up tinged with anxiety. Apprehension discolored your whole life and constituted a hazard to any successful activity. Such a deep thought channel imbedded in the mind is hard to obliterate, but *it can be done*. Indeed you can do anything with your mind *if* – *if* you want to badly enough. It all depends upon the vigor of the desire. If with all your heart – then you are in.

So then the secret is to start a thin trickle of faith, hope, and courage across the mind. It will seem at first woefully ineffective as though it were nothing at all. But just keep at it, reminding yourself of one great and glorious fact that fear is only the second most powerful force in the personality. One is stronger, very much stronger. And that more powerful force is faith. Perseverance in faith will begin to cut a deep channel in the thoughts, and finally it will undercut the old fear-thought channel which, to carry the figure further, will cave in. Then you will have a deep channel of faith into which all your thoughts about yourself, your health, your family, your future will be drained and emerge bright, hopeful, and optimistic. New courage will be yours.

If this procedure should seem a bit incredible, I assure you we have applied it to many over many years and with considerable success. In our American Foundation for Religion and Psychiatry we have taught the skill of revamped thought, the substitution of a pattern of mental emphasis.

I recall the sales manager of a modest-sized company, who developed acute nervous symptoms. He happened to hear a radio talk in which I outlined some of the ideas presented here, including the positive assurance that tension stress and anxiety can be overcome by applying new thought procedures.

This man wrote me asking for an interview, but, realizing his need for professional counseling, I referred him to our clinic. His thinking was analyzed and was found a mass of anxieties traceable to a fear-ridden parental relationship, which had been accentuated with every new and more important responsibility to which he had risen by reason of his extraordinary ability. However, he was terrorized by a haunting fear of failure and of people.

Our counselors revealed the causes of his fear-tension pattern to him and assured him that he could be changed, a fact he accepted. This evidence of faith convinced us that he could make the transition to a healthier thought climate.

We 'fed' him thoughts of hope and courage similar to those included in this chapter, and ultimately he developed an attitude of hope and courage, not fear.

> In the hour of adversity be not without hope
> For crystal rain falls from black clouds.
>
> NIZAMI

Dear Dr Peale:

Friday morning (it was September the 20th) started off as such an ordinary day. After breakfast we held four-year-old Donnie and one-year-old Elizabeth up to the window to wave goodbye as our seven-year-old boy, Scotty, headed off to school. Scotty had just disappeared from sight when Tibby remembered about the ice cream.

'I meant to tell him I'd be at the ice-cream counter today,' she said. Mothers here in Mount Kisco take turns selling ice cream at the school cafeteria. It's just as well Tibby did not tell Scotty; because she never got to the cafeteria.

A few moments later I was upstairs at my typewriter. Spread out on my desk, were the notes I had collected during seven years as a *Guideposts* reporter. People who had found their strength in prayer. Why? It was a fascinating question.

The phone rang. It was my doctor.

'I need to see you,' he said.

'Well, of course, doctor. When?'

'Right now.'

I hung up the phone, mystified. I hadn't been to the doctor's in months, except for a brief session two days earlier, when he had removed a small mole from my ear.

'It's nearly noon,' I called to Tibby. 'Do you want to come along?'

The first inkling we had that something was seriously wrong was when the doctor held my chair for me. He didn't hold Tibby's chair; he held mine.

'I don't know how to tell you this,' the doctor said. 'How can I tell a young husband and father that in all probability he's going to die?'

Shock is an amazing defense, Dr Peale. It allows us to function with perfect calm just after hearing bad news. We sat there and listened to the doctor explain that I had a malignant melanoma. We heard him say, 'It's a particularly vicious kind of cancer, especially if it gets in the blood stream. Without an operation, the statistics say you have one chance in nine of being alive at the end of the year. With an operation, you have one chance in three.'

We said nothing at all. After a moment he went on.

'I don't want you to take my word for this. Get at least two other opinions – from Presbyterian and from Memorial hospitals.'

Tib drove home to start the endless succession of phone calls and I walked over to the Mt Kisco Hospital to have X-rays taken. I walked through the brightly colored trees of our early fall, whistling and humming. I wasn't being heroic. I really felt that way. My body's defenses had set up a wall which the news had not yet breached. With the X-rays under my arm, I walked home. I stopped and chatted idly with some workmen repairing the road. We laughed together over something; I don't remember now what it was. But we laughed.

That afternoon Tibby and I drove into New York City. We took my slide and X-rays to the huge Presbyterian Hospital. But the second report came down: Malignant melanoma. Immediate surgery.

By the time we got to Memorial, its pathology labs were closed until Monday morning. We left the slide and X-rays and drove back out to the country.

As soon as we got home we went upstairs to my office and closed the door, and turned on the air conditioner, because the machine made a buzzing noise that drowned out the house noises below. And then, without warning and without embarrassment, we both suddenly began to cry. It was the moment that we first let reality peek through.

Fear. Fear is such a devastating emotion, Dr Peale. Once it had broken our defenses, it harried us night and day. I woke up in the night and knew that I was afraid. I answered the children's questions automatically; my mind was elsewhere. I spent hours with Tibby going over insurance, wills, finances. Then I tried to force my mind to more healthy matters, but I could not: I was afraid.

And then, Dr Peale, something remarkable happened.

On my desk sat the unfinished manuscript on prayer, 'Why Do Men Pray?' I had come to the conclusion that men always pray in response to a specific need, great or small. As our friends began to hear the news of the cancer, they needed to feel they were helping, and their immediate response was to pray.

The first prayer that we learned about, I think, was the prayer that you said for us from your pulpit that Sunday. After that, prayer rose about us like a flood. There was prayer at *Guideposts*, both in the New York office and the Carmel office. Did you know, Dr Peale, that your friend, Tessie Durlach, asked her synagogue to pray for us, and that she called long distance to the Prayer Tower at Unity? Our assistant art director, Sal Lazzarotti, told me he almost drove off the road saying the rosary on his way home Friday after he heard the news.

'I haven't been saying the rosary too regular, God,' he kept saying. 'But starting tonight it's going to be different.'

Prayer was in the air we breathed. We were surrounded by it, submerged in it. Prayer from trained groups and from people who had never tried it before. Prayer from people we knew well and from people we had never met.

We had known the man who handles our health insurance only as a fun-loving, poker-playing businessman. In a letter explaining our insurance coverage, he told us, 'Don't forget to pray. Remember that with faith all things are possible.' A night-club singer told us she was praying for us after work each night, and a Catholic friend who had left her church when she married admitted that she'd slipped into a chapel and lit candles for us.

On Tuesday we got the report from Memorial. It confirmed the previous reports, and I was admitted to the hospital on Thursday, for an operation on Friday morning.

And to my amazement, the atmosphere at the hospital was one of prayer, too. No sooner had I settled down in my bed in room 609 than I heard a weird and haunting note, almost a cry, permeate the corridor. In the room next to mine an Orthodox Jewish patient was celebrating Rosh Hashana.* The nurse told me I had heard the cry of the ram's horn, which for centuries has been used to call men to prayer.

During all these days, what about my own prayers? They were vibrantly real. But I do not intend to discuss them here, except to say that they were not for myself, they were for others.

* The Jewish New Year, which began September 26.

I must emphasize, Dr Peale, that I am trying simply to report facts. I prayed for others, not from any deliberate selflessness, but because I genuinely did not feel the need to pray for myself. This struck me as a little strange until I realized the reason. Suddenly, on the night before the operation, I was aware that I was free of fear!

Was this the tangible result of all the prayers? I think it was. On the night before the operation I felt such a surge of health that it was hard to realize I was in a hospital.

At six o'clock the next morning a nurse roused me and gave me a needle. 'This will make you sleepy,' she said.

I laughed. 'You wake me up to give me something to make me sleepy?'

They came and wheeled me into the operating room. It was as if I, and the white-masked nurses, and the doctors were in the center of a force that dispelled fear. The closest I can come to describing it is to say that I felt as if I were deeply and personally loved.

And that, of course, must be a perfect condition for healing. . . .

The operation was over.

There was a week of tortuous waiting. Then the doctor brought in his report. He did not tell me the results of the operation right away. He shined a light into my eyes, probed and thumped, and then, in a matter-of-fact voice, he said: 'Your report is the best one I could possibly have for you. There is no evidence of residual melanoma.'

Does this mean that there has been a cure?

I am not a doctor, and I do not pretend to understand the vagaries of cancer. Has it all been removed? Will it come back? No one really knows. But I do know about another kind of cure, one that may be more important.

Before the operation I lived, as I think most of us do, in a kind of twilight fear of cancer. Then, when I learned that I did have cancer, this vague fear blossomed into a monster. The fear had the power to destroy just as surely as did the melanoma.

But after the experience in the hospital, I feel there has been another cure.

With as much honesty as I can possibly muster, I must say that I personally have experienced the power of prayer to heal the most devastating disease of all – the power of prayer to heal fear.*

JOHN SHERRILL

I pray for faith, I long to trust;
I listen with my heart, and hear
A Voice without a sound: 'Be just,

* The writer is now completely healed. N.V.P.

Be true, be merciful, revere
The Word within thee: God is near!

'A light to sky and earth unknown
Pales all their lights: a mightier force
Than theirs the powers of Nature own,
And, to its goal as at its source,
His Spirit moves the Universe.

'Believe and trust. Through stars and suns,
Through life and death, through soul and sense,
His wise, paternal purpose runs;
The darkness of His providence
Is star-lit with benign intents.'

O joy supreme! I know the Voice,
Like none beside on earth or sea;
Yea, more, O soul of mine, rejoice,
By all that He requires of me,
I know what God himself must be. . . .

I fear no more. The clouded face
Of Nature smiles; through all her things
Of time and space and sense I trace
The moving of the Spirit's wings,
And hear the song of hope she sings.

JOHN GREENLEAF WHITTIER

Laura, my friend, suspects that I had arranged the whole affair, just for her benefit. Actually it all happened by coincidence – if there is such a thing, which I am often inclined to doubt.

It began when Laura confided in me. She was, she said, in a predicament.

'The simple fact,' she told me, 'is that I am a coward. Most of my life I have been protected and felt secure. But now, suddenly, my mother and father have been taken from me by death. I am engaged to marry a young man but, although I love him dearly, I am afraid to marry. I feel afraid of life, afraid to face it, afraid of what it will do to me – most of all, I am afraid of death.

'I loved my mother and father and death took them. I love my young man very much, much more – but the thought of being his wife and then having death separate us, sooner or later, fills me with terror. I don't believe in God any more – I just want to run away from everything. How can I find help ?'

I have never fancied myself as a sage, telling other people what to do. Although I tried to help the girl, the words seemed forced and unreal. But presently an idea occurred to me. That same afternoon I was scheduled to speak on a national broadcast presented by *Guideposts*, a non-profit religious magazine for people of all faiths, edited by my good friend Dr Norman Vincent Peale. I knew that some of the other speakers were men of real inspiration, and so I asked my frightened friend to listen in, sure that she would find the answer to her problem.

As the broadcast got under way, the speakers seemed to me to be talking on every other subject in the world except on the conquest of fear. I was feeling quite downhearted, when suddenly a giant of a man was called to the microphone. He was Gene Tunney, undefeated heavyweight champion of the world. As he began to talk, it was as if he were aiming his words directly at my terrified friend.

'People often ask me if I have ever been afraid. They only make me smile. One Eastern philosopher said that any man who boasts that he has never been afraid has never put out a candle with his fingers. We are all afraid. Intelligent people, those with imagination, are the ones who know the most overpowering fears, and there is only one answer to fear – and that is faith. Unless we have something greater than ourselves to believe in, we are lost. We are prey to fears unless we can pray our fears away.

'Talk about dauntless courage makes me smile. I knew what fear was every time I entered the ring. One night I shall never forget I was sound asleep and I woke up in the dark wondering what was wrong with my bed. It was shaking like a 1910 Ford. Then I suddenly realized that it wasn't the bed shaking at all. It was I who was shaking. I was trembling all over with fear. That was the night before my first meeting with Jack Dempsey, and even in my dreams I was thinking of what he was going to do to me the next day. Courage? . . . It is not being fearless, it is finding the strength from God to do what you have to do – whether you are afraid or not.'

My friend Laura still believes I put Gene up to it. But what does it matter? He gave her the answer – and the fact that a prize fighter was not afraid to believe in God sent her back to the faith of her childhood. Her married life has been very happy.

FULTON OURSLER

When you think everything is hopeless
A little ray of light comes from somewhere!
INSCRIPTION IN AN OLD INN,
ST MORITZ, SWITZERLAND

I remember a number of persons who, I am almost certain, died of fright. They died in the operating room, some of them before anything had been done to them, and others with the first whiff of the anaesthetic, which was not enough to have harmed anyone. I remember seeing a rat drop dead when barked at by a dog, and a road runner, a big Arizona bird, drop dead when confronted with a stuffed owl.

A stout, previously healthy man of sixty got so enraged when his daughter sued him for an accounting of her mother's estate that he could think of nothing but his hatred. He immediately lost his health and sense of well-being. His breath became foul, he lost his appetite, quickly lost 60 pounds, his heart and kidneys failed, he became bloated, and soon he died. If ever a man died of hatred and anger, he did.

To show how a strong impression or a panicky fear can make some persons very ill, a stout, healthy, but superstitious young Irishman, when in a cemetery, tripped and fell into an open grave. He was so upset and so filled with fear over what he was sure must be a very bad omen, that overnight he became shaky, sleepless, and so full of pain that he had to stay in his bed. He went on into a miserable nervous breakdown.

When I was a boy in Hawaii, my doctor-father used to see men die who had been told they were being 'prayed to death' by a witch doctor or kahuna. The natives were so firmly convinced that death was inevitable when a kahuna started his incantations directed against them, that they gave up; they sat down on a mat; they refused food and drink, and got it over with as soon as possible. As I remember, they would be dead in about a week. My friend Dr N. P. Larsen, of Honolulu, recently wrote about the many powerfully built and healthy Filipino bachelors who wake out of a fearful nightmare and die – apparently of fright.

These observations show what a powerfully destructive effect the nervous system can have on the chemical functions of the body. . . .

One of the remarkable observations that we doctors keep hearing about all the time is that the letup of strain can cause a distressing and oft-recurrent pain, like that of a bad ulcer in the duodenum (just outside the stomach), to disappear instantly. A few hundred times, I have had a man with an ulcer say to me, 'You know, before I left home to come to see you, I had had weeks of misery in which, because of the pain in my stomach, I walked the floor at night and got little sleep. And then the other day, when I bought a plane ticket to come to you, my pain disappeared and it hasn't come back. This past week, I have been eating all sorts of indigestible foods, but they don't hurt me, and I am sleeping all night.'

I remember a man with a very trying business who walked the floor every night with the severe pain of a 'red-hot' stomach ulcer. When he came to Rochester, Minnesota, to see me, I sent him to a hospital and told the resident to give him all the sedatives he needed to get a bit of rest. I said, 'This fellow will probably keep you up all night with demands for relief of pain.' To my surprise, the resident said next day, 'I didn't see anything peculiar about that chap you sent in; he slept like a baby all night without any help from me.' Actually, he continued without any pain or discomfort the whole time he was in Rochester, because he was at peace. His ulcer was there; it hadn't had time for much healing but he could not feel it. I imagine his nerves had become so much less sensitive that they stopped screaming at his brain. . . .

One of the great difficulties we physicians often have in trying to help nervous patients is their tendency to jump to the conclusion that pains of psychic origin must be mild and wholly imaginary. Actually, I have seen cases in which they were much more severe than the pains that commonly arise in some diseased organ in the abdomen, such as the stomach. To impress a nervous patient with the idea that symptoms produced by nervousness are not imaginary, I remind him that diarrhea due to fright is just as real as is diarrhea due to castor oil.

To further illustrate this point, I often tell a patient the story of two women who, years ago, came into my office. Even yet, I can see them clearly in my mind's eye. One was a sweet old farmer's wife, suffering from a big cancer in the stomach, and the other was her devoted daughter, a 'mama's baby' who had nothing wrong with her except a terrible fear for her mother's health. The older woman said, 'Don't bother with me, I'm not sick, I have no pain, and I'm getting along all right. Just take care of daughter; she is very ill. She has been vomiting steadily for three days, ever since she came home and learned what was wrong with me.'

What a remarkable contrast that was! One woman suffering from the worst possible disease of the stomach, yet perfectly comfortable and unconcerned, and the other with a normal stomach but with great distress referred out from her anguished brain. This story shows how right Cicero was when he said, 'The sufferings of the mind are more severe than the pains of the body.'

WALTER C. ALVAREZ, MD

Keep your fears to yourself, but share your courage with others.

ROBERT LOUIS STEVENSON

Right, but there may come a time when, to be healed of fear, you must talk it out with a wise counselor.

To me it seems basic to the getting rid of fear to know that our trials, of whatever nature, are not motiveless. In our present stage of development we could hardly do without them. So often looking like mere ugly excrescences on, like they are in reality, the branches by which we catch on and climb. They are not obstacles to happiness for the reason that the only satisfying happiness we are equal to as yet is that of wrestling with the difficult and overcoming it. Every call of duty has its place in this ideal; every irksome job, every wearisome responsibility. The fact that we are not always aware of it in no way annuls the other fact, that it is so. . . .

God is with us *to be utilized*. His Power, His Love, His Thought, His Presence must be at our disposal, like other great forces, such as sunshine and wind and rain. We can use them or not, as we please. That we could use them to their full potentiality is, of course, not to be thought of; but we can use them in proportion to our ability. If I, the individual, still lack many things, if I am still a prey to lingering fears, it is probably because I have not yet rooted out a stubborn disbelief in His Power. . . .

I am convinced that absolute confidence in God's overflowing liberality of every sort is essential to the conquest of fear. If we don't profit by that liberality, the fault is not His but our own. . . .

In order to banish fear I think it necessary to train the thought to seeing God as expressing Himself in all the good and pleasant and enjoyable things that come to us. This means forming a habit. It means saying to oneself daily, hourly, 'This is God,' 'That is God,' of incidents, persons, and things we have rarely thought of in that relation. . . .

Meanwhile, it is much for the individual to know that he can act on his own initiative, and that when it comes to making God his refuge he can go into that refuge alone. He needs no nation, or government, or society, or companions before him or behind him. He needs neither leader nor guide nor friend. In the fortress of God he is free to enter merely as himself, and there know that he is safe amid a world in agony.

BASIL KING

Be strong and of a good courage; be not afraid, neither be thou dismayed; for the Lord thy God is with thee whithersoever thou goest.

JOSHUA 1: 9

Wait on the Lord: be of good courage, and he shall strengthen thine heart.

PSALM 27: 14

I see that I am inwardly fashioned for faith and not for fear. Fear is not my native land; faith is. I am so made that worry and anxiety are sand in the machinery of life; faith is oil. I live better by faith and confidence than by fear and doubt and anxiety. In anxiety and worry my being is gasping for breath – these are not my native air. But in faith and confidence I breathe freely – these are my native air. A Johns Hopkins' doctor says that 'we do not know why it is that the worriers die sooner than the non-worriers, but that is a fact.' But I, who am simple of mind, think I know: we are inwardly constructed in nerve and tissue and brain cell and soul, for faith and not for fear. God made us that way. Therefore, the need of faith is not something imposed on us dogmatically, but it is written in us intrinsically. We cannot live without it.

To live by worry is to live against Reality.

E. STANLEY JONES

WE BREAK NEW SEAS TODAY

Each man is Captain of his Soul,
And each man his own Crew,
But the Pilot knows the Unknown Seas,
And he will bring us through.

We break new seas today –
Our eager keels quest unaccustomed waters,
And, from the vast uncharted waste in front,
The mystic circles leap
To greet our prows with mightiest possibilities,
Bringing us – What?

Dread shoals and shifting banks?
And calms and storms?
And clouds and biting gales?
And wreck and loss?
And valiant fighting times?
And, maybe, death! – and so, the Larger Life!

For, should the Pilot deem it best
To cut the voyage short,
He sees beyond the sky-line, and
He'll bring us into Port!

JOHN OXENHAM

May you live all the days of your life.

JONATHAN SWIFT

Have courage for the great sorrows of life and patience for the small ones; and when you have laboriously accomplished your daily tasks, go to sleep in peace. God is awake.

VICTOR HUGO

Let us be of good cheer, remembering that the misfortunes hardest to bear are those which never come.

JAMES RUSSELL LOWELL

For God hath not given us the spirit of fear; but of power, and of love, and of a sound mind.

II TIMOTHY I: 7

Once when I was facing a decision that involved (I thought) considerable risk, I took the problem to a friend much older and wiser than myself. 'I'd go ahead,' I said unhappily, 'if I were *sure* I could swing it. But . . .'

He looked at me for a moment, then scribbled ten words on a piece of paper and pushed it across the desk. I picked it up and read, in a single sentence, the best advice I ever had: *Be bold – and mighty forces will come to your aid.*

It's amazing how even a fragment of truth will illuminate things. The words my friend had written were from a quotation, I discovered later, in a book by Basil King. They made me see clearly that in the past, whenever I had fallen short in almost any undertaking, it was seldom because I had tried and failed. It was because I had let fear of failure stop me from trying at all.

On the other hand, whenever I *had* plunged into deep water, impelled by a momentary flash of courage or just plain pushed by the rude hand of circumstance, I had always been able to swim until I got my feet on the ground again.

Be bold – that was no exhortation to be reckless or foolhardy. Boldness meant a deliberate decision, from time to time, to bite off more than you were sure you could chew. And there was nothing vague or mysterious about the mighty forces referred to. They were the latent powers that all of us possess: energy, skill, sound judgment, creative ideas – yes, even physical strength and endurance in far greater measure than most of us realize.

Boldness, in other words, creates a state of emergency to which the organism will respond. I once heard a famous British mountaineer say that occasionally a climber will get himself into a position where he can't back down, he can only go up. He added that sometimes he put himself into such a spot on purpose. 'When there's nowhere to go but up,' he said, 'you jolly well go up!'

The same principle works, less dramatically but just as surely, in something as commonplace as accepting the chairmanship of some civic committee, or even seeking a more responsible job. In either case, you know you'll have to deliver – or else. And unless you're hopelessly unqualified, you *will* deliver. Your pride, your competitive instinct, and your sense of obligation will see to it that you do.

These are some of the mighty forces that will come to your aid. They are, admittedly, psychic forces. But they are more important than physical ones. It was centrifugal force, in a hurtling pebble, that killed Goliath. But it was courage that enabled David to face the champion of the Philistines in the first place.

It's curious, actually, how spiritual laws often have their counterpart in the physical world. A college classmate of mine was a crack football player, noted particularly for his fierce tackling although he was much lighter than the average varsity player. Someone remarked that it was surprising that he didn't get hurt. 'Well,' he said, 'I think it goes back to something I discovered when I was a somewhat timid youngster playing sandlot football. In one game, playing safety man, I suddenly found myself confronting the opposing fullback, who had nothing but me between him and our goal line. He looked absolutely gigantic! I was so frightened that I closed my eyes and hurled myself at him like a panicky bullet . . . and stopped him cold. Right there I learned that the harder you tackle a bigger player, the less likely you are to be hurt. The reason is simple: momentum equals weight times velocity.'

In other words, if you are bold enough, even the laws of motion will come to your aid.

This personality trait – a willingness to put yourself in a position where you will have to extend yourself to the utmost – is not one that can be acquired overnight. But it can be taught to children and developed in adults. Confidence is a cumulative thing.

To be sure, there will be setbacks and disappointments in any program of expanded living; boldness in itself is no guarantee of success. But, as someone said, the man who tries to do something and fails is a lot better off than the man who tries to do nothing and succeeds.

Boldness, of course, like any other virtue, can be pushed too far. Once, in my more impulsive days, I jumped out of an airplane just to see what it was like. I had a parachute, naturally – two, in fact – but I promptly wound up in a hospital with a broken ankle. I suppose I did achieve my main objective, which was to write a story about paratroopers, with a certain amount of realism. But it was hardly worth it.

Still, for every time you thus overshoot your target, there are a hundred times that you undershoot it. In the famous Parable of the Talents, the servant who buries his master's money in the ground is severely reprimanded for failing to do anything with it or take any risk. And the servant's answer is very significant. It could be summarized in three words: I was afraid. . . .*

* Matthew 25: 25.

Fear, the opposite of boldness, is the most paralyzing of all emotions. It can literally stiffen the muscles, as anyone knows who has ever been really scared. And (again the psychic-physical parallel holds) it can also stupefy the mind and the will. Most of us free-lance writers know this very well. When you are blessed – or cursed – with a vivid imagination, it's all too easy to become convinced that your energy is dwindling, that the flow of ideas is drying up, that your latest effort is also your last. Such thoughts are dangerous. Fears, like hopes and dreams, have a way of clothing themselves ultimately with reality. As Job said, reviewing his troubles (and anticipating the psychiatrists by a couple of millennia), The thing which I greatly feared is come upon me. . . .*

Almost from the beginning of recorded history, mankind has recognized that the surest antidote for fear is religious faith. Belief – and trust – in a personal God makes a man bigger than himself and stronger than himself. Washington bore witness to this repeatedly; so did Lincoln. Joan of Arc was a shining example of the power of faith to transform an individual, and through an individual a whole nation.

This source of power is just as available to the rank and file as to the leaders. The man who believes firmly that the Creator of the universe loves him and cares infinitely what he does with his life – this man is automatically freed from much of the self-distrust that afflicts less certain men. Fear, guilt, hostility, anger – these are the emotions that stifle thought and impede action. By reducing or eliminating them, religious faith makes boldness possible, and boldness makes achievement possible. Over and over again, in both the Old and New Testaments, the Bible hammers this message home: The Lord is my light and my salvation; whom shall I fear?† . . . According to your faith be it unto you.‡

Boldness is not always spectacular; there is also a quiet kind. I knew a city-dwelling family once that wanted to move to the country. They had no financial resources, but plenty of spiritual ones. Instead of counting the pennies and deciding the move was impossible, they calmly drew up a list of six requirements that they considered essential (actually, they agreed they would settle for five of the six). The place, they decided, would have to have a pleasant view, some shade trees, a stream or brook, some arable land to grow things, some pasture for animals, and it had to be near enough to the city for the father to milk the cows every morning and still commute to his job.

They finally found such a place, borrowed the money to make a down payment, and have been living there happily (and boldly, although no doubt the word would astonish them) ever since.

This sort of self-confidence and decisiveness often marks a leader

* Job 3: 25.   † Psalm 27: 1.   ‡ Matthew 9: 29.

in the business world. The best executive I ever worked for was a man who made almost instantaneous decisions. 'At least,' he used to say wryly, 'I make my mistakes quickly.' On one occasion someone asked this man if he didn't believe in the old adage, 'Look before you leap.'

'No,' he said cheerfully, 'I don't.' He thought for a minute, then added, 'The trouble with that axiom is that if you look too long, or too often, you never leap at all.'

A willingness to take chances, a solid faith in the ability of the individual to cope, God helping him, with just about any problem – these characteristics are part of the traditional American heritage. Is that spirit dying out? Some observers claim that our preoccupation with security is weakening it. Initiative, they say, is the instinctive response to lack. Security is the absence of lack. Can the two really exist, side by side?

I think they can, simply because there are always new and more challenging worlds to conquer. We may be remembered as the generation that sought, and provided, material security for many. But we are also the generation that dared to pick the lock of the universe, the generation that invaded the heart of the atom. The risks were, and still are, appalling. But the mighty forces unleashed by our boldness will come to our aid some day in the form of unlimited light and heat and power for all mankind.

One of the best speeches I ever heard was made by a little man who came into our schoolroom one day and was invited to say a few words to us. I don't remember who he was, and probably I am not quoting him verbatim, but what he said was very close to this: Love life. Be grateful for it always. And show your gratitude by not shying away from its challenges. Try always to live a little bit beyond your capacities. You'll find that you never succeed.

ARTHUR GORDON

No soul can be forever banned,
    Eternally bereft,
Whoever falls from God's right hand
    Is caught into his left.

EDWIN MARKHAM

That he would grant you, according to the riches of his glory, to be strengthened with might by his Spirit in the inner man.

EPHESIANS 3: 16

Nay, in all these things we are more than conquerors through him that loved us.

ROMANS 8: 37

Chapter 7

Enthusiasm for Life

I write this at the end of a perfect day, the kind of day that automatically started you saying those vibrant words from the 118th Psalm: 'This is the day which the Lord hath made; we will rejoice and be glad in it.'

The air was crisp and fresh and clear as crystal. The sky, too, was clear except for a few dignified white clouds that sailed like ships with billowing sails across a sea of incredible blue. This July day was a glorious demonstration of the fullness of summer, cornfields stirring to a gentle breeze, the hills standing clear against the horizon.

Tonight, Pete Stewart, my neighbor, whose property adjoins our farm, commented on the glory of the day. He told me, 'We drove this afternoon to the old Hitchcock chair factory forty miles up the valley.'

'Interesting the way they reproduce those fine old chairs isn't it?'

'Yes, indeed,' he replied, 'but it wasn't the chairs, it was the day that got me. It was so very beautiful, so inexpressibly wonderful. In fact, it made me excited to be alive.'

'Excited to be alive' – what a way to be! What feeling, what sensitivity to life itself. And also, what a contrast to the dullness of response that leaves so many unexcited and unenthusiastic. Elizabeth Barrett Browning may have had this pathetic phenomenon in mind when she wrote: 'What frightens me is that men are content with what is not life at all.' Preferable indeed is the enthusiasm of Robert Louis Stevenson: 'The world is so full of a number of things; I am sure we should all be as happy as kings.' Though long ill and confined to bed, Stevenson was excited to be alive and so could write little verses that have sung themselves across the years, such as:

> *The children sing in far Japan,*
> *The children sing in Spain,*
> *The organ and the organman*
> *Are singing in the rain.*

Of course, that is the ultimate secret – not only to be excited on a glorious summer day but also to be able to sing in the rain, to be enthusiastic when the going is hard and the way overshadowed.

But so many miss the art, the skill of having enthusiasm for life. Napoleon said, 'Men grew old quickly on the battlefield.' And so also do they in life unless they are vigilant. Charles Lamb once declared, and truly, that 'our spirits grow gray before our hairs.' And Thoreau said, 'None are so old as those who have outlived enthusiasm.'

Perhaps Wordsworth gives the best description of the sad erosion of delight and enthusiasm that takes place in all too many persons:

> *Heaven lies about us in our infancy !*
> *Shades of the prison-house begin to close*
> *Upon the growing boy,*
> *But he beholds the light, and whence it flows,*
> *He sees it in his joy;*
> *The youth, who daily farther from the east*
> *Must travel, still is Nature's priest,*
> *And by the vision splendid*
> *Is on his way attended;*
> *At length the man perceives it die away,*
> *And fade into the light of common day.*

But enthusiasm for life need not ever fade. On the contrary, it can be stimulated to increase and grow more meaningful despite difficulty or age. As Henry van Dyke said, 'I shall grow old, but never lose life's zest, because the road's last turn will be the best.'

Since enthusiasm is very important indeed, so much so that Charles M. Schwab insisted that 'a man can succeed at almost anything for which he has unlimited enthusiasm,' it behooves us to know how to get and maintain this quality over our lifetimes.

In learning this, I have always set store on the method employed by Robert John, publisher of *Ebony* magazine. Have little goals, he suggests, and, as one is attained, another is always waiting. Thus your interest remains and there is continuing fascination in watching little goals add up to big ones.

Another important fact is that you will never have enthusiasm in your life unless you steadily put some in. This is basic: to have enthusiasm, you must practice enthusiasm. It is based on the 'as if' principle. Act as if, and that which you practice will tend to be. If, for example, you are fearful but want to have courage, act *as if* you did have courage and in time you will have courage. Similarly, if you are lacking in enthusiasm, act as if you were enthusiastic and your personality will begin to be just that.

I once taught a class in public speaking. One man was completely desultory and uninspired in his platform presentation. 'You need enthusiasm,' I said.

'I know,' he replied, 'but you cannot be enthusiastic just by wanting it.'

'Oh, yes you can,' I insisted. 'Next time you speak, act really enthusiastic. Pour it on, give it all you've got.'

'That will be a phony. You can't be enthusiastic just by acting as if you were,' he remonstrated.

I gave him the as if principle. The next time he was the speaker, he really threw himself into his talk and the reaction of his hearers was electric. So inspired was this hitherto dull speaker that he continued to act *as if* he were the most enthusiastic of all speakers until in due course he honestly qualified for that category.

To have enthusiasm for life, act *as if* you did possess it and you shall have it.

When Joseph Haydn was criticized for the 'gaiety' of his church music, he said: 'When I think of God, my heart is so filled with joy that the notes fly off as from a spindle.'

THE BIBLE'S
TIMELESS – AND TIMELY – INSIGHTS*

The other day a new patient noticed a Bible lying on my desk. 'Do you – a psychiatrist – read the Bible?' he asked.

'I not only read it,' I told him, 'I study it. It's the greatest textbook on human behavior ever put together. If people would absorb its message, a lot of us psychiatrists could close our offices and go fishing.'

'You're talking about the Ten Commandments and the Golden Rule?'

'Certainly – but more, too,' I said. 'There are dozens of other insights that have profound psychiatric value. Take your own case. For the past hour you've been telling me how you've done this, tried that, all to no avail. It's pretty obvious that you're worrying yourself into a state of acute anxiety, isn't it?'

'That,' he said dryly, 'is why I'm here.'

I picked up the Bible. 'Here's some advice St Paul gives to the Ephesians. Just four words: *Having done all, stand.* Now, what does that mean? Exactly what it says. You've done your best, what more can you do? Keep running in circles? Plow up the same ground? What you really need – far more than a solution to this particular problem – is peace of mind. And there's the formula: relax, stand quietly, stop trying to lick this thing with your conscious mind. Let

* Reprinted with permission from the August 1966 *Reader's Digest*, copyright, 1966, by the Reader's Digest Association, Inc.

the creative power in your unconscious mind take over. It may solve the whole thing for you, if you'll get out of your own way!'

My patient looked thoughtful. 'Maybe I should do a little Bible reading on my own,' he said.

It does seem foolish not to make use of the distilled wisdom of 3,000 years. Centuries before psychiatry, the Bible knew that 'the kingdom of God is within you.' We psychiatrists call it the unconscious mind – but only the words are new, not the concept. From beginning to end the Bible teaches that the human soul is a battleground where good struggles with evil. We talk about the forces of hostility and aggression contending with the love-impulses in human nature. It's the same thing.

What psychiatry has done is to bring scientific terminology to the truths that the Bible presents in poetry, allegory and parable. What, in essence, did Freud and other pioneers discover? That the human mind functions on the conscious *and* the unconscious level. That the thing we call conscience does, too, and that many emotional pressures and dislocations are caused by its hidden action.

It is tremendously exciting to read the Bible with even this much knowledge of psychiatry. Here are a few of my favorite passages, words so full of insight that I think they might well be memorized and repeated periodically by anyone who values his mental health.

Underneath are the everlasting arms. For hundreds of years, troubled people have found comfort in these words from the Book of Deuteronomy. This is not surprising. One of the few fears we are born with is the fear of falling, so the idea of a pair of loving arms, sustaining and eternal, is an answer to the yearning in all of us to feel safe, to find security. Furthermore, one of the deepest forms of communication is *touch*. And so this Biblical image brings a great sense of peace. If you suffer from tension and insomnia, try repeating these words to yourself at bedtime. You may find them more effective than any sleeping pill.

Love thy neighbor as thyself. Many people think this noble concept comes from the New Testament. Actually you can find it in Leviticus. The remarkable thing, to a psychiatrist, is its recognition that in an emotionally healthy person there must be self-love as well as love of others.

Lack of self-esteem is probably the most common emotional ailment I am called upon to treat. Often pressure from the unconscious mind is causing this sense of unworthiness. Suppose a woman comes to me, weighted down with guilt. I can't undo the things she has done. But perhaps I can help her understand why she did them, and how the mechanism of her conscience, functioning below the conscious level, is paralyzing her. And I can urge her to read and reread the story of the Prodigal Son. How can anyone feel permanently condemned or rejected in a world where this magnificent promise comes ringing down the centuries, the promise that love is stronger than any mistake, any error?

Take no thought for the morrow. A modern rephrasing might well be, 'Stop worrying about the future.' Worry causes tension. Tension blocks the flow or creative energy from the unconscious mind. And when creative energy wanes, problems multiply.

Most of us know perfectly well that worry is a futile process. Yet many people constantly borrow trouble. 'Sufficient unto the day,' says the Bible, 'is the evil thereof.' There are plenty of problems in the here-and-now to tackle and solve. The only moment when you're really alive is the present one, so make the most of it. Have faith that the Power that brought you here will help you through any future crisis, whatever it may be. 'They that wait upon the Lord,' sang Isaiah, 'shall renew their strength; they shall mount up with wings as eagles.' Why? Because their faith makes them non-worriers.

As he thinketh in his heart, so is he. This penetrating phrase from Proverbs implies that what you *think* you think is less important than what you really think. Every day in my office I see illustrations of this. Last week I was talking to a woman who had married during the Korean war. Her husband, a reserve officer, had volunteered for war duty and gone overseas, leaving her pregnant. He had been killed; she was left to bring up their son alone. Eventually she remarried, but now she was having difficulty with the 15-year-old boy.

It was apparent that she treated her son with unusual harshness and severity. 'Why are you so strict with him?' I asked.

'Because I don't want him to grow up spoiled,' she said instantly.

'Did it ever occur to you,' I asked, 'that when this boy's father went away voluntarily, leaving you, and got himself killed, something in you was enraged, something in you hated him? And isn't it just possible that some of this unadmitted hate has been displaced onto the child he left you with, although your unconscious mind doesn't want to admit that either? Look into your heart and search for the truth there, below the rationalizations of your mind. Until you do, we're not going to get anywhere with this problem.'

Where your treasure is, there will your heart be also. Of course! *What* we shall love is the key problem of human existence, because we tend to become the reflection of what we love. Do you love money? Then your values will be materialistic. Do you love power? Then the aggressive instincts in you will slowly become dominant. Do you love God and your neighbor? Then you are not likely to need a psychiatrist!

We psychiatrists warn against sustained anger and hostility; we know that unresolved conflicts in the unconscious mind can make you physically ill. How does the Bible put it? *Let not the sun go down upon your wrath*. And *A merry heart doeth good like a medicine*. Exactly so. These flashing sparks of truth from the pages of the Bible are endless!

If I were asked to choose one Bible passage above all others it would be this: *And ye shall know the truth, and the truth shall make you free*. In one tremendous sentence these words encompass the whole theory and method of psychotherapy.

Nine times out of ten, when people come to me tormented by guilt, racked by anxiety, exhausted by unresolved hate, it is because they don't know the truth about themselves. It is the role of the psychiatrist to remove the camouflage, the self-deception, the rationalizations. It is his job to bring the unconscious conflicts into the conscious mind where reason can deal with them. As Freud said, 'Reason is a small voice, but it is persistent.' Once insight is gained, the cure can begin – because the truth *does* make you free.

We shall never have all the truth. Great questions of life and death, good and evil, remain unanswered – and must so remain, as the book of Job eloquently tells. But this much seems plain to me: locked in the unconscious of each of us are the same elemental forces of love and hate that have haunted and inspired the human race from the beginning. With this hidden area of the human spirit psychiatry concerns itself – sometimes helpfully, sometimes not. But there is also an ancient book that deals with it, that understands it profoundly and intuitively, a book that for 3,000 years has been a help in time of trouble to any person wise enough to use it.

SMILEY BLANTON, MD

Oh, the eagerness and freshness of youth! How the boy enjoys his food, his sleep, his sports, his companions, his truant days! His life is an adventure; he is widening his outlook; he is extending his dominion; he is conquering his kingdom. How cheap are his pleasures; how ready his enthusiasms! In boyhood I have had more delight on a haymow with two companions and a big dog – delight that came nearer intoxication – than I have ever had in all the subsequent holidays of my life. When youth goes, much goes with it. When manhood comes, much comes with it. We exchange a world of delight sensations and impressions for a world of duties and studies and meditations. The youth enjoys what the man tries to understand. Lucky is he who can get his grapes to market and keep the bloom upon them; who can carry some of the freshness and eagerness and simplicity of youth into his later years; who can have a boy's heart below a man's head.

JOHN BURROUGHS

ABRAHAM DAVENPORT

'Twas on a May day of the far old year
Seventeen hundred eighty, that there fell
Over the bloom and sweet life of the Spring,
Over the fresh earth and the heaven of noon,
A horror of great darkness, like the night
In day of which the Norland sagas tell, –
The Twilight of the Gods.
               The low-hung sky
Was black with ominous clouds, save where its rim
Was fringed with a dull glow, like that which climbs
The crater's sides from the red hell below.
Birds ceased to sing, and all the barnyard fowls
Roosted; the cattle at the pasture bars
Lowed, and looked homeward; bats on leathern wings
Flitted abroad; the sounds of labor died;
Men prayed, and women wept; all ears grew sharp
To hear the doom blast of the trumpet shatter
The black sky, that the dreadful face of Christ
Might look from the rent clouds, not as he looked
A loving guest at Bethany, but stern
As Justice and inexorable Law.
Meanwhile in the old Statehouse, dim as ghosts,
Sat the lawgivers of Connecticut,
Trembling beneath their legislative robes.
'It is the Lord's Great Day! Let us adjourn,'
Some said; and then, as if with one accord,
All eyes were turned to Abraham Davenport.

He rose, slow-cleaving with his steady voice
The intolerable hush. 'This well may be
The Day of Judgment which the world awaits;
But be it so or not, I only know
My present duty, and my Lord's command
To occupy till he come. So at the post
Where he hath set me in his providence,
I choose, for one, to meet him face to face, –
No faithless servant frightened from my task,
But ready when the Lord of the harvest calls;
And therefore, with all reverence, I would say
Let God do his work, we will see to ours.
Bring in the candles.' And they brought them in.

Then by the flaring lights the Speaker read,
Albeit with husky voice and shaking hands,
An act to amend an act to regulate
The shad and alewive fisheries. Whereupon,
Wisely and well spake Abraham Davenport,
Straight to the question, with no figures of speech
Save the ten Arab signs, yet not without
The shrewd, dry humor natural to the man:
His awe-struck colleagues listening all the while,
Between the pauses of his argument,
To hear the thunder of the wrath of God
Break from the hollow trumpet of the cloud.

And there he stands in memory to this day,
Erect, self-poised, a rugged face, half seen
Against the background of unnatural dark,
A witness to the ages as they pass,
That simple duty hath no place for fear.

                              JOHN GREENLEAF WHITTIER

Be cheerful – live blithely.

The day returns and brings us the petty round of irritating concerns and duties. Help us to play the man, help us to perform them with laughter and kind faces, let cheerfulness abound with industry. Give us to go blithely on our business all this day, bring us to our beds weary and content and undishonored, and grant us in the end the gift of sleep. Amen.

                              ROBERT LOUIS STEVENSON

Enthusiasm can be cultivated.

Here is good news for those to whom enthusiasm does not come naturally: It can be cultivated.

At first you must consciously put your eyes, your voice, your spirit – in a word, yourself – into your appreciation of people and events and things. Do this around your home, at your work, and in your social contacts, and you will be surprised how quickly it will become second nature. You will find yourself living in a more gracious and enthusiastic world, for your enthusiasm will be reflected back to you from the people to whom you give it.

                              DAVID DUNN

Just get right with life and then you will have life.

Truth is tough. It will not break, like a bubble, at a touch; you may kick it about all day, like a football, and it will be round and full at evening.

OLIVER WENDELL HOLMES

Enthusiasm makes ordinary people extraordinary.

A man had died, and the whole city mourned his going. At a club we were discussing him, reminding ourselves of one characteristic and another that had endeared him to us.

Finally a man whose name is famous spoke:

'You know our friend hardly had a fair start,' he said quietly. 'Nature did not mean to let him be a big man. She equipped him with very ordinary talents.

'I can remember the first time I heard him speak. It was a very stumbling performance. Yet, in his later years, we regarded him as one of the real orators of his generation.

'His mind was neither very original nor very profound, but he managed to build a great institution, and the imprint of his influence is on ten thousand lives.'

The speaker stopped, and we urged him to go on.

'How then do you account for his success?' we asked.

'It is simple,' he replied. '*He merely forgot himself.* When he spoke, his imperfections were lost in the glory of his enthusiasm. When he organized, the fire of his faith burned away all obstacles. He abandoned himself utterly to his task; and the task molded him into greatness.'

BRUCE BARTON

Shortly after I started out as a professional baseball player, I got one of the biggest shocks of my life. That was back in 1907. I was playing for Johnstown, Pennsylvania, in the Tri-State League. I was young and ambitious – wanted to get to the top – and what happened? I was fired! My whole life might have been different if I hadn't gone to the manager and asked him *why* he fired me. . . .

The manager said he fired me because I was lazy! Well, that was the last thing I expected him to say.

'You drag yourself around the field like a veteran who has been playing ball for twenty years,' he told me. 'Why do you act that way if you're not lazy?'

'Well, Bert,' I said, 'I'm nervous, so scared that I want to hide my fears from the crowd, and especially from the other players on the team. Besides, I hope that by taking it easy, I'll get rid of my nervousness.'

'Frank,' he said, 'it will never work. That's the thing that is holding you down. Whatever you do after you leave here, for heaven's sake, wake yourself up, and put some life and enthusiasm into your work!'

I had been making $175 a month at Johnstown. After being fired there, I went down to Chester, Pennsylvania, in the Atlantic League, where they paid me only $25 a month. Well, I couldn't feel very enthusiastic on that kind of money, but I began to *act* enthusiastic. Danny Meehan came to me and said, 'Frank, what in the world are you doing down here in a rank bush league like this?'

'Well, Danny,' I replied, 'if I knew how to get a better job I'd go anywhere.'

A week later Danny induced New Haven, Connecticut, to give me a trial. My first day in New Haven will always stand out in my memory as a great event in my life. No one knew me in that league, so I made a resolution that nobody would ever accuse me of being lazy. I made up my mind to establish a reputation of being the most enthusiastic ballplayer they'd ever seen in the New England League. I thought if I could establish such a reputation, then I'd have to live up to it.

From the minute I appeared on the field, I acted like a man electrified. I acted as though I were alive with a million batteries. I threw the ball around the diamond so fast and so hard that it almost knocked our infielders' hands apart. Once, apparently trapped, I slid into third base with so much energy and force that the third baseman fumbled the ball and I was able to score an important run. Yes, it was all a show, an act I was putting on. The thermometer was nearly 100°. I wouldn't have been surprised if I had dropped over with a sunstroke the way I ran around the field.

Did it work? It worked like magic. Three things happened:

1. My enthusiasm almost entirely overcame my fear. In fact my nervousness began to work *for* me, and I played far better than I ever thought I was capable of playing. (If you are nervous be thankful. Don't hold it back. Turn it on. Let your nerves work *for* you.)

2. My enthusiasm affected the other players on the team, and they too became enthusiastic.

3. Instead of dropping with the heat, I felt better during the game and after it was over than I had ever felt before.

My biggest thrill came the following morning when I read in the New Haven newspaper: 'This new player, Bettger, has a barrel of enthusiasm. He inspired our boys. They not only won the game, but looked better than at any time this season.' . . .

Within ten days *enthusiasm* took me from $25 a month to $185 a month – it increased my income 700 per cent. Let me repeat – nothing but the determination to act enthusiastic increased my income 700 per cent in ten days! I got this stupendous increase in salary not because I could throw a ball better or catch or hit better, not because I had any more ability as a ballplayer. I didn't know any more about baseball than I did before.

Two years later – two years from the time I had been hoping to get $25 a month in that little Chester outfit, I was playing third base for the St Louis Cardinals and had multiplied my income by thirty times. What did it? Enthusiasm alone did it; nothing but enthusiasm.

Two years after that, while playing a game in Chicago against the Chicago Cubs, I had a bad accident. Picking up a swinging bunt while on a full run, I attempted to throw in the opposite direction. Something snapped in my arm. The accident forced me to give up baseball. This seemed like a great tragedy at the time, but I now look back on it as one of the most fortunate events in my life.

I returned home and for the next two years made my living riding around the streets of Philadelphia on a bicycle. I was a collector for an installment furniture concern; one dollar down and the balance in 'uneasy' weekly payments. After two dismal years of collecting installments, I decided to try selling insurance with the Fidelity Mutual Life Insurance Company.

The next ten months were the longest and most disheartening months of my life.

A dismal failure at selling insurance, I finally concluded that I *was never cut out to be a salesman*, and began answering want ads for a job as a shipping clerk. I realized, however, that no matter what work I tried to do, I had to overcome a strange fear complex that possessed me, so I joined one of Dale Carnegie's courses in public speaking. One night, Mr Carnegie stopped me in the middle of a talk.

'Mr Bettger,' he said. 'Just a moment ... just a moment. Are you interested in what you are saying?'

'Yes ... of course I am,' I replied.

'Well, then,' said Mr Carnegie, 'why don't you talk with a little enthusiasm? How do you expect your audience to be interested if you don't put some life and animation into what you say?'

Dale Carnegie then gave our class a stirring talk on the power of enthusiasm. He got so excited during his talk, he threw a chair up against the wall and broke off one of its legs.

Before I went to bed that night, I sat for an hour thinking. My thoughts went back to my baseball days at Johnstown and New Haven. For the first time, I realized that the very fault which had threatened to wreck my career in baseball was now threatening to wreck my career as a salesman.

The decision I made that night was the turning point of my life. That decision was to stay in the insurance business and put the same enthusiasm into selling that I had put into playing baseball when I joined the New Haven team.

I shall never forget the first call I made the next day. It was my first 'crashing through' session. I made up my mind that I was going to show my prospect the most enthusiastic salesman he'd ever seen in his life. As I pounded my fist with excitement, I expected every minute to have the man stop me and ask if there was anything wrong with me, but he didn't.

At one stage of the interview, I noticed he raised himself to a more erect position and opened his eyes wider, but he never stopped me, except to ask questions. Did he throw me out? No, he bought! This man, Al Emmons, a grain merchant in the Bourse Building, Philadelphia, soon became one of my good friends and best boosters.

From that day on I began to sell. The Magic of Enthusiasm began to work for me in business, just as it had in baseball.

FRANK BETTGER

Never minimize life's possibilities.

Eye hath not seen, nor ear heard, neither have entered into the heart of man, the things which God hath prepared for them that love him.

I CORINTHIANS 2: 9

In him was life; and the life was the light of men.

JOHN 1: 4

You have everything to make life happy.

You say that 'this World to you seems drain'd of its sweets!' I don't know what you call sweet. Honey and the honeycomb, roses and violets, are yet in the earth. The sun and moon yet reign in Heaven, and the lesser lights keep up their pretty twinklings. Meats and drinks, sweet sights and sweet smells, a country walk, spring and autumn, follies and repentance, quarrels and reconcilements have all a sweetness by turns. Good humour and good nature, friends at home that love you, and friends abroad that miss you – you possess all these things, and more innumerable, and these are all sweet things. You may extract honey from everything.

CHARLES LAMB

It's wonderful what one person can do when he is dedicated to doing it.

I am only one, but I *am* one. I can't do everything, but I *can* do something. And what I *can* do, that I ought to do. And what I *ought* to do, by the grace of God, I *shall* do.

EDWARD HALE

Two things fill me with constantly increasing admiration and awe, the longer and more earnestly I reflect on them: the starry heavens without and the moral law within.

IMMANUEL KANT

Love every day. Each one is so short and they are so few.

I still find each day too short for all the thoughts I want to think, all the walks I want to take, all the books I want to read, and all the friends I want to see. The longer I live the more my mind dwells upon the beauty and the wonder of the world.

JOHN BURROUGHS

'Beauty is truth, truth beauty,' – that is all
Ye know on earth, and all ye need to know.

JOHN KEATS

Life is a series of surprises, and would not be worth taking or keeping if it were not.

RALPH WALDO EMERSON

APRIL RAIN

It is not raining rain to me,
    It's raining daffodils;
In every dimpled drop I see
    Wild flowers on the hills.

The clouds of gray engulf the day
    And overwhelm the town;
It is not raining rain to me,
    It's raining roses down.

It is not raining rain to me,
    But fields of clover bloom,
Where any buccaneering bee
    May find a bed and room.

A health unto the happy!
    A fig for him who frets! –
It is not raining rain to me,
    It's raining violets.

ROBERT LOVEMAN

Thoreau wrote: 'Only that day dawns to which we are awake.' The art of awareness is the art of learning how to wake up to the eternal miracle of life with its limitless possibilities.

Let any true man go into silence: strip himself of all pretense, and selfishness, and sensuality, and sluggishness of soul; lift off thought after thought, passion after passion, till he reaches the inmost depth of all; remember how short a time and he was not at all; how short a time again, and he will not be here; open his window and look upon the night, how still its breath, how solemn its march, how deep its perspective, how ancient its form of light; and think how little he knows except the perpetuity of God, and the mysteriousness of life: – and it will be strange if he does not feel the Eternal Presence as close upon his soul as the breeze upon his brow; if he does not say, 'O Lord, art thou ever near as this, and have I not known thee ?' – if the true proportions and the genuine spirit of life do not open on his heart with infinite clearness and show him the littleness of his temptations and the grandeur of his trust. He is ashamed to have found weariness in toil so light, and tears where there was no trial to the brave. He discovers with astonishment how small the dust that has blinded him, and from the height of a quiet and holy love looks down with incredulous sorrow on the jealousies and fears and irritations that have vexed his life. A mighty wind of resolution sets in strong upon him and freshens the whole atmosphere of his soul, sweeping down before it the light flakes of difficulty, till they vanish like snow upon the sea. He is imprisoned no more in a small compartment of time, but belongs to an eternity which is now and here. The isolation of his separate spirit passes away; and with the countless multitude of souls akin to God, he is but a wave of his unbounded deep. He is at one with Heaven, and hath found the secret place of the Almighty.

JAMES MARTINEAU

Look for the loveliness everywhere offered.

> Life has loveliness to sell,
>   All beautiful and splendid things,
> Blue waves whitened on a cliff,
>   Soaring fire that sways and sings
> And children's faces looking up
> Holding wonder like a cup.
>
> Life has loveliness to sell,
>   Music like a curve of gold,
> Scent of pine trees in the rain,

Eyes that love you, arms that hold,
And for your spirit's still delight,
Holy thoughts that star the night.

Spend all you have for loveliness,
Buy it and never count the cost;
For one white singing hour of peace
Count many a year of strife well lost,
And for a breath of ecstasy
Give all you have been, or could be.

SARA TEASDALE

What a wonderful thing a day is!

Nothing is more highly to be prized than the value of each day.

JOHANN W. VON GOETHE

Every day is a messenger of God.

RUSSIAN PROVERB

Every day is the best of all.

One of the illusions of life is that the present hour is not the critical, decisive hour. Write it on your heart that every day is the best day of the year.

RALPH WALDO EMERSON

Lost, yesterday, somewhere between sunrise and sunset, two golden hours, each set with sixty diamond minutes. No reward is offered, for they are gone forever.

HORACE MANN

Every great and commanding movement in the annals of the world is the triumph of enthusiasm.

RALPH WALDO EMERSON

Chapter 8

Loving and Being Loved

The first person one must learn to love is oneself. If you do not love yourself, and by that is meant respect and esteem for your own self, you will not be able to love anyone else.

The Scripture teaches this strange but important truth, 'Thou shalt love thy neighbor as thyself,' which is to say, 'Have the same feelings, the same regard for the other fellow that you have for yourself.' Then he will love you as you love him and a real spirit of brotherhood will prevail. Then you will love and be loved.

Of course, there can be and is abnormal self-love. It's called narcissism, in which the individual becomes enamored of himself and totally concerned with himself. This constitutes a personality sickness and results in alienation from the community of men. It is a far cry from that wholesome regard for your own self which leads to a similar regard for all other people, whoever they are, black or white, ignorant or educated, unattractive or attractive.

We have often prescribed love for nervous, tense, unhappy people who have come to us trying to make some sense of life. They always seem to equate love with some perfumed, scented, sophisticated Hollywoodized concept. They inevitably want to romanticize the word when actually it simply means to treat people with common decency, with the respect due to every man as a child of God or, for that matter, as a fellow human and brother.

Go out and get interested in the human problems that are everywhere around us. Help to improve the human lot. This service of love is perhaps the healthiest attitude in this world. It puts one into the main stream of the human race, where the profound problems are, and as one participates and gets involved and learns to know people and they him, one is loving and being loved and life becomes good – very good.

Love is never a soft, genial attitude, indeed it is far from it. For example, when you really love the poor and underprivileged, you will get out and fight for better conditions for all men. The fight is often against prejudice and intrenched greed, and it is no easy struggle to overcome these. But love is tough and never gives up as long as one of God's children is the victim of injustice and mistreatment.

This kind of love is illustrated by the experience of Abraham Lincoln when he saw a slave girl being sold on the block like a horse or cow. She was being sold away from her family and he saw the fright and terror in her eyes. 'This thing must go,' he said. His career from that moment on bore witness to his love of mankind. Today, any injustice to anybody must go and, if we love enough to do something constructive about it, we will receive love even as we love. Loving and being loved are opposite sides of the same coin.

Years ago, there was a man, a member of the Rotary Club of New York, of which I also am a member, who at the weekly luncheons often would sound off about the low quality of American youth. He had no use for them at all. Rough treatment was the old way to handle these 'young jerks', he said.

'Better try to love them, Fred,' I said, 'then you'll understand them. They've got something on their minds.'

'What minds ?' he growled in contempt.

It so happened that shortly thereafter a Rotarian's son from out West was arrested in New York for stealing a car. The judge asked me if I wanted the boy paroled to me as his father had requested. 'No, Judge, please parole him to Fred,' I requested. It was done, and Fred had the boy on his hands. The youngster was really a problem, and no fooling.

But Fred stuck with him and, after a while, told me: 'You wouldn't believe it, but I like that kid, wild as he is. We'll make something of him yet.' Was Fred proud on that day four years later when he was present at the boy's ordination into the ministry!

'And,' said the young fellow, 'if it hadn't been for the love and faith Fred gave me when I was making a complete ass of myself, I would have gone down the drain. That man's love saved me.'

In the following chapter are many more thoughts and ideas on loving and being loved. Taken together, they can mean much to you.

The hardest job in the world, I think, is being a parent. Looking back over my own family life, I often wonder at my parents' patience, understanding, and wisdom. Each of us three children, probably, can find some lack in our family life for which we will have to compensate in other ways. Parents cannot hope to raise perfect families, but I believe the job of parenthood is to help each child develop his personality in such a way that he, in turn, will make an even better parent.

I believe that a good family life is dependent on the family's growing together. Mother and Dad always made us feel that the things which were important to us were also important to them. My two main interests in high school were basketball and singing. An important game would never go by without one or both of my parents there watching me. I never asked them to come, but they knew how much it meant to me, and would always fit it into their busy schedules.

Because our parents liked whomever we liked, a constant stream of friends paraded in and out of the house. One day the door to our apartment opened and John, my brother, stood on the threshold with seven other boys. 'I've brought some friends to spend the night, Mom. That's O.K., isn't it?'

Without batting an eyelash, Mother smiled and said, 'Why, of course, come in.' At that moment she wasn't sure she had extra beds, but John knew she would provide.

Mother and Dad indoctrinated us early with the idea that each member of the family has an equal share in family responsibilities, and that we are a team of five.

Out of this atmosphere grew a feeling of trust. We never had any strict rules of do's and don'ts. We discussed what was right, wrong, and sensible, and then Mother and Dad trusted us to use our own judgment and act accordingly.

Into this atmosphere of family discussion God was brought as a necessary and vital factor. Religion was thus never really taught us; it was just practiced. Perhaps that fact accounted for the lack of rebellion which so many minister's children go through.

An example of how this combination of family closeness and religion works came at the end of my Junior year in college. I was asked to be an advisor to thirty Freshman girls during my Senior year. This required living with the girls, and actually being partly responsible for their adjustment to college. I shied away from the job, actually refusing it once, because I felt I couldn't handle the responsibilities it entailed. Then I called my parents.

Dad said, 'God has given you this chance for a purpose. If you stand still and never take advantage of your opportunities, you won't get anywhere in life. Have the courage to accept the position and God will make known to you the reasons behind it.'

I did as he advised, and it proved to be the most meaningful experience of my college career.

Once, when John and Elizabeth and I were quite young, our favorite pastime was throwing water bombs, sand bombs, and paper airplanes out of our apartment window.

While I am sure it caused Mother and Dad some moments of acute embarrassment, this passing fad was handled with real understanding. We were always punished, usually by cleaning up the mess or by apologizing to the superintendent, but never forbidden to see our friends. Again, a sensible and adult discussion of our actions turned the trick.

Probably the most difficult thing for Mother to face was the time John and I decided we didn't want to go to church any more. This was particularly drastic for a minister's family, but careful searching un-covered the real reason – we didn't want to walk down the aisle and sit in the pastor's pew. In spite of Mother's desire to have the family sit together in church, she said, 'You can sit wherever you like.' So, for years, we sat in the front row of the balcony – the most conspicuous place in the church, I might add – but we went to church.

Probably the hardest thing for parents to do is to let their children go, but it is one of the most important. Recently, when a girl friend and I moved into an apartment of our own, I discovered something. If parents have created a home filled with love, understanding, and trust, and have helped each child develop his own personality and make his own decisions, parents need never fear losing their children.

MARGARET PEALE EVERETT

The old Jewish couple ran a tiny, cluttered Mamma-Papa store near our house. The store was filled with a thousand and one items to excite the taste and smell – lox, halvah, pickles, strudel, and many other delicious things.

On balmy summer days Mama and Papa sometimes sat outside of the store – side by side, in two old rockers – Papa, with his hands folded and head bowed on his gray white whiskers, snoring softly.

And Mama – always sitting on the side nearest his heart, with her small, thin hand resting on his shoulder. From time to time she would look at him tenderly, her smile and the snowy whiteness of her hair making her look like an angel. And she would say, 'Papa – he is such a child.'

When awake, Papa would hold Mama's hand – the one she rested on his shoulder.

And so the peaceful days passed along with these gentle people, and the years melted, one into the other. Then one day I heard the news that is so hard for the very young to comprehend – Mama was gone.

Papa joined her soon afterward, but the day before he died he was sitting outside the store in his old rocker, his hand on his left shoulder – patting it – just as he'd always done when the chair beside him wasn't vacant.

Papa didn't hear the person who came up softly behind him but who left quietly upon hearing Papa say:

'You didn't want me to be afraid, Mama . . . as a small child might be afraid . . . so you went first. . . .'

As you can see, there is really no end to love that is real love, for like two flowers that spring from a single seed, it will always blossom as one . . . even in another world.

MARTIN BUXBAUM

Tears glistened in the eyes of Salvation Army officer Shaw as he looked at the three men before him. Shaw was a medical missionary who had just arrived in India. It was the turn of the century, and the Salvation Army was taking over the care of the leper colony.

But these three lepers had manacles and fetters binding their hands and feet, cutting the diseased flesh. Captain Shaw turned to the guard and said, 'Please unfasten the chains.'

'It isn't safe,' the guard replied. 'These men are dangerous criminals as well as lepers.'

'I'll be responsible. They're suffering enough,' Captain Shaw said, as he put out his hand and took the keys. Then he knelt on the ground, tenderly removed the shackles and treated their bleeding ankles.

About two weeks later Captain Shaw had his first misgivings about freeing the criminals. He had to make an overnight trip and dreaded leaving his wife and child alone.

But his wife was also a Salvation Army officer whose life was dedicated to God. She insisted that she was not afraid.

The next morning when she went to her front door, she was startled to see the three criminals lying on her steps.

One explained, 'We know doctor go. We stay here so no harm come to you.' This was how 'dangerous men' responded to an act of love.

EVELYN WICK SMITH

When Jesus came to Golgotha they hanged Him on a tree,
They drove great nails through hands and feet and made a Calvary;
They crowned Him with a crown of thorns; red were His wounds, and deep,
For those were crude and cruel days, and human flesh was cheap.

When Jesus came to Birmingham they simply passed Him by,
They never hurt a hair of Him, they only let Him die;
For men had grown more tender, and they would not give Him pain,
They only just passed down the street, and left Him in the rain.

Still Jesus cried, 'Forgive them, for they know not what they do,'
And still it rained a wintry rain that drenched Him through and through;
The crowds went home and left the streets without a soul to see,
And Jesus crouched against a wall and cried for Calvary.

G. A. STUDDERT KENNEDY

Speak gently: it is better far
    to rule by love than fear;
Speak gently: let not harsh words mar
    the good we might do here.

Speak gently: love doth whisper low
    the vows that true hearts bind;
And gently friendship's accents flow:
    Affection's voice is kind.

Speak gently to the little child;
    Its love be sure to gain;
Teach it in accents soft and mild:
    It may not long remain.

Speak gently to the aged one;
    Grieve not the careworn heart;
The sands of life are nearly run;
    Let such in peace depart.

Speak gently to the young; for they
    Will have enough to bear;
Pass through this life as best they may,
    'Tis full of anxious care.

Speak gently, kindly, to the poor;
    Let no harsh tone be heard:
They have enough they must endure,
    Without an unkind word.

Speak gently to the erring; know
    They may have toiled in vain;
Perchance unkindness made them so:
    Oh, win them back again.

Speak gently: He who gave his life
    To bend man's stubborn will,
When elements were in fierce strife,
    Said to them, 'Peace, be still!'

Speak gently: 'tis a little thing
    Dropp'd in the heart's deep well;
The good, the joy, which it may bring
    Eternity shall tell.

                                    LEWIS J. BATES

I can claim no scientific basis for the point I now make, but I believe it to be sound: giving-away not only is good for the spirit; it is also a beneficial heart stimulant.

It is my conviction that health is to no small extent conditioned, perhaps even controlled, by the circulation of the blood. That important little circulatory organ located in the left side of the breast is, I believe, influenced to a greater degree than we perhaps realize by that other heart which is described in the dictionary as 'the seat of the affections; the emotional nature.'

When your emotional nature is stirred by something you do, is it not probable that your heart is actually stimulated, so that it quickens the circulation of your blood and makes you feel alive and full of health?

I know that the little surges of happiness I get out of giving-away suffuse me with a momentary sense of glowing health. I have come to believe that my hobby of giving-away, with the flush of pleasure it brings, is the finest heart tonic in the world!

DAVID DUNN

God can use each of us to love and help people.

Suppose an individual is not a doctor or a minister or a teacher, that he has none of the opportunities for direct personal service which come to the men and women in these careers. Can God still use that individual to help other people? Can God (for example) use a businessman, a manufacturer, a police officer? For your answer, study these vivid sentences, written recently by one of our discerning religious leaders: 'In the late 1930's a man who owned a small factory said to me, "Throughout the Depression I've succeeded in giving steady work to every man on my payroll. Nobody has been laid off. Tonight there are in this community sixty-four homes that have food on the table because I've provided employment for sixty-four fathers. Tomorrow morning more than one hundred children will start for school wearing warm coats and good shoes because I've kept sixty-four men steadily at work. Don't think you're the only minister here. I'm a minister too, but I work in a factory rather than a church." A few days later a paper manufacturer said to me, "Every time I see mothers going home with food wrapped in clean paper I thank God He called me into the paper business. It's a service calling, just as the ministry is. Think of the homes in this city where there is little or no chronic sickness because the paper I make keeps dirt off the vegetables. Think of the children who stay well because my paper enables their mothers to get meat home clean. I'm as proud of my contribution to this city's life as you are of yours." But the most vivid statement of the principle was made by a traffic officer at a busy intersection. Someone said to him condescendingly, "Yours must be a dog's life!" The policeman replied sharply, "It would be if I were a dog. But I'm not a dog: I'm a saver of lives. Already I've saved three today, right here at this corner. How many lives have you saved?" '

JAMES GORDON GILKEY

Oh, the world's a curious compound with its honey and its gall,
With its cares and bitter crosses, but a good world after all.
An' a good God must have made it – leastways, that is what I say,
When a hand is on my shoulder in a friendly sort o' way.

JAMES WHITCOMB RILEY

Ye are my friends, if ye do whatsoever I command you.

JOHN 15: 14

Kindness is a language which the blind can see and the deaf can hear.

ANONYMOUS

During the First World War a soldier in the trenches saw his friend
out in no-man's land – the ground between our trenches and those of
the enemy – stumble and fall in a hail of bullets. He said to his officer,
'May I go, sir, and bring him in ?' But the officer refused. 'No one can
live out there,' he said. 'I should only lose you as well.' Disobeying the
order, the man went to try and save his friend, for they had been like
David and Jonathan throughout the whole war. Somehow he got his
friend on his shoulder and staggered back to the trenches, but he himself lay mortally wounded and his friend was dead. The officer was
angry. 'I told you not to go,' he said. 'Now I have lost both of you. It
was not worth it.' With his dying breath the man said, 'But it was
worth it, sir.' 'Worth it!' said the officer. 'How could it be ? Your friend
is dead and you are mortally wounded.' The boy shrank from the
reproach, but looking up into his officer's face he said, 'It was worth it,
sir, because when I got to him he said, "Jim, I knew you'd come." '

LESLIE D. WEATHERHEAD

ABOU BEN ADHEM

Abou Ben Adhem (may his tribe increase!)
Awoke one night from a deep dream of peace,
And saw, within the moonlight in his room,
Making it rich and like a lily in bloom,
An angel writing in a book of gold: –
Exceeding peace had made Ben Adhem bold,
And to the presence in the room he said,
'What writest thou ?' – The vision rais'd its head,
And with a look made of all sweet accord,
Answer'd, 'The names of those who love the Lord.'

'And is mine one ?' said Abou. 'Nay, not so,'
Replied the angel. Abou spoke more low,
But cheerily still; and said, 'I pray thee, then,
Write me as one that loves his fellow men.'

The angel wröte, and vanish'd. The next night
It came again with a great wakening light,
And show'd the names whom love of God has bless'd,
And lo! Ben Adhem's name led all the rest!

LEIGH HUNT

When God measures man, He puts the tape around his heart – not his head.

GUIDEPOSTS

There is no fear in love; but perfect love casteth out fear; because fear hath torment. He that feareth, is not made perfect in love.

I JOHN 4: 18

I sought my soul
    But my soul I could not see
I sought my God,
    But my God eluded me.
I sought my brother,
    And I found all three.

AUTHOR UNKNOWN

For more than forty years I have sat in my office and listened while people of all ages and classes told me of their hopes and fears, their likes and dislikes, and of what they considered good or bad about themselves and the world around them. I have listened while mature people tried to piece together for me the converging patterns of their troubled lives. I have listened while adolescents confided their secret resentments and anxieties, and while very small children told me by indirection where things were going wrong with them. I have listened, too, while the elderly explained where they had failed, where succeeded, and what hopes they still cherished for the future.

As I look back over the long, full years, one truth emerges clearly in my mind – the universal need of love. Whether they think they do or not, all people want love. Their spoken words may tell of other things, but the psychiatrist must listen to their unconscious voice as well. He must probe deeply into the human mind and heart, for it is his function to evaluate the buried urges that determine our lives even though we often have no conscious knowledge of them whatsoever. There he sees that people sit on the threshold of their personalities as Robert Louis Stevenson put it, and call on the world to come and love them. They cannot survive without love; they must have it or they will perish.

For without love, we lose the will to live. Our mental and physical vitality is impaired, our resistance is lowered, and we succumb to illnesses that often prove fatal. We may escape actual death, but what remains is a meager and barren existence, emotionally so impoverished that we can only be called half alive.

The poets and the prophets have defined love and expressed many great truths about it. But the modern studies of the depths of the personality have shown for the first time the structure of this love and the reason why it is so sought after and needed by human beings. It also shows why so many people, though they wish for love and often starve for it, cannot accept it even when it is offered to them.

Love is a very complex emotion, requiring a richness of personality and a great variety of talents. It is first of all the strong feeling of attachment and dependence that one feels for one's parents. This feeling grows, widens, and changes until it develops, correctly, into the many-faceted desire and strong relationships with human beings of any age or sex. It develops also into the abstract feeling for things, or ideas, for beauty and learning, and, finally, into a feeling for the Supreme Being.

Saint Paul describes love in the thirteenth chapter of Corinthians, one of the greatest love poems ever written:

> *Love suffereth long and is kind.*
> *Love envieth not –*
> *Seeketh not her own.*
> *Thinketh no evil,*
> *Beareth all things.*
> *Believeth all things.*
> *Hopeth all things.*
> *Love never faileth.*

I have grown more concerned each year of my life by the fact that so many people live such unsatisfactory lives. To them life is always a battle or a reaction against something; rarely is it an expression of an affirmative feeling that can make for happiness. The person who is afraid of love constantly reacts against it with hatred. In new surroundings he acts as though he were in the old surroundings of his early life. He eternally puts his new wine in old bottles. His behavior may be completely unsuitable to the present, but his real self is smothered by this compulsive necessity to act as though the present were past. . . .

In the deeper levels of the mind are resources of power, strength, and courage hardly imagined. *To each person himself is given the task of tapping these levels,* with what assistance he can muster. There are, fortunately, untold resources in each of us if we will only find and utilize them. . . .

Whatever you do in life, do with love! We have no alternative save to act from motives of hate – yet how doleful to make this our choice! For hate is the destroyer of life, where love is its guardian. Hate blinds our vision and warps our talents; but love releases our energies for the creative action that sustains mankind. While all human behavior springs from a mixture of both these great forces of nature, it is within our power to determine which shall prevail as we journey through life. . . . We must tip the balance ever in favor of love if we wish to hurdle the obstacles before us on the road to normal happiness and success.

SMILEY BLANTON, M.D.

THIS DAY IS MINE TO MAR OR MAKE

This day is mine to mar or make,
 God keep me strong and true;
Let me no erring by-path take,
 No doubtful action do.

Grant me when the setting sun
 This fleeting day shall end,
I may rejoice o'er something done,
 Be richer by a friend.

Let all I meet along the way
 Speak well of me to-night.
I would not have the humblest say
 I'd hurt him by a slight.

Let there be something true and fine
 When night slips down to tell
That I have lived this day of mine
 Not selfishly, but well.

ANONYMOUS

George Gissing was going along the road one day, and he saw a poor little lad, perhaps ten years old, crying bitterly. He had lost sixpence with which he had been sent to pay a debt. 'Sixpence dropped by the wayside, and a whole family made wretched. I put my hand in my pocket, and wrought sixpennyworth of miracle!'

I think Gissing's phrase is very significant. It suggests how easily some miracles can be wrought. How many troubled, crooked, miserable conditions there are which are just awaiting the arrival of some simple, human ministry, and they will be immediately transformed! . . .

John Morel, Mayor of Darlington, was passing through the town and met a fellow citizen who had just been released from gaol, where he had served three years for embezzlement. 'Hallo!' said the Mayor, in his own cheery tone. 'I'm glad to see you! How are you!' Little else was said, for the man seemed ill at ease. Years afterwards, as John Morel told me, the man met him in another town, and immediately said, 'I want to thank you for what you did for me when I came out of prison.' 'What did I do?' 'You spoke a kind word to me and it changed my life!' Sixpennyworth of miracle!

JOHN HENRY JOWETT

What can I give Him,
    Poor as I am?
If I were a shepherd
    I would bring a lamb
If I were a Wise Man
    I would do my part –
Yet what can I give Him,
    Give my heart.

CHRISTINA ROSSETTI

We had been married only a few weeks when I discovered to my joy that Norman had the makings of a real husband. It happened this way:

We had returned from our honeymoon and were settled in our little apartment on Waverly Avenue in Syracuse, New York. I wanted to prepare the most delicious dinner possible for Norman on this first night in our new home, and I planned it very carefully. For dessert I had the audacity to bake an apple pie.

My mother had taught me to cook and I had taken some courses in Home Economics, but this was one of my first attempts at a pie.

I set the table with our best silver and we ate by gleaming candlelight. The meal went very well, and I was delighted. Then I cleared the table, and with fear and trembling brought on the pie and set it before Norman.

Watching his face, I thought I detected a faintly apprehensive expression. But then, bravely, he took a small piece, chewed reflectively for a moment, then broke into a broad smile. 'Say,' he declared, 'this is good!'

Joyfully, I watched him clean up every crumb. I know it wasn't as good as he said. But that incident started our married home life on the right note, because his kindness satisfied the craving every wife has to be appreciated.

Thus, at the top of my list of qualities a good husband should possess, I would place appreciation, chiefly because it has the power to unlock a wife's personality. Lack of appreciation brings a chill upon her spirit and eventually causes her personality to wither and die.

Of course, appreciation is a great deal more than manfully liking a pie. True appreciation includes esteem. A wife wants to be loved in the romantic sense of the word, but she also wants to be esteemed for her own personality value. Therefore, a good husband is one who not only loves his wife in a romantic and tender way, but who also respects her as a person, regards her highly as an individual. He should thoughtfully compliment her, and in general have a genuine respect for her mind and soul.

Still another quality of vital importance is simple politeness. I once saw a sign in an office which read, 'If you can't love your enemies, at least be polite to your friends.' If a husband is consistently polite to his wife, it will do much toward strengthening their marriage.

By politeness, of course, I do not mean stiff formality but an affectionate relationship in which thoughtfulness, kindliness, and gentility are uppermost.

A polite husband will not shout at his wife. He will remember that, in addition to being a wife, she is also a woman and therefore responsive to little niceties and gallantries. It does not take much effort for a husband to open the car door for his wife, or help her on with her coat, or tell her that her hat is pretty. It would be silly for him to bound up every time she comes into the room, because an easy naturalness is important, too. But marriage should never become so humdrum that a couple drop all the amenities when they enter their own home and descend into the unlovely status of two bears growling at each other.

So I would advise any husband to stop now and then and ask himself this rather curious question, 'How polite am I to my wife? Do I accord her the simple respect that I would give to any woman outside the home?'

Try a little gallantry now and then. It may sound 'corny' but sometimes the sweetest things in life are corny, which is why we love them.

One reason I have always considered Norman a good husband is that, from the very beginning, he has tried to bring out the best qualities that are within me. He constantly declares that the purpose of his work in life is to help people find themselves and to develop their personalities to the maximum.

When we first started going together, Norman used to take me to dinner in the charming dining room of old Lincklaen House in Cazenovia, New York. On one of these occasions he said to me, 'Ruth, as I study you, I am convinced that you have some wonderful abilities!' Then he went on to picture what he thought I could do in the world. I was just a young girl of 21, somewhat self-conscious and doubtful of myself. In the presence of strangers I had an annoying tendency to become a bit rigid and to freeze up. No one had ever described me as he did that night, and it had a wonderful effect. Suddenly I felt a conviction that I *could* do creative things and live a life of service.

Under the spell of Norman's enthusiasm a little door within me opened, and my own personality rather timidly looked out upon the broad expanse of life's possibilities. It required a good deal more of his urging and his expressions of faith to bring me completely out of myself. But I will never cease to believe that one of the greatest things my husband did for me was to inspire me to realize my own self, and to be that self completely.

Early in our marriage we moved to New York City where Norman became minister of the historic Marble Collegiate Church on Fifth Avenue, the oldest Protestant church in the United States. So at 25 I had the responsibility of being the wife of the pastor of one of America's great churches. Norman himself was only 33 years old. The minister's wife, by virtue of her position, was likely to be asked to serve on certain committees of the church and local civic groups. I wanted to fulfill my obligations effectively, but still that old perfectionist rigidity plagued me. Norman taught me how to be relaxed, explaining that the personality could not 'flow' and be its best self if it was tied up. Under his patient guidance, I began to overcome this difficulty. I found new joy in work and in association with Christian leaders. Norman enthusiastically supported me, not only because this was an avenue of service but because he felt it would develop me as a person.

He often told me how he 'hated' to be on committees and boards. I shall never forget how touched I was when he told me that in our family 'team' he wanted me to assume these responsibilities because, he said, 'I am not too good at it, and I think you are.'

Thus he made it possible for me to participate in other areas which have meant much in my life.

This concept of marriage as a team has been a vital part of our lives. In all of Norman's activities, as author and preacher, he has included me as a full partner. Across the street from our home we have an office where we each have desks, and we consult constantly.

But, above all, I value my role as wife, mother, and homemaker. And Norman never fails to appreciate his home where he declares he finds 'the greatest peace and joy and rest.'

To husbands and wives everywhere I offer these suggestions: appreciate each other, respect each other, try to bring out the best in each other. Share everything: the good and the bad, the joy and the sorrow. Work at these things through prayer with love and honesty, and your reward will be the highest happiness that we are privileged, in this life, to know.

RUTH S. PEALE

Send out love and build bridges of friendship.

It (*friendship*) redoubleth joys, and cutteth griefs in halves.

FRANCIS BACON

I shot an arrow into the air,
It fell to earth, I knew not where;
For, so swiftly it flew, the sight
Could not follow it in its flight.

I breathed a song into the air,
It fell to earth, I knew not where;
For who has sight so keen and strong,
That it can follow the flight of song?

Long, long afterward, in an oak
I found the arrow, still unbroke;
And the song, from beginning to end,
I found again in the heart of a friend.

HENRY WADSWORTH LONGFELLOW

Where cross the crowded ways of life,
Where sound the cries of race and clan,
Above the noise of selfish strife,
We hear Thy voice O Son of Man. . . .

The cup of water given for Thee
Still holds the freshness of Thy Grace;.
Yet long these multitudes to see
The sweet compassion of Thy face.

O Master, from the mountainside,
Make haste to heal these hearts of pain;
Among these restless throngs abide,
O tread the city's streets again.

FRANK MASON NORTH

God's love forgives and forgets.

Where is the foolish person who would think it in his power to commit more sins than God could forgive? and who will dare to measure by the greatness of his crimes, the immensity of that infinite mercy which casts them all into the depths of the sea of oblivion, when we repent of them with love?

ST. FRANCIS DE SALES

A flock of wild geese had settled to rest on a pond. One of the flock had been captured by a gardener, who had clipped its wings before releasing it. When the geese started to resume their flight, this one tried frantically, but vainly, to lift itself into the air. The others, observing his struggles, flew about in obvious efforts to encourage him; but it was no use. Thereupon, the entire flock settled back on the pond and waited even though the urge to go on was strong within them. For several days they waited until the damaged feather had grown sufficiently to permit the goose to fly. Meanwhile, the unethical gardener, having been converted by the ethical geese, gladly watched them as they finally rose together and all resumed their long flight.

ALBERT SCHWEITZER

If you love do some good. If you do some good you will love.

We have a call to do good, as often as we have the power and occasion.

WILLIAM PENN

TODAY

Mend a quarrel. Search out a forgotten friend. Dismiss suspicion and replace it with trust. Write a love letter. Share some treasure. Give a soft answer. Encourage youth. Manifest your loyalty in a word or deed.

Keep a promise. Find the time. Forego a grudge. Forgive an enemy. Listen. Apologize if you were wrong. Try to understand. Flout envy. Examine your demands on others. Think first of someone else. Appreciate, be kind, be gentle. Laugh a little more.

Deserve confidence. Take up arms against malice. Decry complacency. Express your gratitude. Worship your God. Gladden the heart of a child. Take pleasure in the beauty and wonder of the earth. Speak your love. Speak it again. Speak it still again. Speak it still once again.

AUTHOR UNKNOWN

Do all the good you can,
By all the means you can,
In all the ways you can,
In all the places you can,
At all the times you can,
To all the people you can,
As long as ever you can.

JOHN WESLEY

Now is the time to forget the quarrel and mend the friendship.

You who are letting miserable misunderstandings run on from year to year, meaning to clear them up someday; you who are keeping wretched quarrels alive because you cannot quite make up your mind that now is the day to sacrifice your pride and kill them; you who are passing men sullenly upon the street, not speaking to them out of some silly spite, and yet knowing that it would fill you with shame and remorse if you heard that one of those men were dead tomorrow morning; you who are letting your neighbor starve, till you hear that he is dying of starvation; or letting your friend's heart ache for a word of appreciation or sympathy, which you mean to give him someday; if you could only know and see and feel, all of a sudden, that 'the time is short,' how it would break the spell! How you would go instantly and do the thing which you might never have another chance to do!

PHILLIPS BROOKS

Life is a gift to be used every day,
Not to be smothered and hidden away;
It isn't a thing to be stored in the chest
Where you gather your keepsakes and treasure your best;
It isn't a joy to be sipped now and then
And promptly put back in a dark place again.

Life is a gift that the humblest may boast of
And one that the humblest may well make the most of.
Get out and live it each hour of the day,
Wear it and use it as much as you may;
Don't keep it in niches and corners and grooves,
You'll find that in service its beauty improves.

EDGAR A. GUEST

Love life and live love.

What delightful hosts are they —
   Life and Love!
Lingeringly I turn away,
   This late hour, yet glad enough
They have not withheld from me
   Their high hospitality.
So, with face lit with delight
   And all gratitude, I stay
   Yet to press their hands and say,
'Thanks. — So fine a time! Good night.'

JAMES WHITCOMB RILEY

A STRING OF BLUE BEADS*

No one concerned with this matter likes to talk about it. They are all embarrassed. That is why I have changed the names, and altered the locality. But nothing can disguise the fact that Pete Wakefield was the most friendless man in town, on the day Barbara May opened his door.

Pete's shop had come down to him from his grandfather. The little front window was strewn with a disarray of old-fashioned things: bracelets and lockets worn in days before the Civil War; gold rings and silver boxes, images of jade and ivory, and porcelain figurines.

On this winter's afternoon a child was standing there, her forehead against the glass, earnest and enormous eyes studying each discarded treasure, as if she were looking for something quite special. Now and then she stamped her feet, for the day was bitter cold, Finally, she straightened up with a satisfied air and entered the store.

The shadowy interior of Pete Wakefield's establishment was even more cluttered than his show window. Shelves were stacked with jewel caskets, dueling pistols, clocks and lamps, and the floor was heaped with andirons and mandolins and things hard to find a name for.

Behind the counter stood Pete himself, a man not more than 30 but with hair already turning gray. His eyelids were lowered and there was a bleak air about him as he looked at the small customer who flattened her ungloved hands on the counter.

'Mister,' she began, 'would you please let me look at that string of blue beads in the window?'

Pete Wakefield parted the draperies with his left hand – the right hung helpless from a Normandy fusillade – and lifted out a necklace. The turquoise stones gleamed brightly against the pallor of his palm, as he spread the ornament before her.

'They're just perfect,' said the child, entirely to herself. 'Will you wrap them up pretty for me, please?'

Pete Wakefield studied her with a stony air.

'Are you buying these for someone?'

'They're for my big sister. She takes care of me. You see, we haven't any mother any more. I've been looking for the most wonderful Christmas present for Sis – and this sure is it, mister.'

'How much money do you have?' asked Pete warily.

She had been busy untying the knots in her handkerchief and now she poured out eleven pennies on the counter.

'I emptied my bank,' she explained simply.

Pete Wakefield's good hand drew back the necklace. The price tag

* Reprinted with permission from the December 1951 *Reader's Digest*, copyright, 1951, by the Estate of Fulton Oursler.

was clearly visible to him but not to her. How could he explain the difficulty ? The trusting look of her blue eyes smote him like the pain of an old wound.

'Just a minute,' he said and turned his back. Over his shoulder he called: 'What's your name ?' He was very busy about something.

'Barbara May.'

When Pete faced Barbara May again, a package lay in his hand, wrapped in bright scarlet paper and tied with a bow of green ribbon.

'There you are,' he said shortly. 'Don't lose it on the way home.'

'Don't worry about that!'

And she smiled over her shoulder, as she ran out the door. Through the window he watched her go, while desolation flooded his thoughts. Something about Barbara May and her string of beads had stirred him to the depths of a grief that would not stay buried. The child's hair was wheat yellow, her eyes sea-blue, and once upon a time, not so many years before, Pete had been in love with a girl with hair of the same yellow and with large eyes just as blue.

They had chosen a little house on the eastern edge of town, and named the wedding day. But there had come a rainy night, and a truck skidding on a slippery road, and the life was crushed out of his dream.

Ever since then, Pete Wakefield had lived in solitude. He was politely attentive to customers, but after business hours he preferred his own silent society. Noontimes, in the back of the shop, he ate lunch out of a boarding-house bundle; evenings he dined by himself in a restaurant. Until late at night he sat up in his furnished room, reading tales of Dumas and other romances of a world utterly different from the empty one he knew. He was trying to forget in a haze that deepened day by day.

But the blue gaze of Barbara May had jolted him back to reality, to living remembrance of what he had lost. The pain of it made him recoil from the casual exuberance of holiday shoppers. Trade was brisk during the next ten days, chattering women swarming unto him, fingering trinkets, trying to bargain. When the last customer had gone on Christmas Eve, he sighed with relief. It was over for another year. But for Pete Wakefield, the night was not quite over.

The door opened and a young woman hurried in. With an inexplicable start he realized that she looked familiar to him, yet he could not remember when or where he had seen her before. Her hair was golden and her large eyes were blue. Without speaking she drew from her purse a package loosely unwrapped in its red paper, a bow of green ribbon with it. Presently the string of blue beads lay gleaming before him.

'Did this come from your shop ?' she asked.

Pete Wakefield raised his eyes and answered softly, 'Yes, it did.'

'Are the stones real?'

'Yes. Not the finest quality – but real.'

'Can you remember who it was you sold them to?'

'Of course. To your little sister, Barbara May. She bought them for your Christmas present.'

'How much are they worth?'

'The price,' he told her solemnly, 'was $37.'

'But Barbara May has never had $37! How could she pay for them?'

With amazing skill for a man who had only one hand to use, Pete Wakefield was folding the gay paper back into its creases, rewrapping the little package just as neatly as before.

'She paid the biggest price anyone can ever pay,' he said. 'She gave all she had.'

There was a silence then that filled the little curio shop. In some faraway steeple, a bell began to ring. The sound of the distant chiming, the little package lying on the counter, the question in the eyes of the girl, and the strange feeling of renewal unreasonably struggling in the heart of the man, all had come to be because of the love of a child.

'But why did you do it?'

He held out the gift in his hand.

'It's already Christmas morning,' he said. 'And it's my misfortune that I have no one to give anything to. Now all of a sudden I'm unbearably lonely. Would you let me see you home and let me wish you a Merry Christmas at your door?'

And so, to the sound of many bells and in the midst of many happy people, Pete Wakefield and a girl, whose name he had yet to learn, walked out into the beginning of the great day that brings hope into the world for all.

FULTON OURSLER

We grow as our relationships grow.

I believe that such portion of the psychic universe as is housed in me – that is, my person, myself – will be frustrated and distorted in its growth to the extent that I frustrate and distort other lives. I believe that to do to others as I would have them do to me is not simply a law of duty, it is also a law of health, that we violate at our own risk. Where we violate it, we injure ourselves; inhibit our powers; blunt our sense of reality; condemn ourselves to fear, guilt, and hostility; and progressively isolate ourselves from our human kind, so that we feel alone and under threat. . . .

Where my relationships to others are soundly growing, I am growing.

Where they are halted in their growth, I am halted. Where they are
twisted in their growth, I am twisted in mine.

This belief about human involvements leads to another: that self-
respect and respect for others go together. I do not believe it is possible,
except superficially, to think well of ourselves and ill of our human
fellows, or to think well of them and ill of ourselves. Our attitude
toward ourselves and toward others is one: it is our attitude toward
human nature.

As an extension of this, I believe the best situations for us to live and
grow in are those geared to equality; equality of respect; equality of
rights. I do not believe we can attain our psychological stature, our real
human stature, either by leaning on others or by trying to outdo others
and gain power over them. I am for the level look of equality and the
cordial look of friendliness between man and man.

                                             BONARO W. OVERSTREET

> Before the Cathedral in grandeur rose
> At Ingelburg where the Danube goes;
> Before its forest of silver spires
> Went airily up the clouds and fires;
> Before the oak had ready a beam,
> While yet the arch was stone and dream –
> There where the altar was later laid,
> Conrad, the cobbler, plied his trade. . . .
>
> It happened one day at the year's white end,
> Two neighbors called on their old-time friend;
> And they found the shop, so meager and mean,
> Made gay with a hundred boughs of green.
> Conrad was stitching with face ashine,
> But suddenly stopped as he twitched a twine:
> 'Old friends, good news! At dawn today,
> As the cocks were scaring the night away,
> The Lord appeared in a dream to me,
> And said, "I am coming your Guest to be!"
> So I've been busy with feet astir,
> Strewing the floor with branches of fir.
> The wall is washed and the shelf is shined,
> And over the rafter the holly twined.
> He comes today, and the table is spread
> With milk and honey and wheaten bread.'
>
> His friends went home; and his face grew still
> As he watched for the shadow across the sill.
> He lived all the moments o'er and o'er,

When the Lord should enter the lowly door —
The knock, the call, the latch pulled up,
The lighted face, the offered cup.
He would wash the feet where the spikes had been,
He would kiss the hands where the nails went in,
And then at last would sit with Him
And break the bread as the day grew dim.

While the cobbler mused there passed his pane
A beggar drenched by the driving rain.
He called him in from the stony street
And gave him shoes for his bruisèd feet.
The beggar went and there came a crone,
Her face with wrinkles of sorrow sown.
A bundle of fagots bowed her back,
And she was spent with the wrench and rack.
He gave her his loaf and steadied her load
As she took her way on the weary road.
Then to his door came a little child,
Lost and afraid in the world so wild,
In the big, dark world. Catching it up,
He gave it the milk in the waiting cup,
And led it home to its mother's arms,
Out of the reach of the world's alarms.

The day went down in the crimson west
And with it the hope of the blessed Guest,
And Conrad sighed as the world turned gray:
'Why is it, Lord, that your feet delay?
Did You forget that this was the day?'
Then soft in the silence a Voice he heard:
'Lift up your heart, for I kept my word.
Three times I came to your friendly door;
Three times my shadow was on your floor.
I was the beggar with the bruisèd feet;
I was the woman you gave to eat;
I was the child on the homeless street!'

EDWIN MARKHAM

Not what we give, but what we share, —
For the gift without the giver is bare;
Who gives himself with his alms feeds three, —
Himself, his hungering neighbor, and Me.

JAMES RUSSELL LOWELL

The world is a looking-glass, and gives back to every man the reflection of his own face. Frown at it, and it in turn will look sourly at you; laugh at it, and with it, and it is a jolly, kind companion.

WILLIAM MAKEPEACE THACKERAY

It is great, and there is no other greatness – to make one nook of God's Creation more fruitful, better, more worthy of God; to make some human heart a little wiser, manlier, happier – more blessed.

THOMAS CARLYLE

In men whom men condemn as ill
I find so much of goodness still,
In men whom men pronounce divine
I find so much of sin and blot,
I do not dare to draw a line
Between the two, where God has not.

JOAQUIN MILLER

Every man I meet is my superior in some way. In that, I learn from him

RALPH WALDO EMERSON

That best portion of a good man's life,
His little, nameless, unremembered acts
Of kindness and of love.

WILLIAM WORDSWORTH

Kind words toward those you daily meet,
Kind words and actions right,
Will make this life of ours most sweet,
Turn darkness into light.

ISAAC WATTS

The other day in Emporia, the longest funeral procession that has formed in ten years followed the Rev. John Jones three long miles in the hot July sun out to Dry Creek Cemetery. Now, a funeral procession may mean little or much. When a rich and powerful man dies, the people play politics and attend his funeral for various reasons. But here was the body of a meek, gentle little old man – a man 'without purse or scrip.' It won't take twenty minutes to settle his estate in probate court. He was a preacher of the gospel – but preachers have been buried before this in Emporia without much show or sorrow.

The reason so many people lined up behind the hearse that held the kind old man's mortality was simple: they loved him. He devoted his life to helping people. In a very simple way, without money or worldly power, he gave of the gentleness of his heart to all around him. We are apt to say that money talks, but it speaks a broken, poverty-stricken language. Hearts talk better, clearer, and with a wider intelligence. This old man with the soft voice and the kindly manners knew the language of the heart and he spoke it where it would give zest to joy. He worked manfully and with a will in his section of the vineyard, and against odds and discouragements he won time and again. He was infinitely patient and brave. He held a simple, old-fashioned faith in God and his loving kindness.

When others gave money – which was of their store – he gave prayers and hard work and an inspiring courage. He helped. In his sphere he was a power. And so when he lay down to sleep hundreds of friends trudged out to bid him good-bye with moist eyes and with cramped throats to wish him sweet slumber.

And then they turned back to the world to make money – to make money – what a hollow impotent thing! What is a man profited if he gain the whole world and lose his own soul?

WILLIAM ALLEN WHITE

Open your eyes and look for some man, or some work for the sake of men, which needs a little time, a little friendship, a little sympathy, a little sociability, a little human toil. Perhaps it is a lonely person, or an invalid – or some unfortunate inefficient, to whom you can be something. It may be an old man or it may be a child. Or some good work is in want of volunteers who will devote a free evening to it or will run on errands for it. Who can reckon up all the ways in which that priceless fund of impulse, man, is capable of exploitation! He is needed in every nook and corner. Therefore search and see if there is not some place where you may invest your humanity. Do not be put off if you find that you have to wait and to experiment. Be sure that you will have disappointments to endure. But do not be satisfied without some side line in which you may give yourself out as a man to men. There is one waiting for you if only you are willing to take it up in the right spirit.

ALBERT SCHWEITZER

I often remember with pleasure an encounter one stormy night, many years ago, when an elderly man and his wife entered the lobby of a small hotel in Philadelphia. The couple had no baggage.

'All the big places are filled up,' said the man. 'Can you possibly give us a room here?'

The clerk replied that there were three conventions in town, and no accommodations anywhere.

'Every guest room is taken,' he explained. 'But still I simply can't send a nice couple like you out into the rain at one o'clock in the morning. Would you perhaps be willing to sleep in my room? . . . Oh, I'll make out just fine; don't worry about me.'

The next morning, as he paid his bill, the elderly man said to the clerk:

· 'You are the kind of manager who should be the boss of the best hotel in the United States. Maybe someday I'll build one for you!'

The clerk laughed. And he laughed again when, after two years had passed, he received a letter containing a round-trip ticket to New York and a request that he call upon his guest of that rainy night. In the metropolis the old man led the young clerk to the corner of Fifth Avenue and Thirty-fourth Street and pointed to a vast new building there, a palace of reddish stone, with turrets and watchtowers, like a castle from fairyland cleaving the New York sky.

'That,' he declared, 'is the hotel I have just built for you to manage.'

As if hit by lightning, the young man, George C. Boldt, stood fixed to the ground. His benefactor was William Waldorf Astor – and the hotel, the most famous of its day, the original Waldorf-Astoria.

We should treat well all strangers who seek our help. Under a ragged coat they may hide their wings!

FULTON OURSLER

As a horse when he has run, a dog when he has caught the game, a bee when it has made the honey, so a man when he has done a good act does not call out for others to come and see, but he goes on to another act, as a vine goes on to produce again the grapes in season. Must a man then be one of these, who in a manner acts thus without observing it? Yes. What more doest thou want when thou hast done a man a service? Art thou not content that thou hast done something conformable to thy nature, and doest thou seek to be paid for it, just as if the eye demanded a recompense for seeing, or the feet should demand a recompense for walking?

MARCUS AURELIUS

Fred is a New York linen salesman. He has never earned more than a small salary, but on this he and Clara have bought their home in New Jersey and have sent two boys through college. When I met him one day on Fifth Avenue he was shabbily dressed in a shiny old suit of blue serge – and you know how blue serge can shine. I asked him why he couldn't treat himself a little better, now that the house was all paid for and both of the boys were doing well in their jobs.

'I'm carrying a lot of life insurance,' Fred answered. 'I've got to be awfully sure that Clara's all right when I'm gone.'

He turned away, rather shamefacedly. A stray sunbeam fell across his shoulders and suddenly I saw, not shiny serge, but shining armor. Not Fifth Avenue, but Camelot, and a plumed knight with a sword at his side and his lady's colors worn across his coat of mail.

'What's the difference,' I thought, 'between that man and Lancelot? Those heroes of the lists fought twenty minutes for the women they loved and Fred has fought forty years.' There are millions of Freds all around us. Alexander's army marches into the subway every morning, gives battle, and comes back at night to millions of castles, where some woman has kept the flag flying. That's why we continue to be a nation in spite of the grafters, and the gunmen, and the loose ladies.

Shining armor!

The real romance and adventure are in every little flat and cottage, and in every office and on every farm in America. Times Square and Hollywood continue committed to the kick of that moment in which somebody pokes a pistol into somebody else's belt buckle, and somebody else escapes by deftly tossing the contents of a cigarette paper in the gun toter's eyes. But how many of us ever toted a gun, or had one superimposed upon our belt buckle?

What happens to us is that we fall in love, and marry, and plan for the baby, and sit holding his hot little hand while trying to read the thoughts of the doctor. That's true suspense. There is more honest-to-goodness drama in that dawn by the bedside than in whole life histories of those celluloid ladies who 'played with passion and made men the dangerous toys of soul-searing ecstasy.'

Sentiment and nobility and love are immortal. That may be hokum, but it's true. Tenderness and loyalty, and patience, and self-sacrifice, and devotion to duty – these are life's natural aspirations. The Freds are all around us. Thousands of 'em go to work every morning; to them the whistle of the eight-twenty train isn't really a whistle. It's a trumpet, calling them to battle.

The trouble is that so few of our writers and publishers and producers know shining armor when they see it. Most of them spend their lives within a mile or two of Times Square and, to them, all the rest of America is terra incognita. They never meet the Middle Western farmer whose own family doesn't know that an incurable malady has doomed him to death and who, with set teeth, is trying to leave the land paid for when he goes; or the small-town bank clerk who doesn't falsify books or attempt a killing on Wall Street, but plods on, year after year, paying for the art education of a daughter.

It's the wood haulers and the rail splitters who matter, and we shall be no worse off for a return to the knowledge that they are the wearers of shining armor – 'the little men fighting behind, who win wars.'

A literature that makes their example glamorous is the literature that makes men and women fine – and nations great.

CHANNING POLLOCK

> Be a friend. You don't need money:
> Just a disposition sunny;
> Just the wish to help another
> Get along some way or other;
> Just a kindly hand extended
> Out to one who's unbefriended;
> Just the will to give or lend,
> This will make you someone's friend.
>
> Be a friend. You don't need glory.
> Friendship is a simple story.
> Pass by trifling errors blindly,
> Gaze on honest effort kindly,
> Cheer the youth who's bravely trying,
> Pity him who's sadly sighing;
> Just a little labor spend
> On the duties of a friend.
>
> Be a friend. The pay is bigger
> (Though not written by a figure)
> Than is earned by people clever
> In what's merely self-endeavor.
> You'll have friends instead of neighbors
> For the profits of your labors;
> You'll be richer in the end
> Than a prince, if you're a friend.

EDGAR A. GUEST

If any man is rich and powerful he comes under the law of God by which the higher branches must take the burnings of the sun, and shade those that are lower; by which the tall trees must protect the weak plants beneath them.

HENRY WARD BEECHER

> May every soul that touches mine –
> Be it the slightest contact –
> Get therefrom some good;
> Some little grace; one kindly thought;
> One aspiration yet unfelt;
> One bit of courage

For the darkening sky;
One gleam of faith
To brave the thickening ills of life;
One glimpse of brighter skies
Beyond the gathering mists –
To make this life worth while.

GEORGE ELIOT

Chapter 9

The Art of Thankfulness

'Every morning of the world I give thanks for all the wonderful things in my life,' declared a young man enthusiastically. 'And do you know something? It's strange indeed, but the more I give thanks, the more I have reason to be thankful. For, you see, blessings just pile up on me one after another like nobody's business.'

This exultant expression interested me, for I well remembered this young fellow and the long way he had come in achieving this attitude. In his remarks he had stated a basic law: the more you practice the art of thankfulness, the more you have to be thankful for. This, of course, is a fact. Thankfulness does tend to reproduce in kind. It reverses the flow of life's good away from you and sets flowing in your direction benefits and opportunities. The attitude of gratitude revitalizes the entire mental process by activating all other attitudes, thus stimulating creativity. It focuses the whole personality so that you can work better, think better, get along better with people, and, in short, use your abilities to function more effectively in every respect.

In a speech one night in an East Coast city, I spoke about the limitations we ourselves put on our own potential, how incredibly we shackle and restrict ourselves by our glum and negative thinking. Afterward, a rather impressive young man, the one referred to above, asked to speak with me.

'Theoretically, I agree with what you said, but it just doesn't work out for me,' he declared.

'That's strange,' I replied. 'You look like an intelligent person.'

And when I requested a rundown on his educational experiences, it checked out as top quality; in fact, he had been an honor student. 'Guess you've got the brains all right,' I said. 'But, of course, even the best brains can get fouled up by wrong thinking. Perhaps that is the reason, as you express it, that "everything goes wrong for you".'

That this man had good native ability seemed certain and it appeared that he possessed excellent equipment in the form of training and scholarship. But, when everything consistently goes wrong with any person, the suspicion should be that something is seriously wrong somewhere in the personality pattern. For wrongness inevitably produces wrong results. So, therefore, some procedure is required to correct the wrongness and build up the rightness element. Then presumably, things would no longer go wrong, or at least not so many things, but would, on the contrary, go right.

This rather basic type of reasoning, suggested to this man, got an encouraging response. Pursuing the advantage, I stated that I felt he might be helped by a consistent practice of the art of thankfulness. He looked bewildered, evidently considering the suggestion somewhat irrelevant, but, when the process was outlined, he found he could carry it out faithfully with excellent results.

'Everything is wrong for you?'

'That's right, nothing is right.'

'Isn't something right, just a few things, maybe?'

'No, everything has gone wrong. The outlook is not only dark but black,' he finished gloomily.

I took a large sheet of paper and drew a line down the middle to form two equal columns. Over the left-hand one I wrote, 'Things that are wrong,' and over the other, 'Things that are right.'

'You won't have anything to put in that right-hand column,' he growled.

'O.K., let's see when we come to it. Now start on the things that are wrong.' Quickly and with ease we filled that column.

'Now, what have you to be thankful for. What's one good thing?'

'Can't think of one,' he declared.

'Well, is your wife dead?' I asked.

'Why no, of course not.'

So I wrote in the right-hand column, 'Wife alive and well.'

'How about your house? Has it burned down?'

'Why, of course not.'

So I wrote, 'House not burned.'

'How about yourself? Had a heart attack?'

'Are you kidding?' he asked. 'Do I look like I'd had a heart attack?'

So I wrote, 'No heart attack.'

'Look,' I demanded, 'you told me everything has gone wrong with you. But, without half trying, we've listed three basic facts that are good, very good. Now, what I want you to do is to go on and fill up that column of good things, and every day give thanks for them morning and evening. Talk thankfulness, think thankfulness. See how many things you can be thankful for and go around telling everyone, especially yourself, how thankful you are. You'll be surprised, believe me, for in no time at all you will develop a huge thankfulness psychology.

'And this will start a real turn around for you. It doesn't mean that suddenly everything will be one hundred per cent fine, for it won't. But one thing is sure. The percentage will start growing and keep on increasing until the day will come when you will tell me you're having the time of your life.'

And as you have seen from the opening of this chapter, that is precisely what happened. This man's life was changed, really changed, by practicing the art of thankfulness.

Every day see how many things *you* can be thankful for. Say them over to yourself. Skip the negatives. Accentuate the positives. Face the difficulties. They are real and no illusion; they have to be dealt with. But a positive, thankful psychology has written in it the power to make things good, better, best. Try the art of thankfulness. It works wonders.

There is much more in this chapter about the powerful quality of thankfulness. Read on and build up thankful attitudes of mind. It can stop everything from going wrong with you and start them going right.

None of us is ever too busy to pay his way. It takes only a few seconds to say a heart-warming 'Thank you.' Probably no American of modern times lived a more hurried or hectic life than Theodore Roosevelt. Yet even on political campaign trips, when in the hustle and bustle he might have been excused from thinking of other people, it was his custom as he left his private train to stop and thank the engineer and fireman for a safe and comfortable trip. It took but a fraction of a minute of his time, but he had two more friends for the rest of his life.

'Good politics,' you may say. But good living too – for, after all, isn't having friends the basis of happy living, as well as of successful politics?

Nor have I found any situation in which thanks cannot be given. You can thank even total strangers with a nod of the head, a gesture of the hand, a grateful glance – in jostling street crowds, in swaying subway trains, at the theatre, in the quiet of a church service, anywhere at all, if your heart is saying, 'Thank you.'

DAVID DUNN

Why, who makes much of a miracle?
As to me I know of nothing else but miracles,
Whether I walk the streets of Manhattan,
Or dart my sight over the roofs of houses toward the sky,
Or wade with naked feet along the beach just in the edge of the water,
Or stand under the trees in the woods,
Or talk by day with any one I love, or sleep in the bed at night with any
    one I love,
Or sit at table at dinner with the rest,
Or look at strangers opposite me riding in the car,
Or watch honey-bees busy around the hive of a summer forenoon,
Or animals feeding in the fields,

Or birds, or the wonderfulness of insects in the air,
Or the wonderfulness of the sundown, or of stars shining so quiet and
    bright
Or the exquisite delicate thin curve of the new moon in spring;
These with the rest, one and all, are to me miracles,
The whole referring, yet each distinct and in its place.

To me every hour of the light and dark is a miracle,
Every cubic inch of space is a miracle,
Every square yard of the surface of the earth is spread with the same,
Every foot of the interior swarms with the same.
To me the sea is a continual miracle,
The fishes that swim – the rocks – the motion of the waves – the ships
    with men in them,
What stranger miracles are there?

WALT WHITMAN

If the stars should appear one night in a thousand years, how would
men believe and adore, and preserve for many generations the remembrance of the city of God which had been shown! But every night come
out these envoys of beauty, and light the universe with their admonish-
ing smile.

RALPH WALDO EMERSON

What we see here of this world is but an expression of God's will, so
to speak – a beautiful earth and sky and sea – beautiful affections and
sorrows, wonderful changes and developments of creation, suns rising,
stars shining, birds singing, clouds and shadows changing and fading,
people loving each other, smiling and crying, the multiplied pheno-
mena of Nature, multiplied in fact and fancy, in Art and Science, in
every way that a man's intellect or education or imagination can be
brought to bear. – And who is to say that we are to ignore all this, or
not value them and love them, because there is another unknown world
yet to come? Why that unknown future world is but a manifestation
of God Almighty's will, and a development of Nature, neither more
or less than this in which we are, and an angel glorified or a sparrow on
a gutter are equally parts of His creation. The light upon all the saints
in Heaven is just as much and no more God's work, as the sun which
shall shine tomorrow upon this infinitesimal speck of creation.

WILLIAM MAKEPEACE THACKERAY

Try this experiment today. Select one particular thing in your life
which is not going well and which you wish to make successful. Then
treat it each day with selected thought. Spend from a quarter of an

hour to half an hour reconsidering the matter in the light of your knowledge of God and of prayer. Remind yourself that harmony and true success are the divine purposes of your life. Remind yourself that this particular thing must come under that law. Realize that because there can be no exception to natural law, this thing cannot remain inharmonious or negative once you know the Truth about it. Realize that you are *now* knowing the Truth about it and claim that the Divine Power in you is now healing the condition completely and permanently.

Then give thanks for a complete demonstration. Give thanks, and try to *feel* thankful. Mentally act the part of a person who has received his demonstration and is filled with natural gratitude. Remember that praise and thanksgiving are the most powerful prayers of all. Do not treat the subject again until the next day.

Next day, repeat your treatment, and so on each day until the demonstration comes.

The treatment, however, is only half of the work. In between treatments you must keep your thought right concerning the problem. If it is possible to keep your thought off it altogether in the intervals between treating, so much the better. If for any reason this is not possible, either because you are very much worried concerning it or because the condition is one which you cannot really get away from, the thing to do is to handle it with right thought all day long. This is vital. You must not allow yourself to think wrongly concerning that subject under any circumstances. If other people speak negatively, you cannot help that but you are not obliged to agree with them mentally. Remember that it is your mental agreement or acceptance that controls your life.

This all-day-long guiding of your thought about a particular subject cannot fail to bring your demonstration if you are persistent. . . .

You have a gold mine within more fabulous than the famous mines of King Solomon, or any of those that have been discovered in the Klondike, or California, or the Rand. Of course, the gold mine within does not mean within the body. It certainly does not mean within in any physical sense.

In metaphysics, or the Truth teaching, when we speak of 'within' we mean thought. 'Without' or 'outside' means expression, or manifestation. For instance, we sometimes say, 'As within, so without,' meaning that as we think so do we express.

So the gold mine within means that your power in life lies in your thought. However, to operate this gold mine you need a contact with God. It will be of little avail to reach out for it without that.

Your contact with God lies in recognizing your identity, the 'I am.' The 'I am' is everything you arrogate to yourself in thought. If you say, 'I am sick,' you have ordered your own. If you say, 'I am well, I am one with God,' you have ordered your own.

God is universal – 'I am what I am' – and you as an individual particularize it when you say, 'I am.' When you use your 'I am' in an inverted or negative sense, you are using it against yourself and will bring sickness, poverty, controversy, and fear into your life.

When you particularize, or individualize, Divine Power by using 'I am' constructively, then you will get health, prosperity, and abounding happiness, for you will have identified yourself with God – the gold mine within.

EMMET FOX

If wrinkles must be written upon our brows, let them not be written upon our hearts. The spirit should not grow old.

JAMES A. GARFIELD

To be seventy years young is sometimes far more cheerful and hopeful than to be forty years old.

OLIVER WENDELL HOLMES

FATHER IN HEAVEN, WE THANK THEE

For flowers that bloom about our feet,
For tender grass, so fresh and sweet,
For song of bird and hum of bee,
For all things fair we hear or see –
    Father in heaven, we thank Thee!

For blue of stream, for blue of sky,
For pleasant shade of branches high,
For fragrant air and cooling breeze,
For beauty of the blowing trees –
    Father in heaven, we thank Thee!

For mother-love, for father-care,
For brothers strong and sisters fair,
For love at home and school each day,
For guidance lest we go astray –
    Father in heaven, we thank Thee!

For thy dear, everlasting arms;
That bear us o'er all ills and harms,
For blessed words of long ago,
That help us now Thy will to know –
    Father in heaven, we thank Thee!

RALPH WALDO EMERSON

NEW ENGLAND SABBATH

The smell of pines along the way
To church; a blue glimpse of the sea;
The nearer waters of the bay
Lap at the marsh grass lazily;
Whispering breezes call to me
Soft-voiced across the lowland sod
Like immanent divinity –
'Be still, and know that I am God.'

I catch the scent of ripened hay,
I hear the low drone of the bee;
I watch the tiny insects play
On the warm walls in humble glee;
The lichened rocks, the barberry,
The spires of early goldenrod,
All speak in glowing ecstasy –
'Be still, and know that I am God.'

Why must man meet this lovely day
With solemn face and anxious knee?
All the earth quivers in the ray
Of the kind sun, and only he
Walks down-eyed. More wise than we
Is every bud and bloom and pod.
These hold Creation's secret key –
'Be still, and know that I am God.'

Soul of all growing things, to Thee
I raise my spirit's litany.
You answer me from every clod –
'Be still, and know that I am God.'

                                ANNE HIGGINSON SPICER

God guides always – how thankful we should be.

TO A WATERFOWL

Whither, midst falling dew,
While glow the heavens with the last steps of day
Far, through their rosy depths, dost thou pursue
Thy solitary way? . . .

There is a Power whose care
Teaches thy way along that pathless coast –
The desert and illimitable air –
    Lone wandering, but not lost.

All day thy wings have fanned,
At that far height, the cold, thin atmosphere,
Yet stoop not, weary, to the welcome land,
    Though the dark night is near.

And soon that toil shall end;
Soon shalt thou find a summer home, and rest,
And scream among thy fellows; reeds shall bend
    Soon, o'er thy sheltered nest.

Thou'rt gone, the abyss of heaven
Hath swallowed up thy form; yet, on my heart
Deeply has sunk the lesson thou hast given,
    And shall not soon depart.

He who, from zone to zone,
Guides through the boundless sky thy certain flight,
In the long way that I must tread alone.
    Will lead my steps aright.

                    WILLIAM CULLEN BRYANT

And I say let a man be of good cheer about his soul. When the soul
has been arrayed in her own proper jewels – temperance and justice,
and courage, and nobility and truth – she is ready to go on her journey
when the hour comes.

                    SOCRATES
            (*Minutes before his execution*)

O give thanks unto the Lord; for he is good.
                    PSALM 106:1

GIVE THANKS

For all that God, in mercy, sends;
For health and children, home and friends;
For comfort in the time of need,
For every kindly word and deed,
For happy thoughts and holy talk,
For guidance in our daily walk –
    For everything give thanks!

For beauty in this world of ours,
For verdant grass and lovely flowers,
For song of birds, for hum of bees,
For the refreshing summer breeze,
For hill and plain, for stream and wood,
For the great ocean's mighty flood –
　　For everything give thanks!

For the sweet sleep which comes with night,
For the returning morning's light,
For the bright sun that shines on high,
For the stars glittering in the sky –
For these, and everything we see,
O Lord! our hearts we lift to Thee –
　　For everything give thanks!

ANONYMOUS

Are the growing pains of life at last behind you? Are the uncertainties of old age still far ahead? If so, you should congratulate yourself. You have reached the warm high-noon of living, the magnificent middle years.

Consider! Behind you lie the confusions and inadequacies of that remarkably over-rated period of human existence known as youth. Youth has vitality, it's true; youth has a superabundance of 'free energy.' But it has little else. It lacks poise. It lacks experience. Above all, it has neither judgment nor wisdom, the two qualities that make life supremely worth while.

Consider further Ahead of you, almost certainly, lie several decades of splendid health, years of useful, productive activity in which the decline of vitality is so gradual that it can be ignored. The fantastic march of medical science has made this possible. A hundred years ago, men and women were considered worn out at forty or forty-five. Today at such an age they are just beginning to live.

By this time your education is complete. If you work for your daily bread, your earning power should be rising to a point where you are freed from many of the privations and restrictions of early life. As you move farther into the middle years, you should be able to lift your nose from the grindstone of daily living and look out over a magnificent panorama of art, of music, of literature, of friendship, of great affairs and small – and not only look but choose from such wonderful profusion the most exciting and rewarding and satisfying activities. In short, you should be standing triumphantly at the summit of your full development as a human being.

For more than four decades now, as a practicing psychiatrist, I have been listening to the problems and hopes and fears that beset my fellow-passengers on this complicated speck of dust as it whirls around the sun. . . . The majority of those who come to me for help are neither very young nor very old. They are in the middle years, the years that should be the very best of all. . . .

What is hindering them? What is holding them back?

They are holding themselves back. Not consciously, perhaps. Certainly not intentionally. But with a deadly tenacity all the same.

There is a reason for this. Such people are unhappy, frustrated, sorely puzzled by their failure to make full use of the powers that they sense within themselves, powers that are shackled, somehow, but definitely there. What they almost never realize is that in most cases the shackles have been there for years, unseen, unfelt, unnoticed while the drive and excess energy of youth endured.

But as the exuberant vitality of youth begins to wane, even slightly, as the problems of living become more complex, then the insidious grip of the hidden fetters begin to manifest itself. Conflicts and maladjustments that have lain dormant for years begin to stir into uneasy life. . . .

To some extent, this weakening of psychological defenses takes place in all of us as the fire and optimism of youth begin to die down. These defenses must be reinforced and strengthened if the middle years are to be what they should be – the most rewarding years of life. And there is only one sure way to accomplish this. *We must learn to understand ourselves.* . . .

For the rewards of self-knowledge are enormous. In the last analysis, happiness consists of *balance*, does it not? Balance between the great internal forces of love and aggression that dwell within all of us, balance between our hopeful dreams and harsh reality, balance between selfishness and altruism. Self-knowledge brings such balance within reach, and at the center of this self-knowledge must be a full awareness that in every man's unconscious mind there is a dynamic force that determines much of his daily behavior and ultimately controls his whole life. . . .

People can change when something or somebody gives them new insight into themselves, when they begin at least to understand why they are the way they are, or act the way they do. Professional help is not always necessary. A book can change people, or a sermon, or even a poem, if it leads to new evaluation of self and of things. . . .

The best time for people over thirty to make such a self-examination and reappraisal is now. . . .

They will face the fact that although the middle years are the best years for achieving new goals, the goals are different from those they thought they would have when they were young.

With this in mind, they will realize the importance of making new plans for the future, plans based on a new alignment of their ambitions with their capabilities, plans undistorted by either excessive fears for the future or the rose-colored dreams of youth.

They will be aware that these plans must include a new and mature philosophy of life, a deeper appreciation of their true selves and their relationship to others. They will have learned that although courage is of tremendous importance in living, courage alone is not enough. There must also be self-knowledge, because self-knowledge is the key to self-mastery.

They will discover, sometimes to their amazement and delight, that once they have a degree of self-knowledge, once they understand the hidden forces that make them what they are, they can change – for the better. They can work better, love better, be healthier, happier people. The outside world, the world of reality, may present the same unyielding face as always. But calm, assured, integrated people have a way of making considerable impact on reality. By changing themselves, they change the world around them. . . .

There is one basic and universal enemy who must be unmasked. No real self-understanding is possible without coming to grips with this hidden foe. But to deal with him, you first must understand him.

This demon dwells in all of us. Some of us learn to control him – some of the time. But none of us ever succeeds in eliminating him altogether. Throughout our life he walks one step behind us, and sometimes – especially during the middle years when vitality begins to ebb and problems seem to multiply themselves – he moves close and puts a grim restraining hand on our shoulders.

His name? *Anxiety*.

Everyone knows what anxiety feels like, but it is difficult to define. It is painful, and yet it is not physical pain. It is close to fear, and yet it is different. Fear is an immediate reaction to a specific and actual danger like a car out of control, or a rattlesnake. When we fear something, we know what it is. When we suffer from anxiety, we do not always know the cause – although usually we search about until we find something that looks like a plausible explanation.

Anxiety is a chronic state of mind that may range all the way from a vague uneasiness to unbearable emotional distress. . . .

There are three main types of anxiety that we should learn to distinguish, because recognizing each is the first step in dealing with it.

The first type is inevitable, even in the most sheltered and orderly of lives. We cannot avoid it; it is built into the scheme of things. We have to live with the fact, for example, that sooner or later we are going to die. There is nothing we can do about this. We are going to grow old. There is nothing we can do about that, either. The inevitability of old age or death, the possible loss of health, the gradual decline of vitality and virility – these anxieties are so woven into the fabric of our lives that they might as well be called *existential anxieties*: they are part of the price we pay for the privilege of existence.

Naturally these anxieties tend to grow stronger as we move through life. A man or woman of twenty can afford to be much less concerned with the prospect of death or declining powers than the man or woman of forty. That is why it is so important, as we move into the middle years, to begin to develop a mature philosophy of life, to confirm and strengthen religious beliefs so that we are able to face these existential anxieties squarely and counteract them with the serenity that comes from self-knowledge and a firm faith – however that faith may be expressed – in a power greater than ourselves.

Existential anxieties are with us constantly; they are part and parcel of living. But each of us also faces an endless series of what might be called *situational anxieties*.

They may be minor; worry about an appointment you forgot; the anxiety you feel, lying wide-eyed in the dark, until you hear the crunch of tires on gravel that means Junior has finally brought the family car – and himself – home in one piece.

They may be major; the news that some loved one has incurable cancer; the knowledge that business is going badly and you may have to take a salary cut – or even find yourself out of a job. . . .

Yes, we live in a difficult world full of difficult situations, and the inevitable result – in our vulnerable human hearts – is a certain amount of anxiety. Such anxiety might be called normal so long as it is caused by recognizable problems and impels the anxious person to take action against those problems, or at least to adjust himself to them. But sometimes the anxiety seems to have no visible cause, or is out of all proportion to the cause assigned to it. This is neither existential nor situational anxiety, it is *neurotic* anxiety – and a great deal of the unhappiness in the world stems directly from it.

In all anxiety the sufferer is afraid of something. In neurotic anxiety, *he cannot identify the thing he fears because it is hidden from him.* It is not in his conscious mind at all. It is in his unconscious mind.

SMILEY BLANTON, M.D., WITH ARTHUR GORDON

On a day memorable to me, I boarded a tiny tugboat that I used often in crossing a southern river and saw that we had a new Negro engineer. He sat in the doorway of the engine room reading the Bible; he was fat, squat and black, but immaculate, and in his eyes was the splendor of ancient wisdom and peace with the world. As I paused to talk with him I noticed that the characteristic odors that had always emanated from the engine room were no longer there, and the engine! It gleamed and shone! From beneath its seat all the bilge-water was gone. Instead of grime and filth and stench I found beauty and order. When I asked the engineer how in the world he managed to clean up the old room and the old engine, he answered in words that would go far toward solving life's main problems for many people.

'Cap'n,' he said, nodding fondly in the direction of the engine, 'it's just this way; I got a glory.'

Making that engine the best on the river was his glory in life, and having a glory he had everything. The only sure way out of suffering that I know is to find a glory, and to give it the strength we might otherwise spend in despair.

ARCHIBALD RUTLEDGE

Thanksgiving Day is the one national festival which turns on home life. It is not a day of ecclesiastical saints. It is not a national anniversary. It is not a day celebrating a religious event. It is a day of Nature. It is a day of thanksgiving for the year's history. And it must pivot on the household. It is the one great festival of our American life that pivots on the household. A typical Thanksgiving dinner represents everything that has grown in all the summer, fit to make glad the heart of man. It is not a riotous feast. It is a table piled high, among the group of rollicking young and sober joy of the old, with the treasures of the growing year, accepted with rejoicings and interchange of many festivities as a token of gratitude to Almighty God.

Remember God's bounty in the year. String the pearls of His favor. Hide the dark parts, except so far as they are breaking out in light! Give this one day to thanks, to joy, to gratitude!

HENRY WARD BEECHER

Whereas, it is the duty of all nations to acknowledge the providence of Almighty God, to obey His will, to be grateful for His benefits, and humbly to implore His protection and favor, and;

Whereas, both Houses of Congress have, by their joint committee, requested me 'to recommend to the people of the United States a day of public thanksgiving and prayer, to be observed by acknowledging with grateful hearts the many and signal favors of Almighty God, especially by affording them an opportunity peaceably to establish a form of government for their safety and happiness';

Now, therefore, I do recommend and assign Thursday, the 26th Day of November Next, to be devoted by the people of these states to the service of that great and glorious Being who is the beneficent author of all the good that was, that is, and that will be; that we may then all unite in rendering unto Him our sincere and humble thanks for His kind care and protection of the people of this country previous to their becoming a nation; . . .

to promote
the knowledge and practice of true religion and virtue, and the increase
of science among them and us; and, generally, to grant unto all mankind such a degree of temporal prosperity as He alone knows to be best.

Given under my hand, at the City of New York, the 3rd day of
October, A.D. 1789.

GEORGE WASHINGTON
(*First Thanksgiving Day proclamation*)

When men speak strong for brotherhood,
For peace and universal good;
When miracles are everywhere,
And every inch of common air
Throbs a tremendous prophecy
Of greater marvels yet to be.
Oh, thrilling age!

ANGELA MORGAN

It is the great mystery of human life that old grief passes gradually
into quiet, tender joy. The mild serenity of age takes the place of the
riotous blood of youth. I bless the rising sun each day, and, as before,
my heart sings to meet it, but now I love even more its setting, its long
slanting rays and the soft, tender, gentle memories that come with them,
the dear images from the whole of my long, happy life – and over all
the Divine Truth, softening, reconciling, forgiving! My life is ending,
I know that well, but every day that is left me I feel how my earthly life
is in touch with a new infinite, unknown, but approaching life, the
nearness of which sets my soul quivering with rapture, my mind glowing and my heart weeping with joy.

FYODOR DOSTOEVSKY

Why,
If it's only the strip of sky
Through my open window at dusk,
The intense blue look of outdoors,
There's beauty enough for a night!
Don't you know –
When the room inside is all bright
And you suddenly see through the top of your window
A streak of astounding color –
(When they paint it that way on the stage
We call it exaggeration) . . .
Whatever your rank or station,
Whether your house is a hovel,

A hall or a home . . .
Just try it sometime
When you happen to have a window opened a trifle –
(The closer your quarters, the sooner you do it
Rather than stifle!) . . .
Then – lo!
In the midst of our mean,
Insignificant living
The mad, indescribable color the gods are giving . . .
If God has a garment for clothing His lightning splendor,
If God has a garment for hiding His terrible beauty
While giving that beauty away,
It is blue, it is blue,
It is blue like the look of the sky through my window
At twilight.

ANGELA MORGAN

If, one great day, the God I see
Aflame in blade and bush and tree,
In the white dawn and passing sun –
Shall I not joy in that clear sight
And tell in song my strange delight,
 Tho' come a day when mist and cloud
Shall the celestial presence shroud?
O, shall I not be bold,
And cry, 'Behold!'
Tho' swift the vision darkens and is done?

RICHARD WATSON GILDER

These are the things I prize
And hold of dearest worth:
Light of the sapphire skies,
Peace of the silent hills,
Shelter of the forests, comfort of the grass,
Music of birds, murmur of little rills,
Shadows of cloud that swiftly pass,
 And, after showers,
 The smell of flowers
 And of the good brown earth, –
And best of all, along the way, friendship and mirth

HENRY VAN DYKE

When I would beget content, and increase confidence in the power
and wisdom and providence of Almighty God, I will walk the meadows

of some gliding stream, and there contemplate the lilies that take no care, and those very many other little living creatures that are not only created, but fed (a man knows not how) by the goodness of the God of Nature, and therefore trust in Him.

IZAAK WALTON

I lost my soul to-day
For the sake of scrubbing and buttons and trash.
It was a wonder-day of beauty.
Rapturous leaves afire in the sun besought me;
Butterflies beckoned, birds entreated with song;
The great mother sky, wide and blue as the ocean,
Implored me to drift on the miracle tide
Of gladness and renewing.

But I turned away.
There were chairs to be dusted, floors to be swept. . . .
Floors, mind you! Common boards, dirt-covered,
That must absorb my being.
And the ecstatic world without
Pleaded with me in vain.
A book lay open on the table.
In it were hidden jewel-truths
More wonderful than gems in the depths of the earth.
'Gather us! Take us! Be comforted and inspired!' . . .
But there were buttons to be sewn upon garments,
Buttons to be sorted and stowed in boxes;
Buttons, mind you, that must absorb my soul!

A Master musician there was –
I might have heard him had I paused to think it
This golden afternoon, the music of angels. . . .
But there was trash in the cellar that must be cleared away –
Trash, mind you! Papers and dust and rags
That must smother my soul.
And the great musician played, unheeded.
Had I gone a few rods, I might have listened;
Had I gone a few paces from the fettered path. . . .

But I lost my soul today,
For scrubbing and buttons and trash.
There will be many, many days when I may scrub and sew and clean.
I traded Beauty for an hour of rubbish,
I sold my birthright for a drudge's dole.

O Beauty, stand once more upon my threshold!
O Day of Wonder, beckon me again!
That I, the penitent, may open wide my dwelling
And plead with Loveliness as she has pled with me.

ANGELA MORGAN

I am still rich.
The morning comes with old-time cheer;
The sun breaks through the blurring mist;
And all the sorrows of the night
By newborn rays of hope are kissed.
Up and rejoice! a spirit cries,
What is your loss, with morning skies!

I am still rich.
My friends are faithful, as of old;
They trust me past my poor desert.
They ask no gift of golden gain,
But only love. With their strength girt,
Can I not face the road ahead –
Though some old treasured joys are dead!

I am still rich.
I have my work, which constant calls;
I could not loiter, if I would;
Each moment has some task to speed,
Some work to do. How kind, how good.
Is life that God now grants to me –
A segment of Eternity!

THOMAS CURTIS CLARK

O friends! with whom my feet have trod
    The quiet aisles of prayer.
Glad witness to your zeal for God
    And love of man I bear.

Yet, in the maddening maze of things,
    And tossed by storm and flood,
To one fixed trust my spirit clings;
    I know that God is good. . . .

The wrong that pains my soul below
    I dare not throne above,
I know not of his hate, – I know
    His goodness and his love.

I dimly guess from blessings known
    Of greater out of sight,
And, with the chastened Psalmist, own
    His judgments too are right.

I long for household voices gone,
    For vanished smiles I long
But God hath led my dear ones on,
    And he can do no wrong.

I know not what the future hath
    Of marvel or surprise,
Assured alone that life and death
    His mercy underlies.

And if my heart and flesh are weak
    To bear an untried pain,
The bruised reed he will not break,
    But strengthen and sustain.

No offering of my own I have,
    Nor works my faith to prove;
I can but give the gifts he gave,
    And plead his love for love.

And so beside the Silent Sea
    I wait the muffled oar;
No harm from him can come to me
    On ocean or on shore.

I know not where his islands lift
    Their fronded palms in air;
I only know I cannot drift
    Beyond his love and care.

O brothers! if my faith is vain,
    If hopes like these betray,
Pray for me that my feet may gain
    The sure and safer way.

And Thou, O Lord! by whom are seen
    Thy creatures as they be,
Forgive me if too close I lean
    My human heart on thee!

                    JOHN GREENLEAF WHITTIER

O world, I cannot hold thee close enough!
  Thy winds, thy wide grey skies!
  Thy mists that roll and rise!
Thy woods, this autumn day, that ache and sag
And all but cry with colour! That gaunt crag
To crush! To lift the lean of that black bluff!
World, World, I cannot get thee close enough!

Long have I known a glory in it all,
  But never knew I this;
  Here such a passion is
As stretcheth me apart. Lord, I do fear
Thou'st made the world too beautiful this year.
My soul is all but out of me, – let fall
No burning leaf; prithee, let no bird call.

                    EDNA ST. VINCENT MILLAY

And what is so rare as a day in June?
Then, if ever, come perfect days;
Then Heaven tries earth if it be in tune,
And over it softly her warm ear lays;
Whether we look or whether we listen,
We hear life murmur, or see it glisten;
Every clod feels a stir of might,
An instinct within it that reaches and towers,
And, groping blindly above it for light,
Climbs to a soul in grass and flowers . . .
We sit in the warm shade and feel quite well
How the sap creeps up and the blossoms swell;
We may shut our eyes, but we cannot help knowing
That skies are clear and grass is growing.

                    JAMES RUSSELL LOWELL

In all my perplexities and distresses, the Bible has never failed to give me light and strength.

                    ROBERT E. LEE

The story is told of a man in charge of building a great cathedral who was pestered by an apprentice who wanted to design and arrange the glass for just one of the windows. Although he did not want to discourage so laudable an ambition, neither did the boss want to risk the waste of costly material. Finally he told the apprentice that he could try his hand on one small window, but that he would have to provide the material for it himself.

Undaunted, the apprentice gathered up all the bits of glass that had been cut off and discarded, and with these scraps he worked out a design of rare beauty. When the cathedral was opened to the public, people stood in awe and praise before the one small window designed by the apprentice.

Everyone can put to good use their own little bits of time, talent, influence, ambition, energy, and weave them into lives of beauty and goodness and rare value.

AUTHOR UNKNOWN

The year's at the spring,
And day's at the morn;
Morning's at seven;
The hillside's dew-pearl'd;
The lark's on the wing;
The snail's on the thorn;
God's in His heaven –
All's right with the world.

ROBERT BROWNING

Chapter 10

Finding the Happiness You Want

Suppose someone asked you the question a friend put to me the other day.

'Tell me something,' he asked. 'Are you happy?'

Well, I'd not had a question like that thrown at me before; in fact, I had not considered the matter. What would I say to the question, 'Are you happy?'

Well, my answer is, 'Yes, I am happy. I get a terrific kick out of every day.' Oh, of course, I have problems and setbacks. Everything doesn't go the way I want it to, by a great deal. And I have my share of unpleasant experiences. But, on the whole, life is interesting and exciting and full of satisfaction.

Yes, I would say unequivocally that I'm happy – but not in a cheerio, back-slapping way. Excessive professional cheery people leave me cold. I find them merely happiness simulators; underneath all that showiness, joy and serenity run pretty thin. Their so-called happiness isn't happiness at all but rather a pretense of joy motivated by a desire for the genuine article. Such people are looking for happiness while pathetically pretending that they have it. And it just doesn't come off.

Well, then, how do you find the happiness that you want? I once heard a man say that he goes at this problem experimentally. His idea was to base the secret of happiness upon the things he did from which he got the deepest inner joy. He found, for example, that he enjoyed going out to a charming restaurant for a delicious dinner and a delightful evening with friends. But, when he went out of his way to do something generous and kind and unexpected for someone in deep trouble, he 'felt so good inside that he could sing for joy.' The reaction to the first experience he defined as pleasure and the reaction to the second as happiness. So, to be happy, he concluded, do those things which give you the deepest, most exquisite feelings of joy.

The method has merit in that it points up an old and hackneyed truth but one which needs new currency: that it isn't what you do for yourself that really makes you happy, though it may give you justifiable pleasure, but what you do for others. And it's all the more happiness-producing when it's something you could get away without doing, but you do it, nevertheless, because something in you tells you that you must.

William Lyon Phelps, creative thinker, writer and teacher, once said, 'He is the happiest man who thinks the most interesting thoughts.' There is a type of thinking, if indeed it may be called that, which perpetually revolves around creature comforts. It has exclusively to do with what you eat or wear, how comfortable you are, what she said, what he did, etc., ad infinitum – a monotonized, humdrum series of thoughts that never branch out into fresh or exciting areas.

But a person who reads and studies and converses on current events in science, philosophy, politics will, in the process, escape from dull self-centeredness, and his participatory awareness of life in its infinite vitality will tend to produce the excitement which is inherent in happiness. Unfortunately, thinking the interesting thoughts which create happiness is a disciplinary process which too few people employ.

A man consulted me who complained that he had never been happy since he became a success. 'When younger and looking forward to a business career, I got a lot of fun out of life. But now that I've got it made, the happiness I expected didn't materialize. How come?'

Offering the trite suggestion that things – cars, TV sets, country clubs – do not necessarily guarantee happiness (although why they should be deprecated, I'll never know), I began exploring the things the man was thinking about habitually.

Status was one of them. He was advancing steadily, but so were others and he felt threatened. He became sensitive about his associates, their attitude toward him, what they said and how they said it. If anyone got a raise, how come they passed him by? It got so that if anyone disagreed with an opinion of his he was put out about it and took the gripe to bed with him.

Indeed, he lay awake nights endlessly going over slights and rebuffs, asking himself, 'Why me? Who do they think they are?' and other equally effective sleep disturbers. Naturally, he got up from bed disgruntled, and hurried belligerently downtown to his competitive chip-on-the-shoulder rat race.

I recommended he employ thought therapy. For one thing, I suggested that he turn his thoughts, when going to bed, upon the most pleasant thing that had happened during the day and dwell on that. Such a procedure would tend to 'pleasurize' his attitudes. Next, I urged that he pray specifically and by name for each of his associates, with special emphasis on 'the dirtiest skunks.' He was to pray to understand them, to appreciate their qualities, and to think himself spiritually into good relations with them. Then, he was to dwell on the real things of life, things like love, beauty, health, and God.

Revamp your thoughts from the irritating, agitated, and fulminating whirl to thoughts of peace, forgiveness, love, and appreciation, and

I believe you'll find happiness. The man whose story I have just told did.

This chapter contains other thoughts and suggestions dealing with the happiness you want and seek.

Happiness is as a butterfly, which, when pursued, is always beyond our grasp, but which, if you will sit down quietly, may alight upon you.

NATHANIEL HAWTHORNE

Be ye transformed by the renewing of your mind.

ROMANS 12:2

Take time to laugh
    It is the music of the soul.

Take time to think
    It is the source of power.

Take time to play
    It is the source of perpetual youth.

Take time to read
    It is the fountain of wisdom.

Take time to pray
    It is the greatest power on earth.

Take time to love and be loved
    It is a God-given privilege.

Take time to be friendly
    It is the road to happiness.

Take time to give
    It is too short a day to be selfish.

Take time to work
    It is the price of success.

ANONYMOUS

Oh, the wild joy of living! the leaping from rock up to rock,
The strong rending of boughs from the fir-tree, the cool silver shock
Of the plunge in the pool's living water, the hunt of the bear,
And the sultriness showing the lion couched in his lair.

And the meal, the rich dates yellowed over the gold dust divine,
And the locust-flesh steeped in the pitcher, the full draft of wine,
And the sleep in the dried river-channel where bulrushes tell
That the water was wont to go warbling so softly and well.
How good is man's life, the mere living! how fit to employ.
All the heart and the soul and the senses forever in joy!

ROBERT BROWNING

The things of every day are all so sweet;
    The morning meadows set with dew,
The dance of daisies in the moon, the blue
    Of far-off hills where twilight shadows lie,
The night with all its tender mystery of sound
    And silence, and God's starry sky.
Oh! life – the whole of life – is far too fleet,
    The things of every day are all so sweet.

The common things of life are all so dear;
    The waking in the warm half-gloom
To find again the old familiar room,
    The scents and sights and sounds that never tire,
The homely work, the plans, the lilt of baby's laugh,
    The crackle of the open fire;
The waiting, then the footsteps coming near,
    The opening door, the hand-clasp and the kiss –
Is Heaven not, after all, the Now and Here,
    The common things of life are all so dear.

ALICE ALLEN

THE RAINY DAY

The day is cold, and dark, and dreary;
It rains, and the wind is never weary;
The vine still clings to the mouldering wall,
But at every gust the dead leaves fall,
    And the day is dark and dreary.

My life is cold, and dark, and dreary;
It rains, and the wind is never weary;
My thoughts still cling to the mouldering Past
But the hopes of youth fall thick in the blast,
    And the days are dark and dreary.

Be still, sad heart! and cease repining;
Behind the clouds is the sun still shining;

Thy fate is the common fate of all:
Into each life some rain must fall;
Some days must be dark and dreary.
                    HENRY WADSWORTH LONGFELLOW

He that is of a merry heart hath a continual feast.
                                        PROVERBS 15:15

GOOD-BY, CHILDHOOD*

I can tell you the month (October) and the year (1935) and I am very sure of the day. It was the one on which I learned poignancy and regret, and something new about happiness.

I was nine: fat, freckled, viewing life astigmatically through thumb-printed spectacles. I had grown just old enough to care that on me hair ribbons draggled, dresses assumed odd shapes, socks crawled down at the heel. Yearning for patent-leather Mary Janes with silver buckles, I wore instead blunt, brown oxfords. I hated them. It is the scruffy toes of those plain, practical shoes that I see now, kicking up a rustle of October leaves as, in customary solitude, I walked home from school.

What with the fat and the freckles and such, it was my habit to beguile away the commuting time with make believe. The lesser players in my imaginary extravaganzas varied. If Tarzan didn't suit my mood ('Me Jane'), if I didn't feel like oven-roasting a wicked witch, then I would conjure up a pride of golden lions, tame them, and let them follow me.

But I was the star – magnificent, omnipotent, gowned in gossamer and gilt. Seeing me plod earnestly by, you would not have guessed that you had glimpsed a spy in splendidly effective disguise, or that, by flapping my arms, I could soar like a lark. Nor would I have told you. It was a private, wonderful world I made, in which nothing was impossible. Especially me.

So. There was the day, brilliant with autumn, and I, unseeing, passing through it as usual, lost in my make-believe. But at the turn into my street, when I slowed to admire my Mary Janes, they were brown oxfords. Alarmed, I looked at my gossamer gown, and saw lumps and buttons.

Never had fantasy so failed me.

I stopped at once to consider the strange unease I felt. Try as I would – and I desperately did – I could not summon the certainty that I was gowned in gossamer and capable of flight. No lions padded softly in my footsteps. In a flood of frightened understanding, I discovered that I had outgrown my magical world. I knew that from that moment

* Reprinted with permission from the May 1968 *Reader's Digest*, copyright, 1968, by the Reader's Digest Association, Inc.

I would see it only from a distance, as grownups do. The realization brought me almost to tears. For the first time, I felt that most poignant of adult emotions – regret at the irrevocable passing of a part of one's life.

It surprises me now that I recognized all this so precisely. But I did – and I felt the weight of the occasion. 'I must remember this,' I thought. Rubbing my stomach, where the sorrow seemed to sit, I looked about to fix memory with details of the day.

Only then did I notice how fine a day it was. Before me, trees were letting go of leaves, quietly, one by one. The ground beneath, the path ahead, were layered in autumn's cheerful litter. The circle of the sun made me blink, so yellow-white it was in a sky of perfect clarity. I grew dizzy with looking upward, trying to see through the blue translucence to something I had heard about – infinity.

Nearer to earth (under my nose, in fact), invisible motes of leaf smoke flavored the air. I put out my tongue and tasted them. I sniffed apples – the season's first falls beneath a neighbor's tree – and the ranker odor of frost-nipped mums. A breeze blew lightly, and skittering leaves crackled like paper.

Mistrustful as I am of others' total recall, I hear, see, smell, taste, feel exactly how it was to be me, in that place, at that time, more than 30 years ago. It is out of a child's well-remembered awareness that I report what happened next.

The real world impacted on me. In fragments and pieces, I had realized it before: the fragility of flowers, the raucousness of crows, the sidewise scuttling of baby crabs had all, at one time or another, enchanted me. Tucked into a comfortable hollow of tree roots, I had relished the softness of moss under my hand and the green shade sheltering me.

But not until that day had my every sense been so thoroughly broached. It seemed that I shared with a foraging squirrel the eager lightness with which it leaped down from its tree; that the lift of air on which a leaf drifted supported me; that silence was alive with sound. I saw that the street on which I lived was dazzling.

A queer happiness flowed into me. It settled upon the confused ache that lingered in my middle. I felt sorrow, loss – and love for everything beautiful in the world.

I ran home, raked up a hasty pile of leaves, and burrowed into it to think. Leaves make lovely childnests – weightless, warm and comforting. The light within is dimly, pleasantly mysterious. There are faint friendly noises. (Leaves drying? Bugs exploring?) The smell is good – earthy, clean. A child curled under leaves itches a little, but children enjoy a slight itch. I nestled in. The darkness and the shelter soothed me, and for a while I did not think of anything.

When I was ready, I thought. Wistfully, I thought about being very young (which seemed a long time ago) and growing up (to which I tentatively resigned myself). I considered how nice it was to hide among leaves. Then, cautiously, I thought about the curiously beautiful day outside. Had it changed?

I poked a tiny peephole in my nest. It was only a scrap of lucid sky that I saw, but it reassured me. 'How lucky I am,' I thought, 'to be me in the world right now!'

That's all I remember, but I'm glad I remember it well. One door had shut gently behind me, but another had opened to show that reality can be as magical as dreams and wishes.

It was solace to be nine and know that. It is solace to be 42 and remember it. I have never got over wishful thinking – have you? – but I've never got over marveling at life, either.

Few of us can fully communicate to another our moments of being surprised by this world's sudden joy, but surely we all share them. That unspoken sharing went out from me to my youngest son not long ago when I believe I saw him make his own bittersweet approach to growing up.

Toward dusk of a raw winter day, Chris trotted past the corner of the house, hailing forward a brave band of imaginary companions. 'To the fort, men!' he called, and he tunneled into a snowbank, happy as a mole in summer soil.

I stayed at the kitchen window for the pleasure of watching our last and littlest, enjoying what a funny guy he is, marveling that he could be so blithe about the cold. A flush of pink upon the snow diverted me; rare glory was spreading across the sky. I tapped on the glass and signaled Chris to look.

He popped with a shout from his bunker (frosted like a cupcake, snow even on his lashes) and ran to the top of the bank where the view was grandest. There he slowly circled, seeing it all, his upturned face radiant. Beyond and above him, the whole sky blazed.

Then that roaring, boisterous boy-child of mine sweetly amazed me. He stretched forth his arms, as if in them he could embrace the universe. It was a moving gesture, generations old, of absolute appreciation. Thus the ancients worshiped the sun; thus my son stood until the last flare had faded. He lowered his arms, and then himself, and sat in the snow. Chin in hand, he remained, ·contemplating the early dark.

Chris came quietly to supper, wearing an inward look. I wanted to ask: Was this the day reality happened? I wanted to say: 'I know how it is. I know.'

I said nothing. When I filled his plate, I patted him casually and left him to his thoughts. Poignancy, regret and happiness – if that's what he felt – go along with growing. And growing up is something we must do alone.

JOAN MILLS

No matter what may be one's nationality, sex, age, philosophy, or religion, everyone wishes either to become or to remain happy. Hence definitions of happiness are interesting. One of the best was given in my senior year at college by President Timothy Dwight. 'The happiest person is the person who thinks the most interesting thoughts.'

This definition places happiness where it belongs – within and not without. The principle of happiness should be like the principle of virtue: it should not be dependent upon things, but be a part of personality. . . .

If the happiest person is the person who thinks the most interesting thoughts, we are bound to grow happier as we advance in years, because our minds have more and more interesting thoughts. A well-ordered life is like climbing a tower; the view halfway up is better than the view from the base, and it steadily becomes finer as the horizon expands.

WILLIAM LYON PHELPS

The art of living rightly is like all arts: It must be learned and practiced with incessant care.

JOHANN W. VON GOETHE

If it be possible, as much as lieth in you, live peaceably with all men.

ROMANS 12:18

A GIFT FROM THE HEART*

New York City, where I live, is impressive at any time, but as Christmas approaches it's overwhelming. Store windows blaze with lights and color, furs and jewels. Golden angels, 40 feet tall, hover over Fifth Avenue. Wealth, power, opulence . . . nothing in the world can match this fabulous display.

Through the gleaming canyons people hurry to find last-minute gifts. Money seems to be no problem. If there's a problem, it's that the recipients so often have everything they need or want that it's hard to find anything suitable, anything that will really say, 'I love you.'

Last December, as Christ's birthday drew near, a stranger was faced with just that problem. She had come from Switzerland to live in an

* Reprinted with permission from the January 1968 *Reader's Digest*, copyright, 1967, by the Reader's Digest Association, Inc.; from *Guideposts* (December 1967).

American home and perfect her English. In return, she was willing to act as secretary, mind the grandchildren, do anything she was asked. She was just a girl in her late teens. Her name was Ursula.

One of the tasks her employers gave Ursula was keeping track of Christmas presents as they arrived. There were many, and all would require acknowledgment. Ursula kept a faithful record, but with a growing sense of concern. She was grateful to her American friends; she wanted to show her gratitude by giving them a Christmas present. But nothing that she could buy with her small allowance could compare with the gifts she was recording daily. Besides, even without these gifts, it seemed to her that her employers already had everything.

At night from her window Ursula could see the snowy expanse of Central Park and beyond it the jagged skyline of the city. Far below, taxis hooted and the traffic lights winked red and green. It was so different from the silent majesty of the Alps that at times she had to blink back tears of the homesickness she was careful never to show. It was in the solitude of her little room, a few days before Christmas, that her secret idea came to Ursula.

It was almost as if a voice spoke clearly, inside her head. 'It's true,' said the voice, 'that many people in this city have much more than you do. But surely there are many who have far less. If you will think about this, you may find a solution to what's troubling you.'

Ursula thought long and hard. Finally on her day off, which was Christmas Eve, she went to a large department store. She moved slowly along the crowded aisles, selecting and rejecting things in her mind. At last she bought something and had it wrapped in gaily colored paper. She went out into the gray twilight and looked helplessly around. Finally, she went up to a doorman, resplendent in blue and gold. 'Excuse, please,' she said in her hesitant English, 'can you tell me where to find a poor street?'

'A poor street, Miss?' said the puzzled man.

'Yes, a very poor street. The poorest in the city.'

The doorman looked doubtful. 'Well, you might try Harlem. Or down in the Village. Or the Lower East Side, maybe.'

But these names meant nothing to Ursula. She thanked the doorman and walked along, threading her way through the stream of shoppers until she came to a tall policeman. 'Please,' she said, 'can you direct me to a very poor street . . . in Harlem?'

The policeman looked at her sharply and shook his head. 'Harlem's no place for you, Miss.' And he blew his whistle and sent the traffic swirling past.

Holding her package carefully, Ursula walked on, head bowed against the sharp wind. If a street looked poorer than the one she was on, she took it. But none seemed like the slums she had heard about.

Once she stopped a woman, 'Please, where do the very poor people live?' But the woman gave her a stare and hurried on.

Darkness came sifting from the sky. Ursula was cold and discouraged and afraid of becoming lost. She came to an intersection and stood forlornly on the corner. What she was trying to do suddenly seemed foolish, impulsive, absurd. Then, through the traffic's roar, she heard the cheerful tinkle of a bell. On the corner opposite, a Salvation Army man was making his traditional Christmas appeal.

At once Ursula felt better; the Salvation Army was a part of life in Switzerland too. Surely this man could tell her what she wanted to know. She waited for the light, then crossed over to him. 'Can you help me? I'm looking for a baby. I have here a little present for the poorest baby I can find.' And she held up the package with the green ribbon and the gaily colored paper.

Dressed in gloves and overcoat a size too big for him, he seemed a very ordinary man. But behind his steel-rimmed glasses his eyes were kind. He looked at Ursula and stopped ringing his bell. 'What sort of present?' he asked.

'A little dress. For a small, poor baby. Do you know of one?'

'Oh, yes,' he said. 'Of more than one, I'm afraid.'

'Is it far away? I could take a taxi, maybe?'

The Salvation Army man wrinkled his forehead. Finally he said, 'It's almost six o'clock. My relief will show up then. If you want to wait, and if you can afford a dollar taxi ride, I'll take you to a family in my own neighborhood who needs just about everything.'

'And they have a small baby?'

'A very small baby.'

'Then,' said Ursula joyfully, 'I wait!'

The substitute bell-ringer came. A cruising taxi slowed. In its welcome warmth, Ursula told her new friend about herself, how she came to be in New York, what she was trying to do. He listened in silence, and the taxi driver listened too. When they reached their destination, the driver said, 'Take your time, Miss. I'll wait for you.'

On the sidewalk, Ursula stared up at the forbidding tenement, dark, decaying, saturated with hopelessness. A gust of wind, iron-cold, stirred the refuse in the street and rattled the ashcans. 'They live on the third floor,' the Salvation Army man said. 'Shall we go up?'

But Ursula shook her head. 'They would try to thank me, and this is not from me.' She pressed the package into his hand. 'Take it up for me, please. Say it's from . . . from someone who has everything.'

The taxi bore her swiftly back from dark streets to lighted ones, from misery to abundance. She tried to visualize the Salvation Army man climbing the stairs, the knock, the explanation, the package being opened, the dress on the baby. It was hard to do.

Arriving at the apartment house on Fifth Avenue where she lived, she fumbled in her purse. But the driver flicked the flag up. 'No charge, Miss.'

'No charge?' echoed Ursula, bewildered.

'Don't worry,' the driver said, 'I've been paid.' He smiled at her and drove away.

Ursula was up early the next day. She set the table with special care. By the time she had finished, the family was awake, and there was all the excitement and laughter of Christmas morning. Soon the living room was a sea of gay discarded wrappings. Ursula thanked everyone for the presents she received. Finally, when there was a lull, she began to explain hesitantly why there seemed to be none from her. She told about going to the department store. She told about the Salvation Army man. She told about the taxi driver. When she finished, there was a long silence. No one seemed to trust himself to speak. 'So you see,' said Ursula, 'I try to do a kindness in your name. And this is my Christmas present to you. . . .'

How do I happen to know all this? I know it because ours was the home where Ursula lived. Ours was the Christmas she shared. We were like many Americans, so richly blessed that to this child from across the sea there seemed to be nothing she could add to the material things we already had. And so she offered something of far greater value: a gift of the heart, an act of kindness carried out in our name.

Strange, isn't it? A shy Swiss girl, alone in a great impersonal city. You would think that nothing she could do would affect anyone. And yet, by trying to give away love, she brought the true spirit of Christmas into our lives, the spirit of selfless giving. That was Ursula's secret – and she shared it with us all.

> Let me but live from year to year,
>   With forward face and unreluctant soul;
>   Not hurrying to, nor turning from, the goal;
> Not mourning for the things that disappear
> In the dim past, nor holding back in fear
>   From what the future veils; but with a whole
>   And happy heart, that pays its toll
> To Youth and Age, and travels on with cheer.
> So let the way wind up the hill or down
>   O'er rough or smooth, the journey will be joy:
>   Still seeking what I sought when but a boy,
> New friendship, high adventure, and a crown,
>   My heart will keep the courage of the quest,
>   And hope the road's last turn will be the best.
>
> HENRY VAN DYKE

I believe that we can live on earth according to the teachings of Jesus, and that the greatest happiness will come to the world when man obeys His commandment 'Love ye one another.'

I believe that every question between man and man is a religious question, and that every social wrong is a moral wrong.

I believe that we can live on earth according to the fulfillment of God's will, and that when the will of God is done on earth as it is done in heaven, every man will love his fellow men, and act towards them as he desires they should act towards him. I believe that the welfare of each is bound up in the welfare of all.

I believe that life is given us so we may grow in love, and I believe that God is in me as the sun is in the colour and fragrance of a flower – the Light in my darkness, the Voice in my silence.

I believe that only in broken gleams has the Sun of Truth yet shone upon men. I believe that love will finally establish the Kingdom of God on earth, and the Cornerstones of that Kingdom will be Liberty, Truth, Brotherhood, and Service.

I believe that no good shall be lost, and that all man has willed or hoped or dreamed of good shall exist forever.

I believe in the immortality of the soul because I have within me immortal longings. I believe that the state we enter after death is wrought of our own motives, thoughts, and deeds. I believe that in the life to come I shall have the senses I have not had here, and that my home there will be beautiful with colour, music, and speech of flowers and faces I love.

Without this faith there would be little meaning in my life. I should be 'a mere pillar of darkness in the dark.' Observers in the full enjoyment of their bodily senses pity me, but it is because they do not see the golden chamber in my life where I dwell delighted; for, dark as my path may seem to them, I carry a magic light in my heart. Faith, the spiritual strong searchlight, illumines the way, and although sinister doubts lurk in the shadow, I walk unafraid towards the Enchanted Wood where the foliage is always green, where joy abides, where nightingales nest and sing, and where life and death are one in the Presence of the Lord.

HELEN KELLER

Whatever is to make us better and happy, God has placed either openly before us or close to us.

SENECA

A CHRISTMAS CAROL

'What means this glory round our feet,'
  The Magi mused, 'more bright than morn?'
And voices chanted clear and sweet,
  'Today the Prince of Peace is born!'

'What means that star,' the Shepherds said,
  'That brightens through the rocky glen?'
And angels, answering overhead,
  Sang, 'Peace on earth, good-will to men!'

It's eighteen hundred years and more
  Since those sweet oracles were dumb;
We wait for Him, like them of yore;
  Alas, He seems so slow to come!

But it was said, in words of gold,
  No time or sorrow ever shall dim,
That little children might be bold
  In perfect trust to come to Him.

All around about our feet shall shine
  A light like that the Wise Men saw,
If we our loving wills incline
  To that sweet Life which is the Law.

So shall we learn to understand
  The simple faith of shepherds then,
And, clasping kindly hand in hand,
  Sing, 'Peace on earth, good-will to men!'

And they who do their souls no wrong,
  But keep at eve the faith of morn,
Shall daily hear the angel-song
  'Today the Prince of Peace is born!'

JAMES RUSSELL LOWELL

My sister-in-law and I were getting together some things to contribute to what the village was doing for the Christmas of the poor when old Mrs Merrill appeared at the door with a basket. Taking out glasses of jelly and a pumpkin pie, she said, 'I thought my things could go along with yours.'

She produced something else, a small red knitted cap and mittens, bright scarlet. 'There!' she said. 'I thought mebbe they'd pleasure some little boy. My! I do wish't I could ha' done more.'

Her visit reduced us to the breathless state of astonishment in which Mrs Merrill has for 20 years kept her neighbors. When she left, as we watched the bent old back slowly and stiffly begin the mile-long climb up the ladder-steep mountain road to her home, we began reflecting on Mrs Merrill's life.

Her father was a Hammett, one of those 'born to be bossed.' He had married one of the cranky Meigs, lifelong biters of nails. Old Mrs Merrill has told us that never during her mother's life had she done anything without being told she was dumb and do-less like her father. When she was 10 her father ran away. This new grievance darkened her mother's morose temper. The two older children married 'as soon as they could grab anybody, foot or horse.' So for 11 years sensitive little Sarah Ann was left to bear the irritable gloom which filled the home. When she was 23 her mother died and her father came wandering home, a broken alcoholic. Until she was 38 she waited on him day and night. One of the Dewey boys helped her run the farm on shares; somehow she managed.

When her father died, Sarah Ann, at last trying to have some life of her own, married a lazy, vain, self-pitying veteran of the Spanish War. He had never done a lick of work in his life. He received a pension of $40 a month, spent most of it on chewing tobacco and books by atheists, and never gave his wife more than 50 cents at a time. He had a grudge against life and took it out on his 'old-maid wife.'

Labor was beneath his dignity, and he stormed at his wife when she tried to keep things going, and railed at the ingratitude of a nation that left an old soldier to starve. Finally, when she was 56, he died. Then she held up her gray head and began to live.

The first thing she did was to have the house repaired. Using as security her reputation for honesty and what mountain land was left her, she borrowed $400. Some of the timbers and planks were still sound; with these the little house was made tight and shipshape. Painted too! Every ceiling was freshly plastered, every wall had cheerful new wallpaper – she put it on herself. Then she moved in her freshly oiled tables and chairs and beds, and settled.

She had traded some old harness for a couple of broody hens and now had a flock of 19 chickens. Another neighbor took what sound beams and planks were left over after the repairs and gave her in return three ewes and a ram. She's made regular pets of her flock ever since, shears them herself, scours and cards and spins the wool, knits her own woolen things, and has some extra to trade in at the store for tea and sugar.

She always has a big garden planted with the vegetables she likes. When the dandelion greens are tender in April she starts canning, and she cans her way right through to frost – wild strawberries, raspberries, blackberries, blueberries, applesauce, vegetables. Four times a year she has a lamb butchered, and salts and smokes the meat.

She takes care of the garden meticulously. ' 'Tis like scratching a 40-year itch I never could reach before, to do it *right*! I was on my knees weedin' onions last summer, as lame with stoopin' as an old horse with spavins, and it came over me all of a sudden that there wa'n't a soul in the world that could holler at me to do different. I set back on my heels and started to sing, "Praise God from Whom all blessings flow," till you could ha' heard me on the valley road.'

I thought of what city people who happen to stop for a drink of water say. 'What forlorn old age!' they exclaim. 'Not a chick or a child to look out for her! Has to do all the heavy work in that big garden! And not a pleasure or a diversion in her life!'

But Sarah Merrill's taste for life has been so purified by privation that she gets warm, conscious happiness from simple beauties and satisfactions which we thanklessly take for granted. Peace and order and cleanliness, for instance – she thrills to those great overlooked privileges.

As for taking care of herself, why she trips through that undertaking as if it were a dance. To have, when winter approaches, her woodshed filled with firewood cut, piled and *paid for*; to see those cellar shelves filled with jars of food which she herself has grown and canned; to put on warm garments made from her own wool – that makes her feel rich.

Sometimes she has dreams that they are still alive, her mother, her father, her husband, all in the house, 'hollerin' at me.' She bounds up from bed, goes downstairs, pours herself a glass of currant wine and gets out some doughnuts – no matter if it is half past two of a zero night with a wild wind burying the house in snowclouds. She sits down to the organ and plays and sings hymns, the ones with blazing words like 'Rise, Imperial Salem, rise!'

'How many times in our comfortable lives,' I asked myself, 'have we been moved to rise at half-past two of a winter night to feast and give thanks because we have so lived that we are suddenly pierced to the heart with the sheer blessedness of everyday existence?'

DOROTHY CANFIELD FISHER

When we hate our enemies, we give them power over us – power over our sleep, our appetites, our blood pressure, our health, and our happiness. Our enemies would dance with joy if they surmised that they worry and lacerate us. Our hatred is not hurting them at all; it only turns our own days and nights into a hellish turmoil.

AUTHOR UNKNOWN

MONTANA WIVES

I had to laugh,
For when she said it we were sitting by the door,
And straight down was the Fork
Twisting and turning and gleaming in the sun.
And then your eyes carried across to the purple bench beyond the river
With the Beartooth Mountains fairly screaming with light and blue and
    snow
And fold and turn of rimrock and prairie as far as your eye could go.
And she says: 'Dear Laura, sometimes I feel so sorry for you,
Shut away from everything – eating out your heart with loneliness.
When I think of my own full life I wish that I could share it.
Just pray for happier days to come, and bear it.'
She goes back to Billings to her white stucco house,
And looks through net curtains at another white stucco house,
And a brick house,
And a yellow frame house,
And six trimmed poplar trees,
And little squares of shaved grass.

Oh, dear, she stared at me like I was daft.
I couldn't help it! I just laughed and laughed.

GWENDOLEN HASTE

The way to happiness: keep your heart free from hate, your mind from worry. Live simply, expect little, give much. Fill your life with love. Scatter sunshine. Forget self, think of others. Do as you would be done by. Try this for a week and you will be surprised.

H. C. MATTERN

The Lord is my shepherd; I shall not want.
He maketh me to lie down in green pastures;
    he leadeth me beside the still waters.
He restoreth my soul: he leadeth me in the
    paths of righteousness for his name's sake.
Yea, though I walk through the valley of the
    shadow of death, I will fear no evil: for thou
    art with me; thy rod and thy staff they comfort me.

Thou preparest a table before me in the presence
of mine enemies; thou anointest my
head with oil; my cup runneth over.
Surely goodness and mercy shall follow me
all the days of my life: and I will dwell in the
house of the Lord for ever.

PSALM 23

A man I admire very much came in to see me. Many years ago he started with his company at the bottom but with determination to get to the top. He has unusual abilities and energy, and he used all he had. Today he is president of his company and he has all the things that go with his position.

Yet, along the way, he left out something, and one of the things he did not achieve is happiness. He was a nervous, tense, worried, and sick man. Finally, one of his physicians suggested that he talk with a a minister.

We talked of how his physicians had given him prescriptions and he had taken them. Then I took a sheet of paper and wrote out my prescription for him. I prescribed the Twenty-third Psalm, five times a day for seven days.

I insisted that he take it just as I prescribed. He was to read it the first thing when he awakened in the morning. Read it carefully, meditatively, and prayerfully. Immediately after breakfast, he was to do exactly the same thing. Also immediately after lunch, again after dinner and, finally, the last thing before he went to bed.

It was not to be a quick, hurried reading. He was to think about each phrase, giving his mind time to soak up as much of the meaning as possible. At the end of just one week, I promised, things would be different for him.

That prescription sounds simple, but really isn't. The Twenty-third Psalm is one of the most powerful pieces of writing in existence, and it can do marvelous things for any person. I have suggested this to many people, and in every instance which I know of its being tried it has produced results. It can change your life in seven days.

One man told me that he did not have time to be bothered with reading it during the day, so he just read it five times in the morning. However, when a physician prescribed a medicine after each meal, or every certain number of hours, no right-thinking person would take the full day's dose at one time.

Some have told me that after two or three days they felt they knew it sufficiently, and thus, instead of taking time to read it thoughtfully, they would just think about it through the day. That won't work. To be most effective, it must be taken as prescribed.

Ralph Waldo Emerson said, 'A man is what he thinks about all day long.' Marcus Aurelius said, 'A man's life is what his thoughts make it.' Norman Vincent Peale says, 'Change your thoughts and you change your world.' The Bible says, 'For as he thinketh in his heart, so is he' (Proverbs 23:7).

The Twenty-third Psalm is a pattern of thinking, and when a mind becomes saturated with it, a new way of thinking and a new life are the result. It contains only 118 words. One could memorize it in a short time. In fact, most of us already know it. But its power is not in memorizing the words, but rather in thinking the thoughts.

The power of this Psalm lies in the fact that it represents a positive, hopeful, faith approach to life. We assume it was written by David, the same David who had a black chapter of sin in his life. But he spends no time in useless regret and morbid looking back.

David possesses the same spirit that St. Paul expresses: 'Forgetting those things which are behind, and reaching forth unto those things which are before, I press toward the mark' (Philippians 3:13), or the spirit of our Lord when He said, 'Neither do I condemn thee; go, and sin no more' (John 8:11).

Take it as I prescribe, and in seven days a powerful new way of thinking will be deeply and firmly implanted within your mind that will bring marvelous changes in your thinking and give you a new life.

CHARLES L. ALLEN

Every time you give a bit of yourself you plant a little seed of Future Happiness. All the rest of your life these seeds will keep springing up unexpectedly along your path. When you need a friend to give you a lift in some situation, likely as not along will come a person for whom you did something thoughtful when you were a youngster.

Take up giving-away as a hobby while you are young, and you will have a happy life. What is more, because you do so many thoughtful things on impulse, you will develop a lively and interesting personality – gracious, friendly, and likeable.

DAVID DUNN

NINE KEYS TO CONTENTMENT

Health enough to make work a pleasure.
Wealth enough to support your needs.
Strength enough to battle with difficulties and overcome them.
Grace enough to confess your sins and forsake them.
Patience enough to toil until some good is accomplished.
Charity enough to see some good in your neighbors.
Love enough to move you to be useful and helpful to others.

Faith enough to make real things of God.
Hope enough to remove all anxious fears concerning the future.

JOHANN W. VON GOETHE

I wander'd lonely as a cloud
That floats on high o'er vales and hills,
When all at once I saw a crowd,
A host, of golden daffodils;
Beside the lake, beneath the trees,
Fluttering and dancing in the breeze.

Continuous as the stars that shine
And twinkle on the Milky Way,
They stretch'd in never-ending line
Along the margin of a bay;
Ten thousand saw I at a glance,
Tossing their heads in sprightly dance.

The waves beside them danced; but they
Out-did the sparkling waves in glee:
A poet could not but be gay,
In such a jocund company:
I gazed – and gazed – but little thought
What wealth the show to me had brought:

For oft, when on my couch I lie
In vacant or in pensive mood,
They flash upon that inward eye
Which is the bliss of solitude;
And then my heart with pleasure fills,
And dances with the daffodils.

WILLIAM WORDSWORTH

THE PHILOSOPHER

I saw him sitting in his door,
    Trembling as old men do;
His house was old; his barn was old,
    And yet his eyes seemed new.

His eyes had seen three times my years
    And kept a twinkle still,
Though they had looked at birth and death
    And three graves on a hill.

'I will sit down with you,' I said,
    'And you will make me wise;
Tell me how you have kept the joy
    Still burning in your eyes.'

Then like an old-time orator
    Impressively he rose;
'I make the most of all that comes,
    The least of all that goes.'

The jingling rhythm of his words
    Echoes as old songs do,
Yet this had kept his eyes alight
    Till he was ninety-two.

SARA TEASDALE

To seek pleasure for the sake of pleasure is to avoid reality, the reality of other beings and the reality of ourselves. But only the fulfillment of what we really are can give us joy. Joy is nothing else than the awareness of our being fulfilled in our true being, in our personal center. And this fulfillment is possible only if we unite ourselves with what others really are. It is reality that gives joy, and reality alone. The Bible speaks so often of joy because it is the most realistic of all books. 'Rejoice!' That means: 'Penetrate from what seems to be real to that which is really real.' Mere pleasure, in yourselves and in all other beings, remains in the realm of illusion about reality. Joy is born out of union with reality itself. . . .

Does the Biblical demand for joy prohibit pleasure? Do joy and pleasure exclude each other? By no means! The fulfillment of the center of our being does not exclude partial and peripheral fulfillments. And we must say this with the same emphasis with which we have contrasted joy and pleasure. We must challenge not only those who seek pleasure for pleasure's sake, but also those who reject pleasure because it is pleasure. . . .

Joy has something within itself which is beyond joy and sorrow. This something is called blessedness. . . .

This joy which has in itself the depth of blessedness is asked for and promised in the Bible. It preserves in itself its opposite, sorrow. It provides the the foundation for happiness and pleasure. It is present in all levels of man's striving for fulfillment. It consecrates and directs them. It does not diminish or weaken them. It does not take away the risks and dangers of the joy of life. It makes the joy of life possible in pleasure and pain, in happiness and unhappiness, in ecstasy and sorrow. Where there is joy, there is fulfillment. And where there is fulfillment, there is joy. In fulfillment and joy the inner aim of life, the meaning of creation, and the end of salvation are attained.

PAUL TILLICH

There's too much struggle and opportunity and interest in life not to be a happy person.

Tell me not, in mournful numbers,
    Life is but an empty dream!
For the soul is dead that slumbers,
    And things are not what they seem.

Life is real! Life is earnest!
    And the grave is not its goal;
Dust thou art, to dust returnest,
    Was not spoken of the soul.

Not enjoyment, and not sorrow,
    Is our destined end or way;
But to act, that each to-morrow
    Find us farther than to-day.

Art is long, and Time is fleeting,
    And our hearts, though stout and brave,
Still, like muffled drums, are beating
    Funeral marches to the grave.

In the world's broad field of battle,
    In the bivouac of life,
Be not like dumb, driven cattle!
    Be a hero in the strife!

Trust no Future, howe'er pleasant!
    Let the dead Past bury its dead!
Act – act in the living Present!
    Heart within, and God o'erhead.

Lives of great men all remind us
    We can make our lives sublime,
And, departing, leave behind us
    Footprints on the sands of time; –

Footprints, that perhaps another,
    Sailing o'er life's solemn main,
A forlorn and shipwrecked brother,
    Seeing, shall take heart again.

Let us, then, be up and doing,
   With a heart for any fate;
Still achieving, still pursuing,
   Learn to labor and to wait.

HENRY WADSWORTH LONGFELLOW

Ah! Up then from the ground sprang I
And hailed the earth with such a cry
As is not heard save from a man
Who has been dead, and lives again.
About the trees my arms I wound;
Like one gone mad I hugged the ground;
I raised my quivering arms on high!
I laughed and laughed into the sky,
Till at my throat a strangling sob
Caught fiercely, and a great heart-throb
Sent instant tears into my eyes;
O God, I cried, no dark disguise
Can e'er hereafter hide from me
Thy radiant identity!
Thou canst not move across the grass
But my quick eyes will see Thee pass,
Nor speak, however silently,
But my hushed voice will answer Thee.
I know the path that tells Thy way
Through the cool eve of every day;
God, I can push the grass apart;
And lay my finger on Thy heart!
The world stands out on either side
No wider than the heart is wide;
Above the world is stretched the sky, —
No higher than the soul is high.
The heart can push the sea and land
Farther away on either hand;
The soul can split the sky in two,
And let the face of God shine through.
But East and West will pinch the heart
That cannot keep them pushed apart;
And he whose soul is flat – the sky
Will cave in on him by and by.

EDNA ST. VINCENT MILLAY

Most people are about as happy as they make up their minds to be.

ABRAHAM LINCOLN

Very little is needed to make a happy life. It is all within yourself, in your way of thinking.

MARCUS AURELIUS

Four things come not back – the spoken word, the sped arrow, the past life, and the neglected opportunity.

ARABIAN PROVERB

GIVE US, oh, give us, the man who sings at his work! He will do more in the same time, – he will do it better, – he will persevere longer. One is scarcely sensible of fatigue whilst he marches to music. The very stars are said to make harmony as they revolve in their sphere. Wondrous is the strength of cheerfulness, altogether past calculation in its powers of endurance. Efforts, to be permanently useful, must be uniformly joyous, a spirit all sunshine, graceful from very gladness, beautiful because bright.

THOMAS CARLYLE

If I have faltered more or less
In my great task of happiness;
If I have moved among my race
And shown no shining morning face;
If beams from happy human eyes
Have moved me not; if morning skies,
Books, and my food, and summer rain
Knocked on my sullen heart in vain; –
Lord, thy most pointed pleasure take
And stab my spirit broad awake.

ROBERT LOUIS STEVENSON

If the day and the night are such that you greet them with joy, and life emits a fragrance like flowers and sweet-scented herbs, is more elastic, more starry, more immortal, – that is your success.

HENRY DAVID THOREAU

The air is like a butterfly
With frail blue wings.
The happy earth looks at the sky
And sings.

JOYCE KILMER

I am come that they might have life, and that they might have it more abundantly.

JOHN 10:10

Chapter 11

How to Get the
Help You Need

There are times in life when you just must have help. And this goes
for everyone, no matter how self-sufficient they seem to be. The
significant fact is that such help is always available. The needed help
comes from God who gives it to you in various ways. Sometimes He
gives it through other people.

I well recall a Saturday morning years ago when word came of the
sudden death of my mother. I was, of course, crushed with grief. As
a pastor, I had been privileged to help many in similar circumstances,
but found it difficult to get help for myself that day.

I had a preaching engagement the following Sunday on the New
Jersey coast. I never considered canceling the appointment, knowing
that my mother would want me to carry on. So, feeling inconsolable
and lonely, I boarded a train and there I saw sitting in the coach an
old friend, Colonel Myron W. Robinson, a man prominent in public
life, who told me he was on his way to a seashore picnic of New
Jersey political leaders, and he was looking forward to a pleasant day
with friends.

Sitting beside me, he quickly sensed that something was wrong.
He listened sympathetically as I told him of my mother's sudden
death. He asked where I was going to preach, and when we reached
my station, to my surprise, Myron got off with me. 'I'm skipping the
picnic,' he announced. 'I'm going with you.' Despite my remonstrance,
he stayed with me all day and we rode back to New York together. He
said not one word, just stayed with me. He was inarticulate with words
but his love spoke volumes.

When we separated in the city, I said, 'Myron, I will never forget
the friendship you gave me today.'

He put his arm around my shoulder. 'You've often helped me,' he
said simply. 'Just remember God loves you and . . .' he hesitated,
'I do, too.' And he was gone. But he left a strange comfort in my
heart. Colonel Robinson was God's messenger of help for me on that
day of sadness long ago. So, when you need help, look for the love of
God as it can be ministered through people. God's faithful servants
know how to help because they know God.

Of course, the greatest of all sources of help is the Bible. Indeed, in its inspired pages, is help for everyone to meet every trouble of this earth. This profound book was written by men who knew life because they knew God, and through them His helping word is available to us. Reading the book prayerfully and thoughtfully you will discover in all times of need that God is, for a fact, 'your ever-present help in time of trouble.'

The experience of a woman I knew shows how the Bible can provide help in time of deep need. This woman's daughter, a gay and beautiful girl, who loved to ride her horse, was galloping along a bridle path when suddenly a broken limb fell from a tree, striking her head. She was thrown to the ground and died instantly. What tragedy! From fullness of life, in an instant she was in death.

The grief-stricken mother reached blindly out everywhere for help but nothing eased the pain in her heart. Finally, she went away alone to a little country inn where, as she explained it, she could think and pray and fight the battle of grief and bitterness. Restlessly pacing her room, she picked up a Bible. She opened it at random and started reading the first Psalm. As she continued reading one Psalm after another, the ancient words gripped and fascinated her. The night grew chill, but, drawing a blanket around her shoulders, she read on and on, the great poems of faith reaching deeply into her mind and heart.

Finally, in the early hours of the morning she finished the Psalms, and closing the book, said aloud, 'What wisdom, what understanding! All of life is in these marvelous words, all pain and heartache. God has spoken peace to me.' Comfort came, and with it the strength and understanding she needed.

The Bible can be your help in every time of need and in other crises as well. In its pages, you can find guidance in the ordinary problems as well as in the great problems which come in life.

Take, for example, my friend Go Puang Seng, editor and publisher of the *Fookien Times* of Manila. Mr Go was the one man the invading Japanese wanted to capture and kill because of his vigorous and outspoken opposition to their increasing dominance in the Far East prior to World War II. He escaped into the mountains and for three years was hunted like an animal. Daily in the greatest danger of capture and subject constantly to hunger, cold, and disease, he nevertheless survived, and today his paper is more influential than ever.

Mr Go is a man of great faith. He searched the Bible constantly not only for solace and strength but for specific answers to the vital questions of what he should do next, where he should turn. This insight was all important to his very existence. One marvels, in learning his story, that anyone could make so many right decisions while in such constant jeopardy. But he believes that, in every instance, a verse or verses in the Bible suggested proper actions to take and that God guided him, step by step, every day for those three, long, danger-filled years.

Mr Go's experience brings to mind the case of a prominent business leader who was facing a very great crisis in his affairs and couldn't come up with an answer. He was growing increasingly tense and this probably closed off the flow of insight.

Sitting impatiently at his desk, he began to look at his mother's picture, which he kept there, and to think of her. 'She was a simple but strong woman, a Kansas farmer's wife,' he told me later. 'Her faith was unquestioning. God was like a close friend. Suddenly, I began recalling crises in our family life of the kind that occurs in every family. I remembered how she would take her Bible and go into the parlor. She said she went there to talk the problem over with the Lord. She would always come out with a look of peace on her face. "The Lord will provide; He will show the way," she would say confidently. And He always did.'

So this businessman followed his mother's example. He began 'talking it over with the Lord.' He didn't receive a magic answer right away. But he did get a feeling of peace and quiet and a sense of certainty. Presently, his reoriented mind began to grapple with the problem, and creative and effective answers came. He found a real secret of real help.

In this chapter, I have assembled some thoughts that may serve to open channels of help for you as you may have need of them from time to time.

Among the students at a well-known college was a young man who used crutches. A homely sort of fellow, he had a talent for friendliness and optimism.

He won many scholastic honors and the respect of his classmates. One day a classmate asked the cause of his deformity.

'Infantile paralysis,' was the brief reply.

'But tell me,' said the friend, 'with a misfortune like that, how can you face the world so confidently?'

'Oh,' he replied, smiling, 'the disease never touched my heart.'

THE PENTECOSTAL EVANGEL

Said the Robin to the Sparrow:
  'I should really like to know
Why these anxious human beings
  Rush about and worry so.'

Said the Sparrow to the Robin:
'Friend, I think that it must be
That they have no heavenly Father
Such as cares for you and me.'

ELIZABETH CHENEY

Courage, brother! Do not stumble, though thy path be as dark as night; there's a star to guide the humble. Trust in God and do the right.

NORMAN MACLEOD

Ye shall know the truth, and the truth shall make you free.

JOHN 8: 32

Every morning, lean thine arms awhile
Upon the window-sill of Heaven,
And gaze upon the Lord ...

Then, with that vision in thy heart,
Turn strong to meet the day.

AUTHOR UNKNOWN

There is but one way to tranquility of mind and happiness. Let this therefore be always ready at hand with thee, both when thou wakest early in the morning, and when thou goest late to sleep, to account no external thing thine own, but commit all these to God.

EPICTETUS

For all your days prepare,
And meet them ever alike:
When you are the anvil, bear –
When you are the hammer, strike.

EDWIN MARKHAM

Show me a worrying person and I will show you a person who does not know how to relax.

Our religious faith, Christianity, shows us the complete answer to nervous troubles and tensions. A single constant affirmation that the everlasting arms of God are holding you up, repeated hour by hour until you become convinced that God is now your guide and stay, will often bring you out of worries and fears, but how many Christians will really *let go their fears and let God* handle them ? ...

You have to get into the habit of leaving your troubles with God. The only complete and sure cure for your bad nerves, as you call them, is to relax in the hands of God and know that He is now looking after your troubles, that He is now guiding you into the quiet waters of inner peace. ...

The most wonderful thing that ever happened to me was this: Many years ago *I let go* my past and *let God* take over my life. When I completely surrendered my life to Him, I lost my temper, my fears, my years of deadly illness and sicknesses. It meant facing life every hour with the truth that was in me to replace the negative thinking of a lifetime.

It meant an hourly contact with God, in the street-car, the bus, my own car, my laboratory – no matter where I went I had an appointment with Him. What came of it? Peace of mind, health and spiritual prosperity. . . .

Are you willing to put Him first in your life? Are you willing to *let go*, and *let God* be your mentor from this day on?

Then if you are, you, too, can have no fears, no tensions, no nervous-. ness, no worries. When you take His yoke upon you, your life is a converted one. No longer do the sins of the devil haunt you, no longer can the so-called powers of evil assail you, but you learn to live happily, healthfully, confidently, because you have *let go*, you *let God* and abundant living come into your life. . . .

Peace of mind is the greatest asset we can have for happy, healthy living. This is an inner victory which only comes from knowing God intimately. Then the material things of life do not bother us any longer – we live in a spiritual world, and spiritual values are the only real values in life.

We each have this power within us, and when we learn by faith to control this power, then we know how to use it, how to liberate it for our daily needs. . . .

The answer to all our problems of living is how we face them, not where we were born, not that we have had a poor environment, not that we had no chance of an education. The answer is always within ourselves. Fighting, struggling against life will never win us a victory. You have to make your own inner consciousness a citadel of peace, knowing that Christ lives there. You become a member of the D.W.C. – Don't Worry Club – leaving your worries to Him.

We all need a safety valve every day of our lives, and we find it in our religion. Christ is the safety valve for your emotions, your wrong thinking. You cannot have a nervous condition when you open this safety valve.

ALBERT E. CLIFFE

Not in the clamor of the crowded street,
Not in the shouts and plaudits of the throng,
But in ourselves are triumph and defeat.

HENRY WADSWORTH LONGFELLOW

We do not get faith by arguing about religion; we get faith on our knees, in and through surrender, and prayer. God gives faith to those who need and want it.

ELMER G. HOMRIGHAUSEN

It's good to have money and the things that money can buy, but it's good, too, to check up once in a while and make sure you haven't lost the things money can't buy.

GEORGE HORACE LORIMER

None can do a man so much harm as he doeth himself.

BENJAMIN WHICHCOTE

Unless a man takes himself sometimes out of the world, by retirement and self-reflection, he will be in danger of losing himself in the world.

BENJAMIN WHICHCOTE

Now whether the difficulty is real or whether it is imaginary, the results are the same. You become whatever you think. If God is with you, how can you possibly feel inferior to anyone? You have equal access to all the good that comes from God. You can demonstrate your faith in His ability to give it to you by living His life. So change your thought patterns right now. Make up your mind to beat this feeling by faith in God, and you will.

He can who thinks he can! . . .

If you have thoughts of failure, defeat and inferiority, get this idea now. Simply believe that the Bible means what it says; for when you begin to live right, when you begin to live within the laws of God, you will find that your negative tendencies are gradually overcome, because of the power within you, in which you are now trusting. This power, of course, is God.

With most people it is not the fact that they have had a failure or a defeat which has beaten them; but it has been a holding of negative thoughts, the anticipation of failure in their mind. They convince themselves that they are inferior to certain of their friends, their fellows or their neighbors, and the longer they hold this thought the more inferior they become to everything and everybody. . . .

An inferiority complex is a disbelief in your own self, your own powers of mind. This to me is a sin, for every human being has been made in the image of God and is perfect, whole and complete. We all come across people in our lives who suffer from pride and conceit. Strangely enough, this is usually an indication of an inferiority complex, and they are using this method to hide a feeling of inadequacy. . . .

There is an old hymn which says, 'Come to the Saviour, make no delay'; and if you are willing to believe those words, they will bring you to the fount of joy which will enable you to convert your inferiorities into success, your sickness into health, your poverty of mind into abundant living, your fears, your doubts, and your sorrows into a wonderful awareness of joyful living.

Every one of us as he goes through life must die daily in a mental sense, for his negative or evil thoughts must each day die. New ideas, new thoughts, positive instead of negative, new faith must be born in us from day to day. It matters not what fears have beset you in the past, what inferiorities are holding you back. It matters not what you have reaped in life hitherto, if you are willing today to make a new seeding time and believe that tomorrow holds promise of a harvest that will bring you life more abundantly.

It is the easiest thing in the world to learn how to *let go* your sense of inferiority and *let God*; for if God is for you, what can and who can be against you?

ALBERT E. CLIFFE

But this one thing I do, forgetting those things which are behind, and reaching forth unto those things which are before, I press toward the mark for the prize of the high calling of God in Christ Jesus.

PHILIPPIANS 3: 13–14

Teaching them to observe all things whatsoever I have commanded you: and, lo, I am with you always, even unto the end of the world. Amen.

MATTHEW 28: 20

O Love that will not let me go,
I rest my weary soul in Thee;
I give Thee back the life I owe,
That in Thine ocean depths its flow
May richer, fuller, be.

O Light that followest all my way,
I yield my flickering torch to Thee;
My heart restores its borrowed ray,
That in Thy sunshine's blaze its day
May brighter, fairer, be.

O Joy that seekest me through pain,
I cannot close my heart to Thee;
I trace the rainbow through the rain,
And feel the promise is not vain
That morn shall tearless be.

O Cross that liftest up my head,
I dare not ask to fly from Thee;
I lay in dust life's glory dead,
And from the ground there blossoms red
Life that shall endless be.

GEORGE MATHESON

I make it a practice to avoid hating anyone. If someone's been guilty of despicable actions, especially toward me, I try to forget him. I used to follow a practice – somewhat contrived, I admit – to write the man's name on a piece of scrap paper, drop it into the lowest drawer of my desk, and say to myself: 'That finishes the incident, and so far as I'm concerned, that fellow.'

The drawer became over the years a sort of private wastebasket for crumpled-up spite and discarded personalities. Besides, it seemed to be effective, and helped me avoid harboring useless black feelings.

DWIGHT D. EISENHOWER

Lord, give me faith! – to live from day to day,
With tranquil heart to do my simple part,
And, with my hand in Thine, just go Thy way.

Lord, give me faith! – to trust, if not to know;
With quiet mind in all things Thee to find,
And, child-like, to go where Thou wouldst have me go.

Lord, give me faith! – to leave it all to Thee,
The future is Thy gift, I would not lift
The veil Thy love has hung 'twixt it and me.

JOHN OXENHAM

And when he came to his disciples, he saw a great multitude about them, and the scribes questioning with them.

And straightway all the people, when they beheld him, were greatly amazed, and running to him saluted him.

And he asked the scribes, What question ye with them?

And one of the multitude answered and said, Master, I have brought unto thee my son, which hath a dumb spirit;

And wheresoever he taketh him, he teareth him: and he foameth, and gnasheth with his teeth, and pineth away: and I spake to thy disciples, that they should cast him out; and they could not.

He answereth him, and saith, O faithless generation, how long shall I be with you? how long shall I suffer you? Bring him unto me.

And they brought him unto him: and when he saw him, straightway the spirit tare him; and he fell on the ground, and wallowed foaming.

And he asked his father, How long is it ago since this came unto him? And he said, Of a child.

And ofttimes it hath cast him into the fire, and into the waters, to destroy him: but if thou canst do any thing, have compassion on us, and help us.

Jesus said unto him, If thou canst believe, all things are possible to him that believeth.

And straightway the father of the child cried out, and said with tears, Lord, I believe; help thou mine unbelief.

MARK 9: 14-24

It is a shameful thing for the soul to faint while the body still perseveres.

MARCUS AURELIUS

He lays no great burden upon us; a little remembrance of Him from time to time; a little adoration; sometimes to pray for His grace, sometimes to offer Him your sorrows, and sometimes to offer Him thanks for the benefits He has given you, and still gives you, in the midst of your troubles. He asks you to console yourself with Him the oftenest you can. Lift up your heart to Him even at your meals when you are in company; the least little remembrance will always be acceptable to Him. You need not cry very loud; He is nearer than you think.

BROTHER LAWRENCE

One ship drives east, and another west
With the self-same winds that blow:
'Tis the set of the sails
And not the gales,
Which decides the way we go.

Like the winds of the sea are the ways of fate,
As they voyage along through life;
'Tis the will of the soul
That decides its goal,
And not the calm or the strife.

ELLA WHEELER WILCOX

Sow a Thought, and you reap an Act;
Sow an Act, and you reap a Habit;
Sow a Habit, and you reap a Character;
Sow a Character, and you reap a Destiny.

SAMUEL SMILES

With every rising of the sun,
Think of your life as just begun.
The past has shrived and buried deep
All yesterdays; there let them sleep.

Concern yourself with but today,
Woo it, and teach it to obey
Your will and wish. Since time began
Today has been the friend of man;

But in his blindness and his sorrow,
He looks to yesterday and tomorrow.
You, and today! a soul sublime,
And the great pregnant hour of time,
With God himself to bind the twain!
Go forth, I say – attain, attain!
With God himself to bind the twain!

ELLA WHEELER WILCOX

Sorrow is a fruit: God does not make it grow on limbs too weak to bear it.

VICTOR HUGO

It was high counsel that Jones heard given to a young person – 'Always do well what you are afraid to do.'

RALPH WALDO EMERSON

A man is relieved and gay when he has put his heart into his work and done his best.

RALPH WALDO EMERSON

Let not the sun go down upon your wrath.

EPHESIANS 4: 26

In your patience possess ye your souls.

LUKE 21: 19

In quietness and in confidence shall be your strength.

ISAIAH 30: 15

THE ATHEIST WHO WENT TO THE MOUNTAIN

For years an atheist in a Greek village envied the serenity of a Christian friend. Finally, he asked his friend if he, too, might not find from God the same peace of mind.

'Yes, I believe so,' replied the Christian, 'if you get to know Him.'
'But where can I meet this God?'

The Christian explained that he customarily went out several miles beyond the village and there met and talked to God.

The next morning the atheist walked out of the village until he stood before a mountain, and he cried out, 'Lord God Almighty, discover to me the kind of being you are!'

And when he received no answer he again and again cried out the same words. He repeated this action every morning for several weeks and finally gave up. 'There is no God!' he declared.

When the atheist again encountered his Christian friend he scornfully related his futile experience and alleged the Christian was indulging in self-deception.

'Did you go out of the village, as I directed?' asked the Christian.

'Yes, and I stood before that mountain day after day and called out to your God, and there was no answer.'

'Why, there is no mountain out there,' said the Christian. 'But, anyway, tell me, what did you say to the Lord?'

'I asked Him to tell me the kind of being he is.'

'Well, my friend,' replied the Christian, 'when I go out there I tell God the kind of person I am. I confess I am sinful and I recognize that purity and holiness cannot exist apart from Him. Then God appears to me and I gain a better understanding of Him.'

The next morning the atheist again went out beyond the village, fell on his knees before the mountain, and said, 'Lord, I am a sinful man; forgive me!'

And when the atheist looked up, the mountain had disappeared. It was only the shadow of his own self, and when self had no longer remained between him and God, then he saw the Lord.

RALPH L. WOODS

He who has a thousand friends has not a friend to spare, and he who has one enemy shall meet him everywhere.

ALI BEN ABU TALEB

We search the world for truth. We cull
The good, the true, the beautiful,
From graven stone and written scroll,
And all old flower-fields of the soul;
And, weary seekers of the best,
We come back laden from our quest,
To find that all the sages said
Is in the Book our mothers read.

JOHN GREENLEAF WHITTIER

THE BIBLE

Within this ample volume lies
The mystery of mysteries.
Happiest they of human race
To whom their God has given grace
To read, to fear, to hope, to pray,
To lift the latch, to force the way;
But better had they ne'er been born
That read to doubt or read to scorn.

SIR WALTER SCOTT

Chapter 12

Beyond Life's Horizon

Not too long ago, a gallant lady went beyond the horizon. Her name was Marian Kay, and she followed quickly after her husband, Gordon. Never shall I forget these two, because of the great faith that was theirs, faith of a quality that deepened that of all associated with them.

Gordon Kay telephoned me one day. 'I want you to heal my wife,' he said simply.

'But I am not a healer,' I replied. 'Only God can heal. But I will try to help her as God may will.'

When I went to see her she told me of the cobalt treatment, and said a mark had been put upon her chest and back to indicate where the treatment was to go if in a strange hospital.

Opening the neck of her dress, she revealed a purple mark. I noted that it was in the form of a cross and remarked upon that fact. 'Why, I hadn't realized that!' A wonderful expression of faith crossed her countenance. She, her husband, and I clasped hands to pray. I placed a hand on her back over the cross printed there, and committed her to God.

As the months came and went, Gordon, who always asserted stoutly that the Lord had his wife in His hands, passed on of a sudden heart attack. Marian fought a gallant fight to live. One day, when I entered her hospital room, her eyes opened wide. 'Our Saviour entered with you,' she said, in her incisive, always highly intelligent way. Later she stated that He remained constantly, and, on subsequent visits, she said, 'Our Saviour is here.' From then on she talked less of getting well and more about how she loved 'her Saviour.' And she had not previously been an outwardly pious type. Indeed, she was somewhat of a sophisticated woman of the world, though a fine person. But she was sharp and keen, highly discerning.

When finally the end of the earthly struggle came, she told their dear friend 'Pat' Buckley how peaceful she felt with God. The trumpets sounded as this strong woman of faith passed over to the other side.

In this chapter, I have assembled some of the finest expressions of belief in immortality, in life after death, that have deepened the faith of many. And I hope that as you read and ponder these statements you may have deep within your mind the definite assurance that those whom you have 'loved long since and lost a while' are not lost to you at all, but live forever.

As I write these lines I am looking out over a wide valley set amidst the hills of Dutchess County, New York. Beyond are the rounded highest peaks of the Catskills. It is a glorious evening in midsummer; the declining sun, shining in the west, casts its last long soft rays over the grassy lawns under the gigantic hundred-year-old maples. Thinking of the people of faith whom I have known across the years, my thoughts go to one of the great physicians and surgeons of New York City, my friend the late Dr William Seaman Bainbridge, who practiced medicine for many years on Gramercy Park. He had a country home in Bethel, Connecticut, not far from my own farm in Pawling, New York.

When he was dying in the hospital at Danbury, my wife, Ruth, and I went to see him. He had meant so much to us and our family. His photograph is on my office wall. As this big man, healer of so many, lay in bed, his wife sitting with him, he said, 'I am going to the other side. My Lord is calling me. I am not afraid. I am ready to go.'

Mrs Bainbridge, calling him by the affectionate name she always used, said softly, 'Will, when you reach the other side, please wait for me and meet me there.'

A smile of assurance crossed his face, and his voice, which had become weakened, once again had the old-time strength. 'I'll be there, I'll be there,' he declared.

I turned to leave. His hand rose in the old gesture that we knew so well. 'Good-by, dear old friend,' he said. 'I'll see you over there.' It was just as if we were arranging to meet in some agreed-upon rendezvous on earth. But he felt just as certain about a meeting place in Heaven. This man, one of the most respected scientific and medical men of our time, had faith strong and sure, a faith that admitted of no doubt at all.

What I want to stress is that death is not the end of life. The great and subtle thinkers in every generation have been conscious of the intimations of immortality of which sensitive spirits have ever been aware. Their words, as gathered in this chapter, will, I hope, bring comfort and assurance to you.

> I cannot say, and I will not say
> That he is dead. He is just away.

With a cheery smile, and a wave of the hand,
He has wandered into an unknown land.

And left us dreaming how very fair
It needs must be since he lingers there.

And you – O you, who the wildest yearn
For the old-time step and the glad return –

Think of him faring on, as dear
In the love of there as the love of here;

Think of him still as the same, I say;
He is not dead – he is just away!

JAMES WHITCOMB RILEY

It singeth low in every heart,
  We hear it each and all –
A song of those who answer not,
  However we may call.
They throng the silence of the breast;
  We see them as of yore,
The kind, the brave, the true, the sweet,
  Who walk with us no more.

It's hard to take the burden up
  When these have laid it down;
They brightened all the joys of life,
  They softened every frown.
But oh, 'tis good to think of them
  When we are troubled sore;
Thanks be to God that such have been,
  Although they are no more!

More homelike seems the vast unknown
  Since they have entered there,
To follow them were not so hard
  Wherever they may fare,
They cannot be where God is not
  On any sea or shore;
Whate'er betides, thy love abides,
  Our God, forevermore.

JOHN W. CHADWICK

The soul, secured in her existence, smiles
At the drawn dagger and defies its point.
The stars shall fade away, the sun himself
Grow dim with age, and Nature sink in years;
But thou shalt flourish in immortal youth,
Unhurt amidst the war of elements,
The wrecks of matter, and the crush of worlds.

JOSEPH ADDISON

Death is only an old door
    Set in a garden wall;
On quiet hinges it gives, at dusk
    When the thrushes call.

Along the lintel are green leaves,
    Beyond, the light lies still;
Very weary and willing feet
    Go over that sill.

There is nothing to trouble any heart;
    Nothing to hurt at all.
Death is only an old door
    In a garden wall.

NANCY BYRD TURNER

There is no flock, however watched and tended,
    But one dead lamb is there!
There is no fireside, howsoe'er defended,
    But has one vacant chair! . . .

Let us be patient! These severe afflictions
    Not from the ground arise
But oftentimes celestial benedictions
    Assume this dark disguise.

We see but dimly through the mists and vapors;
    Amid these earthly damps
What seem to us but sad, funeral tapers
    May be heaven's distant lamps.

There is no Death! What seems so is transition;
    This life of mortal breath
Is but a suburb of the life Elysian,
    Whose portal we call Death. . . .

In that great cloister's stillness and seclusion,
  By guardian angels led,
Safe from temptation, safe from sin's pollution,
  She lives, whom we call dead. . . .

But a fair maiden, in her Father's mansion,
  Clothed with celestial grace;
And beautiful with all the soul's expansion
  Shall we behold her face.

And though at times impetuous with emotion
  And anguish long suppressed,
The swelling heart heaves moaning like the ocean,
  That cannot be at rest, –

We will be patient, and assuage the feeling
  We may not wholly stay;
By silence sanctifying, not concealing,
  The grief that must have way.

                HENRY WADSWORTH LONGFELLOW

If you should go before me, dear, walk slowly
Down the ways of death, well worn and wide,
For I would want to overtake you quickly
And seek the journey's ending by your side.

I would be so forlorn not to descry you
Down some shining high road when I came;
Walk slowly, dear, and often look behind you,
And pause to hear if someone calls your name.

                ADELAIDE LOVE

For this corruptible must put on incorruption, and this mortal must put on immortality. So when this corruptible shall have put on incorruption, and this mortal shall have put on immortality, then shall be brought to pass the saying that is written, Death is swallowed up in victory. O death, where is thy sting? O grave, where is thy victory?

                I CORINTHIANS 15: 53–55

When speaking of divine perfection, we signify that God is just and true and loving, the author of order, not disorder, of good, not evil. We signify that he is justice, that he is truth, that he is love, that he is order, that he is the very progress of which we were speaking, and that wherever these qualities exist, whether in the human soul or in the order of nature, there God exists. We might still see him everywhere, if we had not been mistakenly seeking for him apart from us, instead of in us; away from the laws of nature, instead of in them. And we become united, not by mystical absorption, but by partaking of that truth and justice and love which He himself is.

Therefore the belief in immortality depends finally upon the belief in God. If there exists a good and wise God, then there also exists a progress of mankind towards perfection; and if there be no progress of men towards perfection, then there cannot be a good and wise God. We cannot suppose that God's moral government, the beginnings of which we see in the world and in ourselves, will cease when we leave this life.

PLATO

Not by lamentations and mournful chants ought we to celebrate the funeral of a good man, but by hymns; for, in ceasing to be numbered with mortals, he enters upon the heritage of a diviner life. Since he is gone where he feels no pain, let us not indulge in too much grief. The soul is incapable of death. And he like a bird not long enough in his cage to become attached to it, is free to fly away to a purer air. . . . Since we cherish a trust like this, let our outward actions be in accord with it, and let us keep our hearts pure and our minds calm.

PLUTARCH

Out of the hitherwhere into the yon –
The land that the Lord's love rests upon,
Where one may rely on the friends he meets,
And the smiles that greet him along the streets,
Where the mother that left you years ago
Will lift the hands that were folded so,
And put them about you, with all the love
And tenderness you are dreaming of.

Out of the hitherwhere into the yon –
Where all the friends of your youth have gone –
Where the old schoolmate who laughed with you
Will laugh again as he used to do,
Running to meet you, with such a face
As lights like a moon the wondrous place
Where God is living, and glad to live
Since He is the Master and may forgive.

Out of the hitherwhere into the yon –
Stay the hopes we are leaning on –
You, Divine, with Your merciful eyes

Looking down from far-away skies,
Smile upon us and reach and take
Our worn souls Home for the old home's sake –
And so, Amen – for our all seems gone
Out of the hitherwhere into the yon.

JAMES WHITCOMB RILEY

As a personal experience, none of my own ever surpassed in moving power that beautiful and dramatic scene which, though it lies years back in the moonlit land of the past and memory, is vividly alive to me now. It happened at sunrise, and it was of a sunrise.

One dearer to me than all else in life had, for days, lain helpless, speechless. Consciousness was gone. We knew that the mortal mists were fast gathering; that the irremediable river must soon be crossed. The last morning of our watching was misty; the day emerged so wanly that we hardly knew that it had come. Suddenly the one we loved so dearly sat up in bed, a strange light on her face of a happiness past all our mortal joy. She stretched abroad her arms, crying in the radiant abandon of spiritual certainty, 'The Dawn! The beautiful Dawn!'

Those were her dying words – glad, triumphant. And for me they hold the eternal promise of the sunrise. They glow with immortality. In every sense, our mortal dawn that day was anything but beautiful; but she saw the beginning of an immortal day. Believing in a God of infinite love and of infinite power, I find it natural to believe that death is not a disastrous sundown but rather a spiritual sunrise, ushering in the unconjectured splendors of immortality. . . .

Sunrise suggests to me not only the power of God grandly to continue what He has begun but it also conveys the reassurance of the Creator's love returning to us daily, bringing joy and forgiveness; and to any reflective heart it intimates that no night is final; for, since with God all things are possible, His almighty love has, I confidently believe, prepared for us a radiant future beyond the sundown of death. And if I meditate but momentarily upon what He has done and upon what He does do, confidence in immortality is natural, reasonable, and, to my way of believing, to be counted upon as infallible as the sunrise.

ARCHIBALD RUTLEDGE

Lead, kindly Light, amid the encircling gloom,
    Lead Thou me on!
The night is dark, and I am far from home –
    Lead Thou me on!
Keep Thou my feet; I do not ask to see
The distant scene – one step enough for me.

I was not ever thus, nor prayed that Thou
  Shouldst lead me on.
I loved to choose and see my path; but now
  Lead Thou me on!
I loved the garish day, and, spite of fears,
Pride ruled my will: remember not past years.

So long Thy power hath blessed me, sure it still
  Will lead me on,
O'er moors and fen, o'er crag and torrent, till
  The night is gone;
And with the morn those angel faces smile
Which I have loved long since, and lost awhile.

                                    JOHN HENRY NEWMAN

It is the Christian hope that to life lived in the presence of God, death is but the entrance into a larger life. It is the Christian hope that in the larger fellowship of God's sons for time and eternity there is no final separation from those we love. It is the Christian hope that whether death comes early or late, no life is fruitless, no personality prized by God as an infinitely precious creation is snuffed out like a candle in the dark. It is the Christian hope that if atomic or bacteriological warfare or a hydrogen bomb should cause life upon the planet to end in mutual destruction, God would not be ultimately defeated or his Kingdom destroyed. It is the Christian hope that Christ is the resurrection and life, and that neither life nor death can separate us from the love of God which is in Christ Jesus our Lord.

                                    GEORGIA HARKNESS

I have thought much lately of the possibility of my leaving you all and going home. I am come to that stage of my pilgrimage that is within sight of the River of Death, and I feel that now I must have all in readiness day and night for the messenger of the King. I have had sometimes in my sleep strange perceptions of a vivid spiritual life near to and with Christ, and multitudes of holy ones, and the joy of it is like no other joy – it cannot be told in the language of the world. What I have then I know with absolute certainty, yet it is so unlike and above anything we conceive of in this world that it is difficult to put it into words. The inconceivable loveliness of Christ! It seems that about him there is a sphere where the enthusiasm of love is the calm habit of the soul, that without words, without the necessity of demonstrations of affection, heart beats to heart, soul answers soul, we respond to the Infinite Love, and we feel his answer in us, and there is no need of words. All seemed to be busy coming and going on ministries of good, and passing each gave a thrill of joy to each as Jesus, the directing soul, the centre of all, 'over all, in all and through all,' was working his beautiful and merciful will to redeem and save. I was saying as I woke: –

'   'Tis joy enough, my all in all
      At Thy dear feet to lay.'

This was but a glimpse; but it has left a strange sweetness in my mind.

HARRIET BEECHER STOWE

FAITH EASES GRIEF

In the course of World War II, I visited the home of a dear friend, a fellow minister who had just received word that his only son had been killed in the Battle of the Bulge. This boy had decided for the Christian ministry and possessed excellent qualifications for that vocation. His father was brokenhearted. As I sat with him in the comradeship of silence, he began at last to talk very tenderly and lovingly about his boy.

Then he said this: 'I am not going to be bitter or rebellious. He is gone. Some day I hope to meet him again. One thing I will say: I must now be twice as good a minister as I have ever been because my son will not be here. I shall try to do his work as well as my own.' He faced the inevitable bravely and robbed it of its power to destroy him. . . .

Most people have more trouble with grief than with any other problem. Every observant person is aware of the fact that when bereavement visits a home, every member of the family is tested to the core of his being. Whether or not we can handle grief is determined largely by the measure of faith we possess and also by our understanding of the problems that sorrow raises.

Let us look at some of the unconstructive ways that people meet grief. There are, of course, right and wrong ways of dealing with it. One of the most serious mistakes we can make is to refuse to express it, 'to keep a stiff upper lip,' to refuse to admit even to ourselves that we have suffered a crushing loss. It is a totally wrong idea that we ought to be stoical and completely unemotional in the face of death. Nature should be allowed to have its way. The Lord gave to us lachrymal glands that we may use them, and the flow of tears is healing to the spirit.

Another unconstructive response to grief is the development of feelings of guilt. These are almost inseparable from death. Rarely do I find anyone who has suffered a grievous loss in death who does not express some guilt. . . . A measure of this is normal and natural, but when it becomes obsessive, it can be dangerous.

Overactivity is another response that may have harmful results. Tennyson, after the death of his friend Arthur Hallam, declared, 'I must lose myself in action, lest I wither in despair.' Activity of a constructive nature is quite important and beneficial, but when it is just a matter of constant hurrying and bustling in unimportant matters, it is an evidence of grief that has been repressed, that has not been allowed expression. . . .

What I have outlined is drawn from the New Testament attitude toward death and grief. When, for instance, Paul begins to list the powers that might threaten to separate us from Christ, he names death first of all but brushes it quickly aside. This was the spirit of all the apostles and evangelists of the early Church. When Stephen was dying, he said, 'Lord Jesus, receive my spirit.' If we too can enter into a like faith, then solemn, portentous death will be defeated. It will not be necessary for us to preserve the material possessions of loved ones who have gone or to erect around them a sort of shrine at which we engage in what is almost idolatry. . . .

We know that Christ triumphed over death and our dear ones triumph in Him. Wherefore, when death lays its hand on some friend or loved one, we are not plunged into hopeless grief, since faith teaches us that those who have walked with God go from strength to strength in the life of perfect service of his Heavenly Kingdom.

JOHN SUTHERLAND BONNELL

ETERNAL SPRING WITHIN THE HEART

I feel within me the future life. I am like a forest that has once been razed; the new shoots are stronger and brisker. I shall most certainly rise toward the heavens. The sun's rays bathe my head. The earth gives me its generous sap, but the heavens illuminate me with the reflecttion of – of worlds unknown. Some say the soul results merely from bodily powers. Why, then, does my soul become brighter when my bodily powers begin to waste away ? Winter is above me, but eternal spring is within my heart. I inhale even now the fragrance of lilacs, violets, and roses, just as I did when I was twenty.

The nearer my approach to the end, the plainer is the sound of immortal symphonies of worlds which invite me. It is wonderful yet simple. It is a fairy tale; it is history.

For half a century I have been translating my thoughts into prose and verse; history, philosophy, drama, romance, tradition, satire, ode, and song; all of these have I tried. But I feel that I haven't given utterance to the thousandth part of what lies within me. When I go to the grave I can say as others have said, 'My day's work is done.' But I cannot say, 'My life is done.' My day's work will recommence

the next morning. The tomb is not a blind alley; it is a thoroughfare.
It closes upon the twilight, but opens upon the dawn.

VICTOR HUGO

'Why should we fear death?' a man once said. 'It is life's finest
form of adventure.' These words were not uttered by some minister
of religion standing securely in his pulpit on Easter Day, surrounded
by flowers and with joyous anthems sounding in his ears. They were
not spoken before an open fire at the close of a delightful evening by
some man sitting in the easy comfort of his armchair. They were
spoken by Charles Frohman on the deck of the *Lusitania* just as the
great ship settled to her doom. He felt that all earthly hope was gone,
and this was his last word to a group of friends who expected to share
his fate.

CHARLES REYNOLD BROWN

Joy, shipmate, joy!
(Pleased to my soul at death I cry),
Our life is closed, our life begins,
The long, long anchorage we leave,
The ship is clear at last, she leaps!
She swiftly courses from the shore,
Joy, shipmate, joy!

WALT WHITMAN

Waste no tears over the griefs of yesterday.

EURIPIDES

The clouds upon the mountains rest;
    A gloom is on the autumn day;
But down the valley, in the west,
    The hidden sunlight breaks its way –
    A light lies on the farther hills.

Forget thy sorrow, heart of mine!
    Tho' shadows fall and fades the leaf,
Somewhere is joy, tho' 'tis not thine;
    The power that sent can heal thy grief;
    And light lies on the farther hills.

Thou wouldst not with the world be one
    If ne'er thou knewest hurt and wrong;
Take comfort, tho' the darkened sun
    Never again bring gleam or song,
    The light lies on the farther hills.

RICHARD WATSON GILDER

Death is not extinguishing the light; it is only putting out the lamp because the Dawn has come.

RABINDRANATH TAGORE

> Though my soul may set in darkness, it will rise in
>   perfect light;
> I have loved the stars too fondly to be fearful of
>   the night.

ATTRIBUTED TO AN AGED ASTRONOMER

We sometimes congratulate ourselves at the moment of waking from a troubled dream: it may be so at the moment after death.

NATHANIEL HAWTHORNE

> Grow old along with me!
> The best is yet to be,
> The last of life, for which the first was made;
> Our times are in his hand who saith,
> 'A whole I planned,
> Youth shows but half; trust God: See all, nor
>   be afraid!'

ROBERT BROWNING

PAIN – THE BEGINNING OF JOY

To curse grief is easier than to bless it, but to do so is to fall back into the point of view of the earthly, the carnal, the natural man. By what has Christianity subdued the world if not by the apotheosis of grief, by its marvellous transmutation of suffering into triumph, of the crown of thorn into the crown of glory, and of a gibbet into a symbol of salvation? What does the apotheosis of the Cross mean, if not the death of death, the defeat of sin, the beatification of martyrdom, the rising to the skies of voluntary sacrifice, the defiance of pain? . . .

Suffering was a curse from which man fled; now it becomes a purification of the soul, a sacred trial sent by Eternal Love, a divine dispensation meant to sanctify and ennoble us, an acceptable aid to faith, a strange initiation into happiness. Power of belief! All remains the same, and yet all is changed. A new certitude arises to deny the apparent and the tangible; it pierces through the mystery of things, it places an invisible Father behind visible nature, it shows us joy shining through tears, and makes of pain the beginning of joy.

HENRI AMIEL

> The embers of the day are red
> Beyond the murky hill.

The kitchen smokes; the bed
In the darkling house is spread:
The great sky darkens overhead,
And the great woods are shrill.
So far have I been led,
Lord, by Thy will:
So far have I followed, Lord, and wondered still.
The breeze from the embalmed land
Blows sudden towards the shore,
And claps my cottage door.
I hear the signal, Lord – I understand.
The night at Thy command
Comes. I will eat and sleep and will not question more.

ROBERT LOUIS STEVENSON

A LITTLE PARABLE ABOUT MOTHERS

The young mother set her foot on the path of life.
'Is the way long?' she asked.

And the guide said: 'Yes. And the way is hard. And you will be old before you reach the end of it. But the end will be better than the beginning.'

But the young mother was happy, and she would not believe that anything could be better than these years. So she played with her children, and gathered flowers for them along the way, and bathed with them in the clear streams; and the young mother cried, 'Nothing will ever be lovelier than this.'

Then night came, and storm, and the path was dark, and the children shook with fear and cold, and the mother drew them close and covered them with her mantle, and the children said, 'Mother, we are not afraid, for you are near, and no harm can come.' And the mother said, 'This is better than the brightness of day, for I have taught my children courage.'

And the morning came, and there was a hill ahead, and the children climbed and grew weary, and the mother was weary, but at all times she said to the children, 'A little patience and we are there.' So the children climbed and when they reached the top they said, 'Mother, we would not have done it without you.'

And the mother, when she lay down that night, looked up at the stars and said: 'This is a better day than the last, for my children have learned fortitude in the face of hardness. Yesterday I gave them courage. Today I have given them strength.'

And the next day came strange clouds which darkened the earth – clouds of war and hate and evil, and the children groped and stumbled, and the mother said: 'Look up. Lift your eyes to the light.'

And the children looked and saw above the clouds an Everlasting Glory, and it guided them and brought them beyond the darkness. And that night the mother said, 'This is the best day of all, for I have shown my children God.'

And the days went on, and the weeks and the months and the years, and the mother grew old, and was little and bent. But her children were tall and strong, and walked with courage. And when the way was hard, they helped their mother; and when the way was rough, they lifted her; for she was as light as a feather, and at last they came to a hill, and beyond they could see a shining road and golden gates flung wide.

And the mother said: 'I have reached the end of my journey. And now I know that the end is better than the beginning, for my children can walk alone, and their children after them.' And the children said, 'You will always walk with us, Mother, even when you have gone through the gates.'

And they stood and watched her as she went on alone, and the gates closed after her. And they said: 'We cannot see her, but she is with us still. A mother like ours is more than a memory. She is a living presence.'

TEMPLE BAILEY

Let not your heart be troubled: ye believe in God, believe also in me. In my Father's house are many mansions: if it were not so, I would have told you. I go to prepare a place for you. And if I go and prepare a place for you, I will come again, and receive you unto myself; that where I am, there ye may be also.

JOHN 14: 1–3

Because I live, ye shall live also.

JOHN 14: 19

I am the resurrection, and the life: he that believeth in me, though he were dead, yet shall he live.

JOHN 11: 25

They that love beyond the world cannot be separated by it. Death cannot kill what never dies, nor can spirits ever be divided that love and live in the same divine principle.

WILLIAM PENN

It is impossible that anything so natural, so necessary, and so universal as death should ever have been designed by Providence as an evil to mankind.

JONATHAN SWIFT

I ask no risen dust to teach me immortality;
I am *conscious* of eternal life.

THEODORE PARKER

I shall not live 'till I see God; and when I have seen Him, I shall never die.

JOHN DONNE

God never promises exemption. He does promise companionship, which is better. He does not promise to deliver you or me or any other individual from pain, sorrow, or economic disaster, but He does give assurance that He will help us through and that there will be compensations. 'I will not leave you comfortless, I will come to you.' These are the words of Jesus.

And this also needs to be said: Nowhere in either the Old Testament or the New are we assured special well-being because of piety. Indeed there are instances, as in the great drama of Job, when goodness itself is tested and made a vehicle of trial. Even Paul cried to be relieved of his 'thorn in the flesh,' but cried in vain; and his contemporaries, the disciples, including Peter and the faithful who were hunted through the Roman catacombs and burned along the Appian Way and fed to the lions in the Colosseum, were not relieved of their physical ordeals because they were holy. But that never-disregarded promise 'I will come to you' was kept with each of them, and it is written that they chose – it was their choice – to suffer affliction as the faithful had suffered in earlier times rather than to enjoy what Rome at her voluptuous best had to offer.

It is even more boldly stated, if you please: 'For whom the Lord loveth he chasteneth, and scourgeth every son whom he receiveth.' Surely, these are hard words to understand. The problem of human suffering remains one of the great mysteries, but this I do know: God comes to His people and grants them mercies and foreglimpses of that which will be theirs to possess. I have seen the evidence of such grantings in the veritable ecstasies of some sufferers upon their deathbeds. We might reasonably curse and die, as Job's wife recommended to him, if this life were all. Those who believe it to be all and who so insist are to be understood when they curse. But this life is definitely not all!

I believe in eternal life because it became a vivid personal experience for me on a certain February morning in 1918. With an orderly I waited in the rain at the head of a communicating trench north of Toul in France. A platoon of American machine-gun company was coming out. The first lieutenant, bringing up the rear, recognized my uniform and stopped to ask the way to the nearest canteen. Fever burned in his tired face. 'Tonsilitis,' he croaked, as he leaned on his stick, 'and trench foot.' Then, pulling himself together, he stumbled on after his men. When he had gone a short distance, a shell exploded in the middle of the platoon. Hearing it coming, the orderly and I flung ourselves flat in the mud. Then the screams of agony called us to the wounded and dead. First looking after those who still needed the little we could do for them, we began gathering the shattered bodies of the others.

There on the blood-soaked bit of French soil I experienced the comprehension of immortality. I knew that the lieutenant with the aching throat, the lad whose sick eyes had looked into mine, the boy with whom I had just talked, was not in what I had just picked up. I had not talked to *that*. But also I knew he was somewhere. I knew that there had been authority enough to begin his life, to carry it from his mother's womb to this awful end. Short of immortality, I had the choice of just two conclusions: Either the great creative authority had willed that this young personality be extinguished there in the blood and muck, willed to end it in such a sorry fashion, or the same authority was able to create but unable to continue, was helpless before the event.

My heart and mind rejected both conclusions. I knew then that the young life did not stop where I picked up his body. I knew then, as I know now, that he went on. It was a conviction, an experience so real that it left me at the moment all but unconcerned about the pitifully broken body.

DANIEL A. POLING

In the bottom of an old pond lived some grubs who could not understand why none of their groups ever came back after crawling up the stems of the lilies to the top of the water. They promised each other that the next one who was called to make the upward climb would return and tell what happened to him. Soon one of them felt an urgent impulse to seek the surface; he rested himself on the top of a lily pad and went through a glorious transformation which made him a dragonfly with beautiful wings. In vain he tried to keep his promise. Flying back and forth over the pond, he peered down at his friends below. Then he realized that even if they could see him they would not recognize such a radiant creature as one of their number.

The fact that we cannot see our friends or communicate with them after the transformation, which we call death, is no proof that they cease to exist.

WALTER DUDLEY CAVERT

She has only gone on a little ahead
To fashion a home for me.
There will be curtains blowing,
And books, as there used to be;
Pictures, a desk, and tables fair
Where friends shall love to come. . . .
She has only gone on as a mother would
To find me a new home.

She has only gone on as others have
Who vanished from our sight,
Others whose lives with ours were wed
Till that mysterious flight.
None shall declare her death to me,
My loneliness deplore –
Oh, it is like her to go ahead
To open the new door.

She has only gone on a little ahead
To find me the loveliest place;
There will be golden roses there
Abloom in an azure space;
Poppies, pansies, and daffodils
And moss I shall love to tread –
O mother! Now it is clear to me,
You've only gone on ahead.

ANGELA MORGAN

Nearer, my God, to Thee,
Nearer to Thee!
E'en though it be a cross
That raiseth me;
Still all my song shall be,
Nearer, my God, to Thee –
Nearer to Thee!

Though like a wanderer,
The sun gone down,
Darkness comes over me,
My rest a stone;
Yet in my dreams I'd be
Nearer, my God, to Thee –
Nearer to Thee!

There let the way appear,
  Steps unto heaven;
All that Thou sendest me,
  In mercy given;
Angels to beckon me
Nearer, my God, to Thee –
  Nearer to Thee!

Then, with my waking thoughts
  Bright with Thy praise,
Out of my stony griefs
  Bethel I'll raise;
So by my woes to be
Nearer, my God, to Thee –
  Nearer to Thee!

Or, if on joyful wing
  Cleaving the sky,
Sun, moon, and stars forgot,
  Upward I fly,
Still all my song shall be,
Nearer, my God, to Thee –
  Nearer to Thee!

                    SARAH FLOWER ADAMS

A good man never dies –
  In worthy deed and prayer
And helpful hands, and honest eyes,
  If smiles or tears be there;
Who lives for you and me –
  Lives for the world he tries
To help – he lives eternally.
  A good man never dies.

Who lives to bravely take
  His share of toil and stress
And, for his weaker fellows' sake,
  Makes every burden less –
He may, at last, seem worn –
  Lie fallen – hands and eyes
Folded – yet, though we mourn and mourn,
  A good man never dies.

                    JAMES WHITCOMB RILEY

Yet Love will dream, and Faith will trust,
(Since He who knows our need is just),
That somehow, somewhere, meet we must.
Alas for him who never sees
The stars shine through his cypress-trees!
Who, hopeless, lays his dead away,
Nor looks to see the breaking day
Across the mournful marbles play!
Who hath not learned, in hours of faith,
   The truth to flesh and sense unknown,
That Life is ever lord of Death,
   And Love can never lose its own!

JOHN GREENLEAF WHITTIER

When on my day of life the night is falling,
   And, in the winds from unsunned spaces blown,
I hear far voices out of darkness calling
   My feet to paths unknown.

Thou who has made my home of life so pleasant,
   Leave not its tenant when its walls decay;
O Love divine, O Helper ever present,
   Be Thou my strength and stay!

Be near me when all else is from me drifting:
   Earth, sky, home's pictures, days of shade and shine,
And kindly faces to my own uplifting
   The love which answers mine.

I have but Thee, my Father! Let Thy spirit
   Be with me then to comfort and uphold;
No gate of pearl, no branch of palm I merit,
   Nor street of shining gold.

Suffice it if — my good and ill unreckoned,
   And both forgiven through Thy abounding grace —
I find myself by hands familiar beckoned
   Unto my fitting place.

Some humble door among Thy many mansions
   Some sheltering shade where sin and striving cease,
And flows forever through heaven's green expansions
   The river of Thy peace.

There, from the music round about me stealing,
    I fain would learn the new and holy song,
And find at last, beneath Thy trees of healing,
    The life for which I long.

JOHN GREENLEAF WHITTIER

Don't dread. God loves you. He will take care of you.

Many live in dread of what is coming. Why should we? The unknown puts adventure into life. It gives us someth ng to sharpen our
souls on. The unexpected around the corner gives a sense of anticipation and surprise. Thank God for the unknown future. If we saw all
good things which are coming to us, we would sit down and degener-
ate. If we saw all the evil things, we would be paralyzed. How merciful
God is to lift the curtain on today; and as we get strength today to
meet tomorrow, then to lift the curtain on the morrow. He is a
considerate God.

E. STANLEY JONES

As a fond mother, when the day is o'er,
    Leads by the hand her little child to bed
    Half willing, half reluctant to be led,
    And leave his broken playthings on the floor,
Still gazing at them through the open door,
    Nor wholly reassured and comforted
    By promises of others in their stead,
    Which, though more splendid, may
        not please him more;
So Nature deals with us, and takes away
    Our playthings one by one, and by hand
    Leads us to rest so gently, that we go
Scarce knowing if we wish to go or stay,
    Being too full of sleep to understand
    How far the unknown transcends the
        what we know.

HENRY WADSWORTH LONGFELLOW

For we know that if our earthly house of this tabernacle were
dissolved, we have a building of God, an house not made with hands,
eternal in the heavens.

II CORINTHIANS 5: I

I never saw a moor,
I never saw the sea;
Yet know I how the heather looks,
And what a wave must be.

I never spoke with God,
Nor visited in heaven;
Yet certain am I of the spot
As if the chart were given.

EMILY DICKINSON

O friends, we are drawing nearer home
As day by day goes by;
Nearer the fields of fadeless bloom,
The joys that never die.

Ye doubting souls, from doubt be free –
Ye mourners, mourn no more,
For every wave of Death's dark sea
Breaks on that blissful shore.

God's ways are high above our ways –
So shall we learn at length,
And tune our lives to sing His praise
With all our mind, might, strength.

About our devious paths of ill
He sets His stern decrees,
And works the wonders of His will
Through pains and promises.

Strange are the mysteries He employs,
Yet we His love will trust,
Though it should blight our dearest joys,
And bruise us into dust.

ALICE CARY

Many a life has been injured by the constant expectation of death. It is life we have to do with, not death. The best preparation for the night is to work diligently while the day lasts. The best preparation for death is life.

GEORGE MACDONALD

Spend your brief moment according to nature's law, and serenely

greet the journey's end as an olive falls when it is ripe, blessing the
branch that bare it, and giving thanks to the tree that gave it life.

                                                              MARCUS AURELIUS

All plants, animals, and men are already in eternity, traveling across
the face of time. Whence we know not. Whither, who is able to say?
Let us have one world at a time, and let us make the journey one of
joy to our fellow passengers, and just as convenient and happy for
them as we can, and trust the rest as we trust life.

                                                              LUTHER BURBANK

May 16 [1826] – She died at nine in the morning, after being ill
for two days – easy at last. I arrived here late last night. For myself,
I scarce know how I feel – sometimes as firm as the Bass Rock,
sometimes as weak as the waters that break on it. . . .

May 18 – Another day, and a bright one to the external world,
again opens on us; the air soft, and the flowers smiling, and the
leaves glittering. They cannot refresh her to whom mild weather was
a natural enjoyment. Cerements of lead and wood already hold her;
cold earth must have her soon. But it is not my Charlotte, it is not
the bride of my youth, the mother of my children, that will be laid
among the ruins of Cryburgh, which we have so often visited in gaiety
and pastime. No, no. She is sentient and conscious of my emotions
somewhere – somehow; where we cannot tell – how we cannot tell;
yet would I not this moment renounce the mysterious yet certain
hope that I shall see her in a better world, for all that this world can
give me.

                                                              SIR WALTER SCOTT

We do not believe in immortality because we have proved it, but
we forever try to prove it because we believe it.

                                                              JAMES MARTINEAU

> Remember me when I am gone away,
> Gone far away into the silent land;
> When you can no more hold me by the hand,
> Nor I half turn to go, yet turning stay.
> Remember me when no more, day by day,
> You tell me of our future that you planned;
> Only remember me; you understand
> It will be late to counsel then or pray.
> Yet if you should forget me for a while
> And afterwards remember, do not grieve;
> For if the darkness and corruption leave

A vestige of the thoughts that once I had,
Better by far you should forget and smile
Than that you should remember and be sad.

CHRISTINA ROSSETTI

Old age hath yet his honour and his toil;
Death closes all: but something ere the end,
Some work of noble note, may yet be done,
Not unbecoming men that strove with the Gods.
The lights begin to twinkle from the rocks:
The long day wanes: the slow moon climbs: the deep
Moans round with many voices. Come, my friends,
'Tis not too late to seek a newer world.
Push off, and sitting well in order smite
The sounding furrows; for my purpose holds
To sail beyond the sunset, and the paths
Of all the western stars, until I die.
It may be that the gulfs will wash us down:
It may be we shall touch the Happy Isles,
And see the great Achilles, whom we knew;
Tho' much is taken, much abides; and tho'
We are not now that strength which in old days
Moved earth and heaven; that which we are, we are;
One equal temper of heroic hearts,
Made weak by time and fate, but strong in will
To strive, to seek, to find, and not to yield.

ALFRED, LORD TENNYSON

O never star
Was lost; here
We all aspire to heaven and there is heaven
Above us.
If I stoop
Into a dark tremendous sea of cloud,
It is but for a time; I press God's lamp
Close to my breast; its splendor soon or late
Will pierce the gloom. I shall emerge some day.

ROBERT BROWNING

Strong Son of God, immortal Love,
    Whom we, that have not seen Thy face,
    By faith and faith alone, embrace,
Believing where we cannot prove;

Thine are these orbs of light and shade;
   Thou madest life in man and brute;
   Thou madest death; and lo, Thy foot
Is on the skull which Thou has made.

Thou wilt not leave us in the dust;
   Thou madest man, he knows not why;
   He thinks he was not made to die;
And Thou hast made him: Thou art just.

Thou seemest human and divine,
   The highest, holiest manhood Thou:
   Our wills are ours, we know not how:
Our will are ours to make them Thine.

Our little systems have their day;
   They have their day and cease to be:
   They are but broken lights of Thee,
And Thou, O Lord, art more than they.

We have but faith: we cannot know;
   For knowledge is of things we see;
   And yet we trust it comes from Thee,
A beam in darkness: let it grow.

Let knowledge grow from more to more,
   But more of reverence in us dwell;
   That mind and soul, according well,
May make one music as before,

But vaster. We are fools and slight;
   We mock Thee, when we do not fear;
   But help Thy foolish ones to bear;
Help Thy vain world to bear Thy light.

Forgive what seem'd my sin in me;
   What seemed my worth since I began;
   For merit lives from man to man;
And not from man, O Lord, to Thee.

Forgive my grief for one removed,
   Thy creature, whom I found so fair.
   I trust he lives in Thee, and there
I find him worthier to be loved.

Forgive these wild and wandering cries,
  Confusions of a wasted youth;
  Forgive them where they fail in truth,
And in Thy wisdom make me wise.

ALFRED, LORD TENNYSON

We pray Thee, O Christ, to keep us under the spell of immortality.
May we never again think and act as if Thou were dead. Let us more and more come to know Thee as a living Lord who hath promised to them that believe: 'Because I live, ye shall live also.'

Help us to remember that we are praying to the Conqueror of Death, that we may no longer be afraid nor dismayed by the world's problems and threats, since Thou hast overcome the world.

In Thy strong name, we ask for Thy living presence and Thy victorious power. Amen.

PETER MARSHALL

Index of Authors

More Books from Vermilion

The prices below were correct at the time of going to press

☐ 07493 0791 9 **New Arthritis and Common Sense: A Complex Guide to Effective Relief** Dale Alexander £6.99

☐ 07493 0938 5 **The Courage to Heal** Ellen Bass and Laura Davis £10.99

☐ 07493 0856 7 **The Body Has Its Reason: Anti-exercise and Self-Awareness** Therese Bertherat and Carol Bernstein £4.99

☐ 07493 0579 7 **How to Develop Self-Confidence and Influence People by Public Speaking** Dale Carnegie £7.99

☐ 07493 0593 2 **How to Enjoy Your Life and Your Job** Dale Carnegie £7.99

☐ 07493 0723 4 **How to Stop Worrying and Start Living** Dale Carnegie £7.99

☐ 07493 0784 6 **How to Win Friends and Influence People** Dale Carnegie £7.99

☐ 07493 0577 0 **The Quick and Easy Way to Effective Speaking** Dale Carnegie £7.99

☐ 07493 0246 1 **Overcoming Overeating** Jane Hirschmann & Carol Munter £6.99

☐ 07493 0713 7 **Living Together Feeling Alone** Dr Dan Kiley £6.99

☐ 07493 0933 4 **The Amazing Results of Positive Thinking** Norman Vincent Peale £7.99

☐ 07493 1341 2 **Courage and Confidence** Norman Vincent Peale £7.99

☐ 07493 0719 6 **Inspiring Messages for Daily Living** Norman Vincent Peale £7.99

☐ 07493 0858 3 **The Positive Way to Change Your Life** Norman Vincent Peale £7.99

☐ 07493 0821 4 **The Power of Positive Living** Norman Vincent Peale £7.99

☐ 07493 0715 3 **The Power of Positive Thinking** Norman Vincent Peale £7.99

☐ 07493 0567 3 **The Power of Positive Thinking for Young People** Norman Vincent Peale £7.99

☐ 07493 0254 2 **Families and How to Survive Them** Robin Skinner and John Cleese £7.99

☐ 07493 2320 5 **Life and How to Survive It** Robin Skinner and John Cleese £7.99

☐ 07493 1041 3 **How to Survive in Spite of Your Parents** Dr Margaret Reihnhold £7.99

☐ 07493 1264 5 **Living with ME: A Self Help Guide** Dr Charles Shepherd £7.99

☐ 07493 1656 X **Victims No Longer** Mike Lew £9.99

☐ 07493 2665 4 **The Handbook of Alternative and Complementary Medicine** Stephen Fulder £12.99

☐ 07493 2289 6 **Your Child's Symptoms Explained** Dr David Haslam £7.99

☐ 07493 0936 9 **The Courage to Grieve** Judith Tatelbaum £6.99